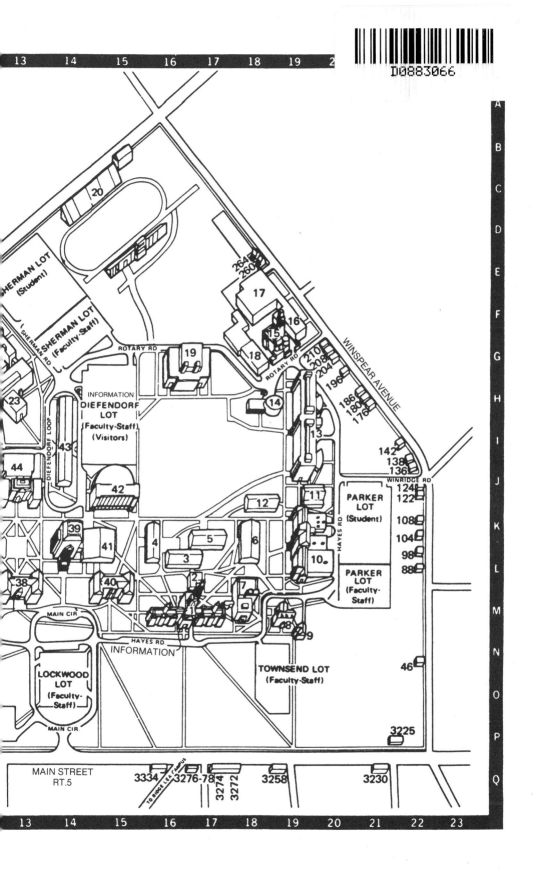

DISSENT
AND
DISRUPTION

To Genevieve,
Fondly,
Dick Siggelkow

DISSENT
AND A UNIVERSITY UNDER SIEGE
DISRUPTION

Richard A. Siggelkow

Prometheus Books
Buffalo, New York

Published 1991 by Prometheus Books.

96 95 94 93 92   5 4 3 2 1

Library of Congress Cataloging-in-Publication Data

Siggelkow, Richard A.
    Dissent and disruption : a university under siege / by Richard A. Siggelkow.
        p.   cm.
    Includes bibliographical references.
    ISBN 0-87975-681-0
    1. State University of New York at Buffalo—History—20th century. 2. Student movements—New York (State)—Buffalo—History—20th century. 3. State University of New York at Buffalo—Students—History—20th century. 4. Student-administrator relationships—New York (State)—Buffalo—History—20th century. I. Title.
LD701.B42S54   1992
378.747'97—dc20   91-17099
                                                                        CIP

#23732534

Printed in the United States of America on acid-free paper.

Contents

Preface

University administrators have generally remained silent about their personal experiences during the period of strident campus unrest that began in the mid-1960s and ended in 1972. As we mark the twentieth anniversary of the student movement the most significant accounts about its impact and influence have come primarily from former radical activist leaders or disillusioned faculty members.

Administrators may have found it too painful during the last twenty years to recall objectively their inability to resolve intractable problems and cope with unpredictable excesses of some student dissidents who seemed determined to destroy the entire academic enterprise.

This book is intended to help readers better understand how students, faculty, administrators, and the outside community were touched by and reacted to expressions of dissent and disruption that were generated at one large, urban university.

The author wishes to acknowledge the following sources that helped to overcome some natural inclinations toward subjectivity and administrative bias:

Professor Dean G. Pruitt deserves special recognition for unselfishly releasing a wealth of previously unpublished research conducted while specific events took place; included is an invaluable daily log he maintained during the crucial spring term of 1970.

Insights and responses from approximately 250 faculty and other observers, reflecting broad ranges of opinion, provide further balance. Quoted statements released by respondents insured greater accuracy in reporting on the period.

Rufus E. Miles, an important outside source, contributed vital understandings into the pathology of institutional breakdown to clarify the sequence of events that took place at many educational institutions during the period.

Comments from law enforcement officials, including such normally overlooked resources as undercover deputies, offer yet another perspective on campus unrest.

UB archivists Shonnie Finnegan and Christopher Densmore were invariably helpful. Dennis R. Black's research and expertise on legal cases and Prometheus editor Jeanne O'Day's unlimited patience and thoughtful suggestions were equally appreciated.

Bantam Books and the National Association of Student Personnel Administrators are thanked for granting approval to incorporate significant background materials related to broader aspects of the period.

Reactions from students who represented the vast majority of college youth who neither supported nor subscribed to extremist tactics of disruption provide further objectivity. In a larger sense, the author is primarily indebted to the many students, whether protestors or not, with whom he has been privileged to interact as a teacher and administrator for almost forty years.

The author would also be derelict if he failed to thank members of his immediate family who must often have silently wished that he had never become a university administrator.

Introduction

The "good old times"—all times, when old, are good.

—Byron

Student indignation [at Columbia University] crystallized on the Monday after the expulsion when a mass meeting was held [in April 1932] on the library steps with more than 4,000 students. Columbia had never witnessed . . . so impressive an outpouring from serious and determined students. And there a University strike of major proportions was voted, to take place on Wednesday. . . .

Policemen sit in the shade of the trees [at CCNY]. . . . Faculty members walk rapidly and cringe at their own shadows. It is only the policemen who are self-confident and sure of themselves [in May 1933]. It is they who have inherited the college. . . .

In response to a call for a nationwide strike against the war preparations of the United States government, 25,000 students left their classrooms on April 13, 1934. The demonstration was unprecedented; nothing in the history of American undergraduate life was equivalent to it. Twelve months later on April 12, 1935, there were 175,000 participants in similar demonstrations throughout the country.

—From *Revolt on the Campus,* by James A.
Wechsler (1973), originally published in 1935

Unpredictable circumstances, complicated by national and international events, could return college student unrest in the United States to levels exceeding the turmoil of the late 1960s and early 1970s.

Interest in reviving the period is a recurrent and nostalgic theme. The sixties are often presented in film and television—accompanied by a period rock music sound track—as youthful optimism in the best of times, but the era had violent undertones. It was scarred by tragedy and violence and remembered for the deaths of the Kennedys and Martin Luther King, battles for civil rights, LBJ, anti-war protests, Richard Nixon, Kent State, police batons, tear gas—and Vietnam.

What stuns 1960s activist Todd Gitlen is the ignorance present-day college students have about the decade in which they were born. "The 60's seem completely other to them—unfathomable," Gitlen tells Katherine Bishop (1988) in a *New York Times* article about "The 60s Legacy." "Until now they have never heard about it except in lurid images—Jerry Rubin, hippies. . . . It's very odd to them, but it's odd enough if you lived through it."

Several recognized journalists sadly agree that the return of the sixties is imminent, if not already upon us. "It would be difficult to think of a more depressing piece of news," observes Jonathan Yardley (1988) in the *Washington Post*. "But there you have it," he maintains, "the Sixties are back." He labels as "baloney" a *New York Times* claim that the era was important to adolescents as a period of ideological commitment.

"The most intense self indulgence," on the part of the privileged children of the American middle class, was fueled, he believes, by the following:

A generation of parents who sought to provide their children with comforts and privileges they thought had been denied.

The attainment of college ages by the first baby boomers.

The largest "youth culture" in history.

The unprecedented expansion of American higher education and the commitment to make it available to all.

The gradual relaxation of sexual mores and the easy availability of drugs.

The creation of a new form of popular music.

The decision by Lyndon Johnson to commit American troops to Vietnam.

Entering the Vietnam War was a colossal mistake for the American government, Yardley maintains, "but the movement that rose up against it on the campuses had far less to do with principles of reasoned resistance than with the avoidance of military service." He deplores "the wholesale capitulation of university administrators and faculty members to the demands of the Sixties 'rebels.' " It was "one of the truly unedifying spectacles in American history, and the repercussions are still being felt."

Under the heading "Incivility of '60s Rears Its Ugly Head," Haynes Johnson (1988) recalls the 1960s:

Once again, the nation is awash in nostalgia for supposedly vanished glories of a decade remembered as more wonderful than it was. . . . The nation experienced a similar glow about the '50s, which Hollywood movies and television sitcoms still depict as a benign, happy time when all America was innocent, tranquil, and content. The '50s were anything but—a terrible decade marked by character assassination, racism and sexism, pathological fears of aliens, and thus dangerous doctrines growing out of the worst of Cold War mentality; digging of bomb shelters; bloody beginnings of the civil rights revolution with sit-ins and freedom marches in the South; no-win war in Korea that left its veterans feeling at least as unappreciated by the country at large as those who later served in Vietnam.

"Much the same can be said about the '60s, but more so," Johnson continues:

> It was our most turbulent and violent decade and, for millions of Americans, a destroyer of hopes and dreams. Twenty years later, we're still digging our way out of the social and political wreckage of that time.
>
> A new intolerance arose in the '60s that stood in marked contrast to earlier gains in civil rights and liberties. It was self-righteous intolerance, born of fury and hatred and hurt, that led otherwise intelligent people to brand anyone they didn't agree with—college presidents, deans, professors, soldiers, police officers—as evil. Filled with a self-vindicating sense of their superiority, they believed they had a right to take matters into their own hands. Some of the aftereffects of that pervasive ugliness and divisiveness, the sheer incivility and know-nothingism of it, are with us still.

Allan Bloom's *The Closing of the American Mind* is labeled by reviewer R. D. Pohl as the most uncanny literary phenomenon of the last decade, "a severe and decidedly highbrow critique of the contemporary state of higher education and intellectual life in the United States. . . . Observers from the political left have almost uniformly panned the book as an anti-democratic, reactionary argument in defense of educational elitism and plutocracy," notes Pohl (1988). "Commentators on the right generally accept Bloom's diagnoses of moral relativism, the politicization of the social sciences and the humanities, and the capitulation of moral authority on college campuses by faculty and administrators during the 1960s as the principal factors underlying the precipitous decline in the quality of higher education in America over the past two decades," Pohl concludes.

Bloom blames presidents and other administrators for abdicating leadership roles and charges faculty members with individually and collectively jumping ship in the sixties. Singled out are his colleagues in the humanities, "who pusillanimously surrendered to the most radical students. At many universities professors all but abandoned the old learning in order to embrace trendy new courses on Black Studies, Women's Studies, and Peace Studies." As Bloom (1987) puts it, "Humanists ran like lemmings into the sea, thinking they would refresh and revitalize themselves in it. They drowned" (p. 353).

Bloom charges that universities have continued to fail in their essential mission ever since that period and are unable to imbue students with a clear idea of what an educated human being is. "Even the greatest of our universities cannot generate a modest program of general education for undergraduate students," he maintains (p. 22). Bloom suggests that we may never fully recover from mistakes of the sixties and doubts if we can recapture an atmosphere in which serious teaching is really possible. He points out that the university epitomizes the very spirit of free inquiry, which in turn is at the root of a free society, concluding that "a crisis in the university, the home of reason, is perhaps the profoundest crisis" for a modern democratic nation.

Seymour Lipset (1989) observes that the special international role of students in fostering rebellion and radical politics, both of the left and right, is an old and continuing story. Historians of youth movements, he explains, note similarities in expressive style, romanticism, and idealism that have occurred among groups that vary considerably in their social and political views. Some psychologists see a special contemporary disposition toward excessive anxiety and commitment in the strains of adolescence, a period that in modern society prolongs education and career preparation into their twenties for college students.

Sociologists explain that youth, and students in particular, are marginal people, Lipset continues. "They are in transition between having been dependent on their families for income, status, and various forms of security and protection, and taking up their own role in jobs and families. . . . As compared to other groups, students simply have fewer responsibilities in the form of obligations to families and jobs. Thus, punitive sanctions against activism are less likely to affect students than those with greater responsibility to others."

College protest movements are not historically unique. Outbursts vary in form, purpose, and number of protesters, but generally a portion of the student body periodically engages in group actions that make matters uncomfortable for administrators, faculty members, alumni, the general public —and fellow students. Causes of unrest today do not differ basically from what caused it in the past, although youthful participants often view their roles as never previously played by anyone else. Reasons for dissent are so varied and numerous, however, it is surprising how well higher education has survived.

Dissent at universities can be traced to "privileges" enjoyed by students in medieval society. "In his famous document of 1231 Pope Gregory IX listed reasons why students might suspend lectures and impose a right to strike. These included refusal of the right to fix ceiling prices for lodgings, an injury or mutilation of a student for which suitable satisfaction had not been given within 15 days, and the unlawful imprisonment of a student. Concluding his caveat, the Pope passed along the following advice: 'Unless the injury ceases when you remonstrate, you may, if you judge it wise, suspend your lectures immediately' " (*California Monthly* 1965).

Dissent also flourished in colonial days when Harvard students expressed dissatisfaction with Nathaniel Eaton's discipline and his wife's cooking, which consisted of "mouldy bread, spoiled beef, and sour beer—when there was beer" (Morison 1970, p. 30). Higher education in colonial America was designed primarily for the upper class, and students—generally only fourteen or fifteen years old—attended religiously oriented institutions that were dedicated entirely to moral values. *In loco parentis* was at full strength—and adolescent rebellions pepper the annals of early American colleges. Strikes and riots were common, and students sometimes fought back when punishment was attempted. Administrators followed the pattern of English schools where corporal punishment was the rule. In England hired bullies often did the beatings, but in America such pummeling generally fell to the president, usually a minister, in the church-sponsored institutions. The pattern of religious influences and strict monastic discipline marked college life up to the Civil War.

Violence was prevalent in student protests during the early nineteenth century, ranging from destruction of property at Princeton to the shooting death of a professor by a student at the University of Virginia. By the middle of the century college students, although older than their colonial counterparts, still represented a small minority from upper-class families.

Impelled by an instinct for a participatory role with adults, students tolerated few restrictions on their own lifestyles. Faculty and administrators, lacking the ability to govern in such areas as dress and sleeping hours, slowly granted many requests after riotous student protests. Poor food, inadequate housing, and incompetent faculty were popular targets of protesters.

According to W. H. Cowley (1949), Princeton University students dynamited Nassau Hall three times in the 1850s; during the same period Yale students set fire to the college coal pile each spring and hurled glowing embers into the rooms of unpopular professors. Cowley also refers to a "horning" tradition at Dartmouth, which involved relays of students blowing tin horns night and day under the windows of their most detested faculty. "Thus did students respond to the paternalism of the old-time college and to the bad instruction to which they were subjected," Cowley explains (p. 20).

By the 1920s student criticism began to include charges that the curriculum was not relevant to social issues, report Margolda and Margolda (1988). Students questioned the role of higher education in society and became concerned about academic freedom. The tenor of campus life changed significantly in the shadow of the major economic depression, and increasing opposition to the threat of another world war resulted in the peace strikes of the 1930s. Many colleges remained cloistered, but others produced enthusiastic activists. Pacifists fought with ROTC members and formed organizations such as the Future Gold Star Mothers of America.

Protests and campus strikes against "War and Fascism" were periodically mounted throughout the 1930s. "There is no question that more students were involved in activism as a percentage of the student population than at any other time in American history, including the 1960s," maintains Philip G. Altbach (1974, p. 102). The widespread nature of antiwar sentiment allowed a temporary alliance of numerous political groups into organizations like the American Student Union, increasing the numbers of students involved in campus unrest. Margolda and Margolda (1988) note, however, that a divisive pattern of different political ideologies—which would be repeated in the 1960s—led to splits among the various student groups. By the time America entered the war in late 1941 the peace movement was near collapse.

During and immediately following World War II, campuses were generally quiet everywhere. Enthusiasm for demonstrations was temporarily inhibited as higher education fell under the influence of returning war veterans. The 1950s produced much to be concerned about, including McCarthyism, but students of that decade are remembered as "The Silent Generation." Thoughtful elders condemned them for inactivity and complacency, but within a few years the same critics would complain that too many college youth were overly preoccupied with social issues. (All was not lost during the fifties. Near the end of that decade large numbers of male students at most large universities, including the University of Buffalo, energetically engaged in massive crowd behavior by storming women's dormitories as participants in "panty raids.")

In the late 1950s and early 1960s, student activism was rekindled with civil rights as the initial impetus for renewed protest. Escalation of the Cold War and nuclear-weapons testing revived antiwar sentiment and restimulated the peace movement. Disorder began in the summer of 1964, six months after President Kennedy's assassination. Sit-ins and demonstrations in the fall of 1964 marked the beginning of a new period of nationwide student action. Margolda and Margolda (1988) identify four intertwined themes that impacted collectively on higher education and characterized activism of the 1960s: civil rights, civil liberties, the peace movement, and the quality of student life.

"Oh, How I Miss the Revolution," bemoans Benjamin J. Stein (1988): "It meant a great many things that now sound silly and even embarrassing. It meant well-to-do white kids masquerading as radicals. It meant pretending to be risking something in a completely risk-free environment. It meant all of the exhilaration of danger without the danger. I want the Revolution back. I don't know why it ever left, but it's time to have it back."

His major theme is understandable: "We have hundreds of thousands of homeless. We have a third world nation inside America, growing radically poorer, more violent, and more helpless as the rest of America gets the BMW's. We have one-fourth of America's children living in single-parent homes. We have a virus as frightening as any illness has ever been. Where's the Revolution? Where is the music in the cafes at night and the Revolution in the air? Where is the whole idea that life should be lived together?" Stein accurately identifies current problems, but radical activists of yesteryear were a divided minority, unable—because of methodolgy and lack of any real program—to capture permanent support from the mainstream population.

Stein's column inspired reactions, two of which illustrate the polarization of the period and the divisions that still exist today. Pat Taub (1988) from Syracuse announces that "Every inch of me resonated with Benjamin Stein's Op-Ed article. How I miss the revolution, too. I marched over and over for peace and women's rights and proudly became a founder of Students for a Democratic Society at George Washington University. I was more alive than at any other time of my life. Benjamin Stein, you are not alone. I hunger for that era as much as you. Here's to a generation of newly respectable revolutionaries in their forties longing to march again." Nostalgic, subjective recollections about the 1960s can be reinforced by the optimism of memory, which makes keeping that unique period of mass radicalization in perspective difficult.

Another reaction to Stein's article comes from Ruth Thompson (1988) of Berkeley, California:

> Just as Mr. Stein is now 43 years old, so was I 43 years old 20 years ago at the time of the "revolution." As a university faculty member I stood helplessly by watching as affluent students indulged themselves in an upper-middle-class orgy, which would have been amusing except for its disastrous aftereffects.
>
> They have to their credit the selection of Richard M. Nixon as President of the United States, a Nixon who said, "Give me another Columbia, and I don't care who the Democrats nominate for President." It is they who gave a political start to Ronald Reagan and his henchman, Edward Meese 3d, for without the riots at Berkeley Ronald Reagan would never have become President. I watched the "revolutionists" try to tear apart the fabric of our greatest universities, which, next to the Constitution, do most to protect intellectual freedom.

Simultaneously conservative and progressive, universities transmit a heritage and produce ideas that influence social growth and alter society. Struggling to resolve old problems, scholars are constantly beset by new ones. Different ways of thinking, coupled with the inquiring nature of higher education, sometimes provoke challenges to strongly held beliefs and to the opinions of contiguous, outside communities.

Universities are typically located in tranquil, parklike settings where courtyards and stately trees are populated by birds, chipmunks, squirrels, and people. These centers of independent thought and academic prestige are usually sheltered in confusing combinations of futuristic and hallowed ivy-covered buildings. As transplanted urban suburbia, colleges and universities reflect, at least outwardly, unique values and a vision of "the good life" to which many Americans aspire. Theoretically emerging from such places is an informed citizenry that has been exposed to knowledge on which to base wise decisions.

Many nonacademics expect too much from the community's best minds being concentrated daily within a small geographically bounded area. People are disappointed by learned professors who are as unable as local and national leaders to resolve intractable problems of racism, poverty, unemployment, corruption, illiteracy, health, economic depression, the environment, crime, world conflict, and the continued deprivation of human rights in the United States and around the world.

Much public confusion exists about the nature and functions of universities. Academics and laymen live in different settings, think differently, speak differently, and react differently to given situations. Parents of students, confused by youthful lifestyles and countercultures, often expect educational institutions to discipline offspring whom they cannot themselves control. Some politicians and their constituents, deploring "permissiveness," join in moralizing about lifestyles of college youth.

Moving uneasily among those who teach and those being taught are administrators, charged with protecting and maintaining the institution's educational purposes. They must lead and follow, teach and be taught, and frequently try to keep the peace, especially when the university is severely threatened by polarized internal or unsympathetic external forces.

The University of Buffalo began as a private institution in 1846. UB is now the most comprehensive research unit within SUNY (the State University of New York), which is the largest university system in the world. Our nation's thirteenth president, Millard Fillmore, for nearly thirty years until his death in 1874, was the first chancellor of the privately endowed institution. It began as a medical school in a downtown building with a faculty of six men. Pharmacy was added in 1886, followed by Law in 1891, Dentistry in 1892, the College of Arts and Sciences in 1919, Business Administration in 1927, a Graduate School of Arts and Sciences in 1939, Nursing in 1940, and Engineering in 1948.

University units were scattered throughout the city until 1909 when a 150-acre site of the Erie County Almshouse and Hospital at the extreme northern edge of the city was acquired. Now known as the Main Street or South Campus, all of the action during the 1960s took place there. After merging with SUNY late in 1962, enrollment at UB mushroomed. In 1968 ground was broken for the present North Campus, a 1,500-acre plot of land in suburban Amherst, three miles north of the original Main Street location.

As the 1960s began there were no indications that higher education would soon be in turmoil. William Manchester (1973) notes that Clark Kerr, newly installed as the president of the University of California at Berkeley, "took a close look at college students in 1959 and said, 'The employers will love this generation. . . . They are going to be easy to handle. There aren't going to be any riots' " (p. 847).

In the May 16, 1959, issue of *The Nation* the editor acknowledged the standard generalization that "the present generation—youth in college and just graduated—has been called apathetic, silent, conformists, indifferent, confused" (p. 440). Another sign of the times was the relative ease with which President Harold M. Stokes of Queens University calmly and single-handedly vetoed a speaking invitation his students had extended to Benjamin Davis, Secretary of the U.S. Communist Party. "The notion that colleges are forums from which everyone has a 'right' to advance his ideas is, in my judgment, questionable on both practical and intellectual grounds," Dr. Stokes said in a press release that appeared in *The Buffalo Evening News* (1961).

In an attempt "to explore some urgent questions which have too long been evaded," a special October 1961 issue of *Harper's Magazine,* titled "The College Scene," was devoted entirely to higher education. The lead article by Christopher Jencks (1961) identifies the same college and university concerns that prevail today: the need for better teaching, curricular innovation, the serious decline of general education, the alarming drop-out rate, "half educated undergraduates," and the lack of incentives for good teaching. Some things never change.

What follows centers around how beleaguered administrators—frequently the only members of the university family remaining on duty at besieged institutions during the often dangerous sixties—tried to preserve ongoing educational processes. Similar problems plagued college and university adminstrators throughout higher education. They tried to cope, not always successfully, with disruption, mass radicalization, political cant, hostile subpublics—all threats to traditional education.

This reconstruction of events at the State University of New York at Buffalo during the 1960s discusses student activism and the antiwar movement, protest tactics and strategies, faculty and administrative responses to dissent and disruption, myths and misperceptions about campus unrest, the polarization of campus constituencies, faculty/administrative/student leadership problems, the impact of dissent on politicians and outside publics, internal and external threats to academic freedom, the role and influence of law enforcement personnel, the power of the press, and underlying causes of student discontent.

References

Altbach, Philip G. (1974). *Student Politics in America: A Historical Analysis.* (New York: McGraw-Hill).

Bishop, Katherine. (1989). "From the Inside Out: The 60s Legacy," *Education Life, New York Times.* January 8.

Bloom, Allan. (1987). *The Closing of the American Mind: How Higher Education Has Failed Democracy and Impoverished the Souls of Today's Students.* (New York: Simon and Schuster).

Buffalo Evening News. (1961). "College Head Explains Killing of Speaking Bid to U.S. Red," November 16.

California Monthly. (1965). "A Season of Discontent," February.

Cowley, W. H. (1949). "Some History and a Venture in Prophecy," *Trends in Student Personnel Work,* E. G. Williamson, ed. (Minneapolis: University of Minnesota Press).

Jencks, Christopher. (1961). "The Next Thirty Years in the Colleges," *Harper's Magazine,* October.

Johnson, Haynes. (1988). "Incivility of '60s Rears Its Ugly Head," *The Buffalo News,* May 26.

Lipset, Seymour. (1989). "Chinese Youth Are New Chapter in an Old Story," *The Buffalo News,* June 4.

Manchester, William. (1973). *The Glory and the Dream: A Narrative History of America, 1932–1972.* (New York: Little, Brown and Company).

Margolda, Marcia B. Baxter, and Margolda, Peter M. (1988). "Student Activism: A Historical Perspective," *Student Affairs and Campus Dissent: Reflection of the Past and Challenge for the Future,* Keith M. Miser, ed., NASPA Monograph Series, Volume 8, March. Reprinted by permission of the National Association of Student Personnel Administrators.

Morison, Samuel Eliot. (1970). *The Intellectual Life of Colonial New England.* (New York: New York University Press).

The Nation. (1959). Editor's note, "Campus Report No. 3, Tension Beneath Apathy," May 16.

Pohl, R. D. (1988). "Some Further Thoughts on Closing of Minds," *The Buffalo News,* July 3.

Stein, Benjamin J. (1988). "Oh, How I Miss the Revolution," Op-Ed, *New York Times,* April 4.

Taub, Pat. (1988). Letters, *New York Times,* April 17.

Thompson, Ruth. (1988). Letters, *New York Times,* April 17.

Wechsler, James A. (1973). *Revolt on the Campus,* Covice and Friede, New York, 1935; reissued in 1973 (Seattle: University of Washington Press, pp. 115, 387–88, 171).

Yardley, Jonathan. (1988). "Revival of Interest in the 60s Produces a Lot of 'Baloney,' " *The Buffalo News,* from *The Washington Post,* July 26.

CHAPTER I

Academic Freedom—A University's Legacy

I foresee the coming of a storm perhaps more severe than any to which our institutions have been subjected for years. The forces bent on challenging the intellectual integrity of colleges and universities are gathering.

—Samuel P. Capen, Chancellor,
The University of Buffalo, 1922–1950

One common misperception about the formerly private University of Buffalo is that it was a conservative institution that catered exclusively to the children of the area's urban blue collar workers until officially adopted by the SUNY system late in 1962. Yet, there were few other private or public universities of larger or comparable size that nurtured and as vigorously defended as strong a tradition of academic freedom.

Uninformed outside observers consistently ignore UB's history, maintaining that its liberal reputation developed only after the school became part of SUNY and students from areas other than Western New York enrolled in ever-increasing number. Mark Goldman (1983) in *High Hopes: The Rise and Decline of Buffalo* conjures up a unique view of UB and directly attributes the university's activist tendencies to its absorption into Governor Rockefeller's massive state system.

Goldman overlooks the leanings of a strong, liberally oriented faculty, attracted by Chancellor Samuel P. Capen, who was far ahead of his academic peers in understanding and espousing the principle of academic freedom. Goldman incompletely describes the privately endowed University of Buffalo as "a place that could be trusted to educate the children of the city's upwardly mobile middle class without shaking them up too much" (p. 248), counted on to reinforce the values and expectations of parents who sent their children there. This assessment is incorrect.

"An increased number of New York Jews," Goldman continues, "now poured into Buffalo, bringing with them the excitement, color, and creative dynamism of their culture and their city" (pp. 252–3). The truth is that prior to the merger approximately one-fourth of UB undergraduates—including the influx of a large contingent from "The City" that coincided with a premerger residence hall building program—were Jewish. (In those days religious preference cards were routinely filled out during registration.) Sadly, many members of the community—despite Buffalo's own proportionately large and influential Jewish population—openly expressed anti-Semitic feelings about "Jew B" long before the merger with State University of New York.

Buffalo has always had a strong Catholic population base of around 50 percent, and university attendance reflected a similar percentage of Catholic undergraduates. However, many parish priests and nuns strongly advised parents of local high-school graduates, for more than religious reasons, against sending their son or daughter to UB. They recommended instead, as a safer alternative, the area's small Catholic colleges.

The university's long tradition of academic freedom is emphasized by Professor Emeritus Henry T. E. Perry (1962) in an issue of the *Buffalo Alumnus,* which was devoted almost exclusvely to a defense of that concept. Controversy, therefore, was a firmly established institutional hallmark. Perry recalls "the intense opposition that was often aroused by the ideas of members of the university faculty, so much so that at one time it was considered by the community at large to be composed solely of atheists, communists, and advocates of free love."

The university's proud heritage of the often misunderstood principle of academic freedom was consistently and unequivocally defended by Samuel P. Capen during his twenty-eight years as chancellor. It remained his chief preoccupation until he died. "When Samuel Paul Capen assumed the chancellorship in 1922 he made academic freedom one of the chief planks in his platform," Perry writes. Capen fervently believed that "all conclusions must be heard if one is to approximate the truth, but truth is not concerned with perpetuating the status quo, whether in church or state; rather, it must push forward ruthlessly to its end, without regard for existing institutions or vested interests." It was a legacy the university would have to keep in mind during its subsequent and inevitably difficult transition into a public institution.

In his 1950 baccalaureate address Capen summarized his ideas about the commitment of a university to inquiry and intellectual creation. "It is and must be wholly free to prosecute the search for truth unhampered from without and from within. . . . Those who pursue the truth under its sponsorship, whether they be teachers or students, must not live in fear of discipline would they chance to offend some institutional official or even an influential segment of the general public" (Perry 1962).

Perry recalled one occasion when the university council asked the chancellor to dismiss an especially recalcitrant and controversial faculty member. "Dr. Capen replied, 'Of course I shall dismiss Mr. X if you so instruct me, but you must realize that if I do so, I must at the same time hand in my resignation from the chancellorship.' " How often would trustees encounter this presidential response today?

Capen left a precious legacy to faculty and students with the hope that freedom would not become a license. Responsibility is the correlate of academic freedom. There is no clearer statement about academic freedom for faculty and students than Capen's own words:

> Acceptance by an institution of the principle of academic freedom implies that teachers in that institution are free to investigate any subject no matter how much it may be hedged about by taboos; that they are free to make known the results of their investigation, and their reflection by word of mouth or in writing, before their classes or elsewhere; that they are free to differ with their colleagues and to present the ground of their difference in their classes or elsewhere; that they are free as citizens to take part in any public controversy outside the institution; that no repressive measure, direct or indirect, will be applied to them no matter how unpopular they may become through opposing powerful interests or jostling established prejudices, and no matter how mistaken they may appear to be in the eyes of members and friends of the institution; that their continuance in office will be in all instances governed by the prevailing rules of tenure and that their academic advancement will be dependent on their scientific competence and will be in no wise affected by the popularity or unpopularity of their opinions or utterances. . . .
>
> That students in the institution are free, insofar as the requirements of the several curricula permits, to inquire into any subject that interests them, to organize discussion groups, or study clubs for the consideration of any subject, and to invite to address them any speaker they choose; that censorship of student publications shall be based on precisely the same grounds and shall extend no further than that exercised by the United States Postal authorities. . . .
>
> Indeed the consistent defense of academic freedom is a costly business. Is it worth the price? . . . Yes, it is worth the price, any price. Higher institutions are by definition committed to the search for truth and to the dissemination of the results of the search. The question is nearly always futile if the inquiry is circumscribed in advance. The search for truth inevitably leads one far from his starting point. In the course of it the preconceptions with which the investigator begins his task generally have to be modified or abandoned. The truth when found—if it concerns the cherished beliefs and habits of society—is almost certain to be unpalatable. . . . (Capen 1953, pp. 25–28).

Since academic freedom was deeply rooted at UB, the Student Senate Convocation Committee and its adviser, the respected and conservative chair of the department of History and Government, Professor John T. Horton, anticipated little trouble when the committee decided in November 1961— well before the merger with SUNY—to invite five speakers to lecture in a 1962 series titled, "A Political Spectrum of a Contemporary World." The purpose (according to Perry, who quotes Richard Erb, President of the Student

Association, who later served in Washington with the Nixon administration and is now with the International Monetary Fund) was "to offer students the opportunity to examine and compare various political ideologies." The speakers, scheduled between September 26 and October 31, were selected after consultation with faculty members to lecture on "The Role of the State." Included were Sir Oswald Mosley, fascism; Russell Kirk, conservatism; Senator Eugene J. McCarthy, liberalism; Norman Thomas, socialism; and Dr. Herbert Aptheker, communism.

After each lecture a faculty-student panel was to question the speaker. Reactions would then be solicited from the audience, which was initially limited to students and faculty. A suggestion to hold individual press conferences was rejected to avoid any "circus atmosphere."

In October 1961, the same Convocations Committee had invited the controversial president of the International Brotherhood of Teamsters, James R. Hoffa, to speak on campus. Although Hoffa eventually cancelled his scheduled visit because he "was heavily engaged in negotiations," student Convocation Committee chairman Elmer Bertsch (1961) remembers the administration's revealing response when the Student Senate requested approval of the invitation. "This is a matter to be decided by the students," Vice Chancellor Claude E. Puffer said. "However, one result may be that several hundred students will decide to join the Teamsters Union," he added.

Immediately following the news release announcing the program, however, a furor erupted over the scheduled visits of Sir Oswald Mosley and Dr. Aptheker. Despite "academic freedom" and ACLU guidelines, neither speaker would then have been invited or permitted to appear at an overwhelming majority of institutions of higher learning. This conclusion was confirmed in an extensive 1965 research study, "The Role of the President in the Desirable Treatment of Academic Freedom for Students," by John L. Cowan and E. G. Williamson at the University of Minnesota, which included responses from 757 college presidents.

The Cowan-Williamson question concerning campus speakers was the most specific of all the questionnaire items, listing the names and identities of seventeen persons, each of whom had been the cause of controversy on some campuses. Four of the listed speakers—George Lincoln Rockwell, Sir Oswald Mosley, Daniel Rubin, and Malcolm X (who had spoken twice at the pre-merger UB campus and had an even greater impact proportionately when compared with today's similarly controversial Islam leader Louis B. Farrakhan)—"represent the extremes that are generally considered outside the limits of acceptable student academic freedom. An invitation to any one of them to address campus audiences is almost certain to involve the institution in a storm of protest, and we may safely say that students who invite any of these speakers are testing the limits of their freedom on even the most open campuses. Yet, students do sometimes invite them to speak and 17 percent would grant permission for all of them to speak according to the presidents" (only 19 percent would have allowed Hoffa to speak on campus) (Cowan and Williamson 1965). The report strongly hints at the possibility of student irresponsibility: "We must give attention to the reality of the psychology of the collegiate adolescent, who is revolting against arbitrary symbols. Sometimes the form of revolt results from an overgeneralization of his resentment of parents or sometimes it originates in riot 'just for the hell of it' or even because it is springtime." British fascist Sir Oswald Mosley's appearance on September 26, 1962, at the University of Buffalo almost resulted in a full-scale riot.

After a distinguished career during World War I in government and with the British Flying Corps, Sir Oswald left the Labour Party in 1931 to lead the British Union of Fascists, also called the Blackshirts. He was held in custody by the government for the duration of World War II. Now in his sixties, he was still actively promoting fascism.

Although UB was still a private institution, the Buffalo area's powerful state senator, the late Walter J. Mahoney (1962), publicly pledged that he "would fight to keep any person who advocated the overthrow of the government from speaking at state supported schools." Since delicate UB-SUNY merger negotiations were just underway, his implication was clear. Chancellor from 1954 to 1966 Clifford C. Furnas (1964) refused to cancel the speech, however, responding that "the basic purpose of a university—service in the public interest through research and teaching—is the same whatever the source of income. The greatest universities of the nation are those that have stated and maintained the right to deal with controversial issues in an objective manner. The list of those greatest institutions includes several state universities and several private ones." He informed the senator that "We all realize that the true strength of America lies in the freedom which we still have to exchange ideas and to analyze different points of view, however unpopular they may be in a particular time or place. If we lose that ability and privilege, then of course we are well down the path to tyranny. I am certain that we all agree that this must be avoided at all costs."

As Sir Oswald's appearance grew near, tension rose in the community, ranging from deeply concerned conservative Jewish groups to such far left organizations as YAWF (Youth Against War and Fascism). UB students discussed whether they should stage a walkout, remain completely silent, turn their chairs around and listen backwards, or not show up at all. The inevitable letters appeared in the local press with increasing frequency; almost all protested the speaker's appearance and called on the administration to revoke the invitation.

Professor Horton's hate mail was matched by negative press coverage as far away as New York City. His name was cast in headlines by columnist Victor Riesel (1962) in *The New York Daily Mirror*. After writing about Mosley's role as a fascist leader in London, where he pushed his "national union" and "Black Shirt" movements, Riesel castigates Horton as an "objective little man":

I would like to take on Prof. Dr. Horton who believes it "liberal" to hear the views of one who has seared the souls of many. If this be free speech, to hell with it. Listen, Dr. Horton, what do you know of Sir Oswald? . . .

Now along comes Dr. Horton and a student who was yet to be born when Hitler and Goering and Goebbels and Himmler and Streicher and Rosenberg were putting pins into the map for the routing of death trains. And the Professor and the students invite the Black Shirt over two days before the high holidays. This is not liberalism. This is dilettantism. If Professor Horton doesn't want to be beastly to the Black Shirtist let him do it privately and not where the visage of Mosley brings back the memory of swastikas.

For several weeks preceding Sir Oswald's highly publicized visit UB had been subjected to daily bomb scares and anonymous messages threatening his life. Two hours before his speech in the university's jammed multipurpose room in Norton Union, an estimated 1,500 to 2,000 angry demonstrators—many representing the area's Jewish community—were already on campus, milling around Norton Hall and Lockwood Library.

Statements on carefully prepared signs read "Stop Mosley," "Smash Fascism," "Go Home, Nazi," "Fascism Means Genocide," and "OH! GOD, help us destroy people like MOSLEY." A dummy representing Sir Oswald was hanged in effigy from a pole in front of Norton.

My staff and I were catapulted into leadership roles. An inbred and then ineffective campus security was not a significant force at this time, and we were wary about calling in uniformed Buffalo police. We were expected to insure the peace without advice or counsel from the president's office.

The original intent to limit the audience exclusively to students and faculty was not fulfilled. Members of one outside group presented counterfeit tickets at the door. Although these were quickly identified through our screening techniques, some legitimate ticketholders were deprived of their seats. Other outsiders flashed $5 and $10 bills in attempts to purchase tickets from incoming faculty and students. For sufficient manpower to contain the situation, we enlisted student officer cadets from the Air Science Department and drew on the membership of a male service fraternity (Alpha Phi Omega). Staff and faculty volunteers filled in the gaps. We assigned one person to sit unobtrusively behind a wheelchair-bound student, with instructions to insure her safety in the event of a riot. Although it was late September we turned water sprinklers on full force to discourage curious onlookers from climbing up to peer in through the several banks of large bay windows that flanked the lecture room. All persons attending were required to check topcoats and briefcases.

Two Buffalo plainclothes police officers, two students, and I guided our despised guest speaker safely from Harriman Hall—along a circuitous, undisclosed route—to the lecture room. Not one word was spoken by any member of our tight little group as we walked through a tunnel connecting Harriman and the Union, edged past startled food-service employees in the narrow confines of the cafeteria food-preparation area, and rode up one flight in a freight elevator that resembled a padded cell. As we moved briskly over a series of wooden, concrete, corrugated iron, and marble floorways, I wondered what the tall man in a dark suit was thinking about.

Sir Oswald was greeted by boos and hissing when he entered the room. The press reported that he concentrated on how Great Britain should improve economic relationships with the United States and said nothing about the virtues of fascism. (I concentrated on the audience and do not recall anything he said.) During the question-and-answer period the atmosphere heated up. After one tense moment, when shouts of "Liar!", "Nazi!", and "Idiot!" arose from members of the audience, one faculty panel-member angrily left the room in protest against such outbursts.

Mosley managed to complete his presentation and no serious incidents developed, but his visit deeply offended Buffalo's Jewish community, and UB's revered historian Selig Adler reported that for some time overt hostility was directed at him by members of his own temple. Academic freedom can exact unforeseen costs.

We breathed a collective sigh of relief when the car carrying our speaker left the campus for the airport and his return flight to London. "University officials would comment only that Sir Oswald 'is out of our jurisdiction now," Frank Buell (1962) reported in the September 27 *Courier-Express*.

A *Buffalo Evening News* (1962a) editorial noted that "UB, having taken in stride the views of sundry other extremists over the years, has now heard from an avowed English fascist. By all indications the city and the university will survive this ordeal too—although this particular character's contribution to the community may now be seen (even by the most gullible freshman we would hope) to have been less than nil. . . .

"Just as we hope no UB student is so naive that he will expect—now that he has 'heard all about fascism' from Mosley—to learn anything about communism from a spokesman at the other end of this series."

Favorable editorial comment about how the event was conducted appeared in Buffalo and New York papers. Dr. Thomas H. Hamilton, then Chancellor of SUNY, publicly supported the still private university.

The series continued quietly for several weeks, until shortly before the scheduled appearance of the final speaker, Dr. Herbert Aptheker. UB's merger with SUNY was now legally assured when Senator Mahoney, the temporary president and majority leader of the New York State Senate, wrote the trustees. Referring to Mosley and Aptheker as "political activists rather than political scientists," he warned that Aptheker's appearance "could well lead to outbreaks of violence. Only the good sense of the people of Buffalo prevented such violence when Mosley appeared. It may be unwise, unfair, and unrealistic to expect that such good sense and tolerance can again be maintained without incident" (Mahoney 1962).

Law professor William Van Alstyne (1962) maintained that "discrimination against speakers because of their beliefs or associations constitutes an abridgement of freedom of speech provided under the First and Fourteenth Amendments to the Constitution" and that "with respect to speakers of a political persuasion, the Constitution permits a state to ban only those who would exhort the audience to unlawful actions and even then it needs to be reasonably clear that they will succeed in their attempts if allowed to appear."

In his formal reply to Senator Mahoney, Trustee Chairman Frank C. Moore (1962) noted that U.S. Supreme Court decisions had established that "mere membership in the Communist Party is not proof that a person advocates the overthrow of the government by force or violence." The fifteen trustees, he continued, "are no less conscious of their obligation to safeguard our precious American heritage without infringing upon the rights of a university to free and unhampered inquiry. . . . We also have confidence that our students . . . can listen, question, and cope with the proponents of all political philosophies, separate the truth from fallacy, and through knowledge itself based on independent inquiry adhere to and even more effectively support the fundamental beliefs which are basic to a strong America."

Two hours prior to the Aptheker lecture on October 31 a temporary order banning his appearance was brought against the trustees by William E. Egan, a Democratic candidate for Congress from a newly established district in northeastern New York. Efforts failed to have the order lifted immediately.

State Supreme Court Justice Russell G. Hunt, writes Perry (1962), held that Senator Mahoney "as a prominent legislator" was "entitled through his standing in the legislature to a great deal more consideration than the Board has given his request." Judge Hunt also quoted Senator Mahoney's public letter to the chairman of the governing board of the University of Buffalo, which held that "It is the established policy of our government . . . that membership in the Communist Party U.S.A. automatically entails advocacy of the overthrow of our government by force and violence."

Egan's attorney, who argued for the injunction, informed the court that Dr. Aptheker required a police escort to reach the university safely after his arrival that morning in Buffalo, according to *The Buffalo Evening News* (1962b), which also reported the opposite: " 'Aptheker arrived on the campus alone,' said Lt. Winthrop H. Phelps, head of the police subversive squad. 'No one even recognized him. He had to ask for directions to the student union.' " A public address announcement in Norton Hall at 2:45 P.M. informed the quietly waiting audience that the Aptheker talk had been postponed, and that they should hold on to their tickets. Dr. Furnas expressed extreme disappointment and Mr. Moore pledged to continue to defend the lawful freedom of inqiury.

The postponement prompted an even greater flood of letters to the local press, 90 percent in support of the ban. Examples from *The Courier-Express* (1962) follow:

In ignoring Senator Walter Mahoney's protests, the Board of Trustees of the State University was ignoring the protests of the majority of taxpayers of New York. It seems to me that too much money has gone into building ivory towers. . . . Western New Yorkers are fortunate in having public servants of such stature as Senator Mahoney, and also Reps. Miller (the later vice-presidential candidate on the Goldwater ticket who had rejected an invitation to be one of the speakers in the series), and Pillion.

Does anyone in possession of the smallest grain of common sense wish to expose vulnerable youth to such vermin? . . . Yes, my dear, gullible citizens, you may practice your freedom of speech. However, please do so on your own time. Do not, under cover of democracy, expose our students to possible contamination.

Impressionable youth are not sufficiently endowed to distinguish truth from falsehood and propaganda from information.

It ought to be remembered that the primary purpose of students coming to and living at the university is to learn and study rather than invoke nonexisting rights.

Many college and university graduates wonder why the student organization invited Sir Mosley and Dr. Aptheker. . . . Learn all you can about the Nazis and Communists but please do not insist that we have one of these outlaws appear personally.

My definition of academic freedom: letting our enemies use our constitutional rights to destroy our Constitution.

Rather ironic: a Communist is allowed on the campus of a secular institution. A prayer is not. Senator Mahoney is right. Our college students cannot combat an experienced teacher or a skilled propagandist. Our campuses allow falsehoods to be preached. These untruths are being thrown at minds which cannot distinguish a "non-sequitur" from an undistributed middle. A falsehood can get on campus. A prayer cannot.

Does it really make sense, by admitting a Communist speaker to the campus, to strengthen the over-all position of the enemy, who is also sworn and dedicated to the overthrow of all existing political, economic, and social institutions not only in the United States, but of all countries where freedom still prevails?

In contrast to the generally negative community reactions, the American Association of University Professors (1962) sent a telegram to Mr. Moore and Chancellor Furnas on November 5 congratulating them on their plans to appeal the ruling, and the local and New York City press praised the university's stand.

Following the Aptheker ban several UB deans and faculty members were asked for their views on academic freedom. Portions of their responses appeared in the *Buffalo Alumnus* (1962) that December. One wonders if faculty members and administrators would be as forthcoming today:

Indeed, the very spirit of democracy may fail unless educational institutions and the academic professions themselves maintain and foster academic freedom (p. 9).

—Dean Milton C. Albrecht (Arts and Sciences)

Although there are people in the society who question the right of an individual or an institution to perpetuate this balance of action, there fortunately is a large number who uphold individuals and institutions in this right. Academic freedom is to the education profession what the Bill of Rights is to emigrants from a closed society (p. 9).

—Dean Robert S. Fisk (School of Education)

The term academic freedom is used today in a larger sense of reference than in my undergraduate days. Most of us thought of it in connection with faculty freedoms. . . . Today we accept the use of the term with reference to the entire academic community: faculty and students (p. 10).

—Professor Harriet F. Montague (Mathematics)

Any idea which purports to solve a problem is fit fodder for the university community. Herein lies the real meaning of academic freedom: The unrestricted privilege of examining, testing, evaluating all such ideas and systems of thought and conducted under the bright light of objective, critical intelligence. This will inevitably mean that certain entrenched interests may be offered and certain legislators become unduly alarmed because they fear "political subverison." . . . It behooves us to allow our students and faculty to examine and test ideas of all sorts and we must stoutly defend this privilege as a free university (pp. 10–11).

—Professor W. Leslie Barnette (Psychology)

In order to assist the progress of a complete educational system, it is the responsibility of all universities to present without bias every aspect of their subject and to be prepared to discuss freely and openly even the most controversial topics (p. 11).

—Professor Peter Hebborn (Medicinal Chemistry)

Freedom of speech . . . is a right accorded to the citizen in simple consequence of his citizenship. . . . The right to freedom is a very general principle blanketing all citizens in a wide sphere of activity.

Academic freedom, on the other hand, is a more particularized right, selectively granted, and having its point of application in a more circumscribed context . . . applying to students and faculty alike. . . .

It should be apparent, that in the episodes surrounding the recent appearance of Sir Oswald Mosley, it was not freedom of speech that was at issue, but academic freedom. The principle at stake was not Mosley's right to speak, but the right of the academic community to hear him as part of a legitimate intellectual pursuit. For that purpose, there needed to be no real interest in the speaker as a particular individual. He was a "specimen" to be examined for what he might reveal about a class of phenomena. . . . Sir Oswald Mosley had no right to speak at this University, but all of us as members of the academic society, did (and do) have a right to hear him speak and query him. . . . This is academic freedom (p. 12).

—Professor Raymond Hunt (Psychology)

"Academic freedom ranks with freedom of speech, freedom of the press, and freedom of worship as an essential characteristic of democratic society," William C. Brickman (1988, p. 532) writes in the *Encyclopedia Americana.* Difficult to define because it rests almost exclusively on traditional long usage, academic freedom is the right of a teacher to teach and of a learner to study without unreasonable restraint or interference. Teachers must be at liberty to pursue scholarly inquiry to any honest conclusion, free to present their findings and judgments about a field of specialization, and free to publish the results of research and reflection so that colleges and the general public can benefit by and criticize their work, Brickman explains.

Following World War II students in the United States and various countries in Europe and Latin America began to demand a much larger share in making and administering university rules and in planning the curriculum. Such student movements greatly enlarged the meaning of student academic freedom. "For the student, academic freedom includes the right to have honest instruction, the right to form his own conclusions on the basis of his studies, the right to hear and express opinions, and the right to a reasonable voice in deciding what he is to study," Brickman notes.

"What must be remembered," he warns, is that "neither students nor teachers can expect academic freedom to be unlimited. The right to exercise liberty implies the right to use freedom responsibly." There must be differentiation between educators and indoctrinators.

"Freedom to teach does not give a professor a right to present views in such a way as to delude students or colleagues," Brickman concludes. "Freedom without responsibility becomes license and interferes with the freedom of others."

Freedom of speech is enshrined in the Bill of Rights, but academic freedom is defined in various ways through by-laws of many universities. Definitions recognize exceptions, including ethical violations like plagiarism or blatantly penalizing students for refusing to agree with a point of view. In a *New York Times* article by Samuel Weiss (1991), reference is made to a definition developed by Dr. Arthur O. Lovejoy, who helped found the American Association of University Professors in 1915. "He said a professor is protected by academic freedom 'unless his methods are found by qualified bodies of his own profession to be clearly incompetent or contrary to professional ethics,' " Weiss reports. "There are grounds for removing even tenured professors: gross neglect of duty, immorality or professional incompetence."

The principle of academic freedom is not a value for which the general public has great enthusiasm or understanding. Test cases usually center around activities that are strongly counter to community attitudes, but freedom does not exist if not protected in such instances. UB Sociologist Lionel Lewis reminds us that, historically, public relations considerations have too often taken precedence over any desires to achieve genuine academic freedom. Lewis (1988) maintains that the cases he studied made all too clear "the limits of academic freedom in a time of national insecurity. Academic administrators may give lip service to academic freedom, but they are not always committed to maintaining the ideal" (p. 5).

The danger to academic freedom is not only from outside interference, but stems from an institutional desire to please, motivated in part by the actual or presumed need of the university to maintain the good opinion of those who support it financially. In the United States neither people nor their institutions like to be out of step with public opinion. Universities remain deeply concerned about their public image, a tendency that may contribute to restrictions and violations of the academic freedom of professors and departments who exercise it to profess views that, however legitimate, may adversely influence "public relations." Reaching out too aggressively for financial support and concentrating too heavily on professional areas may contribute to an atmosphere that further weakens academic freedom.

The most controversial issues are precisely those that should be discussed in a college setting. Understanding the importance of maintaining and protecting this vital principle of academic freedom involves re-educating students, faculty, and the outside world.

UB had drawn sufficient attention to itself so that it was not likely accidental that the Committee on Un-American Activities of the House of Representatives chose to hold hearings—even before Aptheker's return engagment in November was announced—in Buffalo from April 29 to 30, 1964.

By 1960 the House Un-American Activities Committee (HUAC) was the symbol of restraints on free speech and the repressive nature of the 1950s, Altbach (1974) points out. Disruption of an HUAC meeting by student demonstrators in San Francisco was followed by an HUAC-produced film that accused the demonstrators of violence and set the stage for unrest at the University of California-Berkeley campus.

The *Courier-Express* (1964a) charged that "at least three UB faculty members marched in anti-HUAC picket lines, which also included about 100 students." By May 6 the *Buffalo Evening News* (1964a) received so much mail about the hearings (HUAC was "praised in about two-thirds of the letters sent") that space was given only for excerpts, such as "University officials should be more careful of what influences they allow students to be infiltrated with," and "It is deplorable for the University to condone student demonstrations against a Congressional Committee." The full impact of UB's merger with SUNY could hardly have been evidenced after only one year, but a letter in the *News* establishes an underlying tone—especially prevalent during the 1960s—among some community members:

Anyone who saw those picketing children (and let's remember that they ARE just children) must have been struck by their slovenly, unkempt appearance. Girls and boys alike looked as if they hadn't been near soap and water, or a comb, for months. And, like the "educators" under whose influence they have fallen, they never quite made it either. . . . They are looked upon as freaks.

Although inconclusive at best, the hearings produced back-to-back articles in the May 12 *Courier-Express,* headlined "State University Red Hunt Urged" and "Possible Activities by Reds Probed on UB Campus." The first item reported that "Rep. John R. Pillion Monday urged either Gov. Rockefeller or the State Legislature, or both, to investigate the possibility of Communist infiltration of the State University of New York, specifically including the Buffalo branch.

"The Hamburg Republican claimed that testimony produced at the recent Buffalo hearings of the House Un-American Activities Committee revealed a serious and increasing infiltration by Communists in both the faculty and the student body [at UB]." (*Courier-Express* 1964b).

Pillion charged that Communist agitators at the University are victimizing students and exploiting their idealism, their enthusiasm, and their sense of social justice, and raised these questions:

Is there a pipeline for the Communist Party into the faculty?

Why are teachers with uncontradicted pro-Comumnist backgrounds retained on the faculty?

Is there a Communist pipeline for admission to the university?

Are rabble-rousing radicals being improperly allowed to address university groups under the cloak of academic freedom?

The second article included a paragraph stating that "student applicants for admission to State University units are not queried about membership or activities in communist organizations" (*Courier-Express* 1964c).

The specter of HUAC did not easily disappear. Persistent innuendoes and charges caused President Furnas to respond, on May 26, to the newspapers, radios, and TV stations in the Buffalo area. Included was this reminder:

For more than a century, the University of Buffalo as a private institution had a proud heritage of academic freedom. This served as a key to its greatness. This was the legacy of Dr. Samuel Paul Capen, Chancellor of the University for 28 years. Julian Park, University Historian, in his history of Dr. Capen's life, said: ". . . his constant devotion to academic freedom was a shield that hundreds of spears came to be broken against. To his successors it is a precious legacy." The University is proud that this heritage continues under State University. (Furnas 1964)

The Aptheker case was significant as the first legal involvement in the academic freedom issue for SUNY since its founding in 1948. Educational Management Consultant Thomas E. Blackwell (1964), who covered legal stories for *College and University Business,* reported in June that Counsel John C. Crary, Jr., called the SUNY appeal of the ban of primary importance to the state university. His brief included the charge that there had been interference with the constitutional guarantee of free speech, and stated that freedom of intellectual inquiry in a university is vital and essential in a free society. He argued further that freedom of intellectual inquiry in a university is vital to its being and essential to its function in a democratic society.

The State Supreme Court's Appellate Division, third department, unanimously upheld the rights of a Communist Party member to lecture at the State University of Buffalo, Blackwell explained. The five-member appellate court emphasized that the university could explore and expose students to controversial ideas without governmental interference in the name of academic freedom.

"Furthermore," the court added, "membership in the Communist Party does not automatically entail illegal advocacy. . . . There is no contention that Dr. Aptheker advocates, has advocated, or will advocate at the lecture in question, the forcible overthrow of our government as any more than abstract doctrine." Blackwell notes that spokesmen for the state university called the decision "an historic one that protects the principle of freedom of inquiry which is basic to a university's ability to serve mankind" (p. 66).

On June 5 the *News* (1964b) and the *Courier* (1964c) reported the state's highest tribunal ruling that an avowed Communist could lecture at a state university campus. The *News* noted that "Mr. Egan was reversed last December in the Appellate Division and brought the case to the highest court. It is not expected that he will take the matter to the U.S. Supreme Court, though it is always a possibility."

Aptheker returned to the campus to deliver his speech, "Marxism, Its Relevance to the United States Today." An "Extra" edition of *The Midnight Oil* (1964), the university's evening division's weekly newspaper, evaluated the overdue presentation. "The unanimous decision was that his talk was low key and not particularly exciting and there was no evidence of outside protests by those who may have been still opposed to his using the campus." Speaking for the university community, *The Midnight Oil* added the following to summarize the event editorially: "On Friday, November 13th, Herbert Aptheker appeared on campus to deliver a speech which had been two years in suspension. His opposition need not have worried."

During the 1980s small groups of students have deprived their peers of the opportunity and right to judge for themselves an invited guest lecturer's message. Demonstrators have succeeded in silencing such speakers as former United Nations' Chief Delegate Jeane Kirkpatrick at Berkeley, Secretary of

Defense Casper Weinberger at Harvard, and Chief Justice William Rehnquist at Indiana.

John H. Bunzel (1981) points out that those who violated Ms. Kirkpatrick's right to express her views belonged to those on the left who believe that there are times when issues of greater urgency and higher purpose must override concerns about civil liberties.

> The arrogance of the demonstrators—which is always paraded as truth and virtue—is quickly revealed when they explain why they were justified in their obstructionist tactics. "This wasn't a free speech issue." "We were protesting the honor accorded her." Or: "She represented only one point of view. The format should have been a debate." Or, "Since she would provoke a confrontation, she should never have been invited." The "explanations" are not only self-serving, but betray a cynicism about democratic principles that they profess to embrace. It is the kind of sophistry that subverts democracy in the name of democracy.
>
> Freedom of expression is not something to be protested; it is an intellectual necessity. The shouting and sloganeering of self-proclaimed moralists are not substitutes for thought and reflection.
>
> Very simply, the academic community has a special responsibility to expose mindless behavior whenever it is disguised as freedom.

Robert F. Goldberger (1987), provost of Columbia University (one of the nation's foremost academic institutions hurt by the protests of the sixties), is deeply concerned about present activist trends.

During 1987, "in protest against fairness, stupidity, and danger in our society," he notes, "outraged students have raised a number of issues on campuses throughout the country." Yet, "the form of some of these protests is disturbing. It exhibits a narrowness of mind usually associated with totalitarian ideologies of the right or left and . . . undercuts the academic freedom and constitutional protection they would claim to hold dear." Citing current attempts to bar military and CIA recruitment on college campuses, he raises the same question posed throughout higher education two decades ago. "If the military is to be barred," he asks, "what other organizations should be included? And who should decide? After all, there is something among the great variety of potential employers to displease almost everyone. . . .

"Today students and some faculty members seem confused about what a free society and a free university should be. Time and again we have seen instances when speakers have been shouted down and prevented from speaking on campuses. And students have demanded that the university deny the use of its facilities for such speakers," Goldberger concludes.

Similar concerns were expressed during the 1960s, when some radicals imposed their values and self-selected morals on the academic community. Democracy was invoked when it suited them without respecting what it requires. The right to speak is meaningless if no one is willing to listen. If we are unwilling to hear that with which we most violently disagree we are not free at all.

Some administrators and faculty have already reverted to the confusion of the sixties by failing to recognize basic principles. They are succumbing to an unwillingness to stand up for academic freedom, overlooking trends among college youth who verbally (or physically) make it impossible to hear opposing views. William F. Buckley, Jr. (1986) recently invoked Sidney Hook's warning that "a host of speakers think twice about accepting invitations to speak . . . and very successful disruption increases the likelihood of self-censorship on the part of the faculty, not inviting those who may be regarded as objectionable to the farthest left." Or right.

Are academic leaders unprepared to cope with serious episodes of student dissent? How many will recognize the importance of academic freedom when faced by renewed student activism? What will they say if students decide it is not worth their time to learn anything about opinions counter to theirs? How can students intelligently argue their own cause without listening to opposing views?

In 1962 UB had the institutional courage to defend and preserve a vital principle despite powerful political and community opposition. Will the concept of academic freedom that was so severely challenged during the 1960s be less treasured today by administrators and faculty at UB, or elsewhere?

"Will academic adminstrators be able to contend with the forces of social and economic change in society any better than they were able to contend with the winds of political change in the decade after World War II?" Lionel Lewis (1988) asks today. "The evidence," he predicts, "would suggest that there is considerable risk in trusting them" (p. 6).

Lewis is not optimistic about the future and maintains that there were not enough instances after World War II when administrators met their responsibilities and too many instances when they did not. A surprising number, he charges, showed little capacity to stand up to the pressures of the cold war: "Rarely did an administrator explain to the public the risks inherent in any assault on academic freedom, and why it might be necessary to defend it without compromise" (p. 5).

References

American Association of University Professors. (1962). Telegram to Frank Moore and Clifford C. Furnas, November 5.
ACLU. (1961). Pamphlet, "Academic Freedom and Civil Liberties of Students in Colleges and Universities," November.
Altbach, Philip G. (1974). *Student Politics in America: A Historical Analysis* (New York: McGraw-Hill).
Bertsch, Elmer. (1961). Speech before Student Senate of UB, October 3.
Blackwell, Thomas E. (1964). "Should a Communist Be Permitted to Address Campus Audiences: New York Case Involves Academic Freedom Principle," *College and University Business,* June.
Brickman, William C. (1988). "Academic Freedom," *Encyclopedia Americana.*

Buckley, William F., Jr. (1986). "Free Speech Loses Ground on Campus," *The Buffalo Evening News,* May 29.

Buell, Frank. (1962). "War Atrocities Didn't Stem from Fascism, Mosley Says," *Courier-Express,* September 7.

Buffalo Alumnus. (1962). "Faculty Statements on Academic Freedom," December.

Buffalo Evening News. (1962a). "Call in the Truth Squad," September 27.

———. (1962b). "Aptheker Can't Speak at UB, Justice Hunt Rules in Albany," December 19.

———. (1964a). "Letters on HUAC Hearings Here," May 6.

———. (1964b). "Court Upholds UB's Right to Invite Aptheker to Speak," June 5.

Bunzel, John M. (1981). "Campus 'Free Speech,' " Op-Ed, *New York Times,* March 19.

Capen, Samuel P. (1953). *The Management of Universities,* O. A. Silverman, ed. (Buffalo, New York: Foster & Stewart Publishing Corporation).

Courier-Express. (1962). "Morning Mail," November 4.

———. (1964a). "UB Faculty Join Protest March," May 5.

———. (1964b). "State University Red Hunt Urged," May 12.

———. (1964c). "Possible Activities by Reds Probed on UB Campus," May 12.

Cowan, John L., and Williamson, E. G. (1965). "The Role of the President in the Desirable Treatment of Academic Freedom for Students," *The Educational Record,* fall.

Furnas, C. C. (1964). "Allegations About UB Answered by Dr. Furnas," *Courier-Express,* May 27.

Goldberger, Robert F. (1987). "College Protests Today Show a Narrowness of Mind," *The Buffalo News,* May 13.

Goldman, Mark. (1983). "Paranoia: The Fear of Outsiders and Radicals During the 1930s and 60s," *High Hopes: The Rise and Decline of Buffalo* (Albany, New York: SUNY Press).

Lewis, Lionel. (1988). *Cold War on Campus: A Study of the Politics of Organizational Controls* (New Brunswick, USA: Transaction Books).

Mahoney, Walter J. (1962). Letter to UB trustees, October.

The Midnight Oil. (1964). "Editorial Comments: Aptheker, Kremlin Love Old Chestnuts," extra edition, November 14.

Moore, Frank C. (1962). "Mr. Moore Replies to Senator Mahoney's Letter on Speaker," in SUNY Newsletter, December 5.

Perry, Henry T. E. (1962). "Dr. Capen and Academic Freedom," *Buffalo Alumnus,* December 5.

Riesel, Victor. (1962). "Do You Remember, Professor Horton?" *The New York Daily Mirror,* September 3.

Van Alstyne, William. (1962). "Speaker's Rights Examined by Van Alstyne in Report," *Ohio State University Lantern,* October 29.

Weiss, Samuel. (1991). "The Jeffries Case: Are There Any Enforceable Limits on Academic Freedom of Speech?" *New York Times,* November 10.

CHAPTER II

The Lull Before the Storm: Aveillugd Urubod and the Press

You should always believe all you read in the newspapers, as this makes them more interesting.

—Dame Rose Macaulay

UB has been no stranger to serious student protests or student pranks that have been strongly entrenched throughout the history of American university life. Even as Mario Savio's Free Speech Movement was flourishing at Berkeley in 1964, students there and elsewhere were simultaneously competing for their place in the *Guinness Book of Records*—by pushing beds along city streets for more miles than anyone else, attempting to ascertain how long it is humanly possible to remain continuously under a running shower, or trying to better the existing record for cramming human bodies into a telephone booth.

One UB student hoax in 1964 is worth noting, in part because it was reasonably ingenious. More important, it graphically illustrates how the news media, intentionally or not, distorts even minor events that involve mass behavior.

The hoax was launched when the *Buffalo Evening News* was tricked into running the following item of two modest column inches on December 15, 1964:

RULER DUE HERE FROM MARCHANTIA

Aveillugd Urubod, the Thallus or ruling monarch of the principality of Marchantia, will arrive at Greater Buffalo Airport at 1:48 tomorrow afternoon on a two-day visit to the Buffalo area.

The Thallus of the principality, about the size of Buffalo in the southwestern section of the Arabian Peninsula, will be here until Friday morning when he leaves for Chicago. He is on a State Department tour of this country. (*Buffalo Evening News* 1964a)

Among the various motives later advanced by the perpetrators of the hoax was a desire to relieve the pressure of a difficult examination period. An unappreciated examination accounts for terminology in the original article—Thallus (stalk), and Marchantia (liverwort, plants resembling mosses), along with other technical terms obscure to the layman. The instigators claimed that they were seeking to test the gullibility of local news media, while also proving that most people believe what they read in print. There was the further thought of mocking the Berkeley revolts, coupled with a perennial attempt to reinforce that nebulous concept, "school spirit." For their part, the conspirators quickly disappeared, especially after learning that giving a newspaper false information is a violation of New York State law, punishable by a prison term not to exceed one year, a $500 fine, or both.

Once the story appeared, student interest in "picketing" and "a demonstration" spread rapidly. By the time the plane was due a crowd of approximately 1,000 at most was waiting (although almost every news report initially doubled that number); whatever the total, however, it was in sharp contrast with the twenty-five to thirty students who, based on our past experience, were regularly turning out for *bona fide* civil rights demonstrations on the UB campus during the 1964–65 school year.

The "demonstrators" were amiable, orderly, good-natured, and remarkably well disciplined. Their signs reflected unusually good taste, with statements like "Thallus, Return to Your Palace," "No Malice Toward Thallus," and "Arab, Go Home." The Thallus, a seventeen-year-old first-year student, wearing a dark business suit under a white trench coat, was winging his way back to Buffalo after having used the first half of a round-trip ticket—purchased the same day—which allowed for a forty-minute stopover at Newark. In his briefcase he carried a pen, a notebook, a pair of dark sunglasses, and an authentic kiffiyeh for headwear. Lt. Benedict Kostizewski of the Cheektowaga Police Department, which had jurisdiction over the airport area, was later to describe the visiting potentate's headgear to the *New York Herald Tribune* (1964) as "some strange sort of flowing headdress."

A bugler mysteriously appeared at the airport. After sounding a few notes for attention, announcements followed, such as "the Thallus requests that you sit" and "the Thallus asks that you walk backwards." The assembled group, well aware of the situation even if members of the onlooking police detachment were not, cheerfully complied. The Thallus, after adjusting his costume prior to getting off the plane, may have been more surprised than pleased at the size of the crowd assembled for his heralded arrival. The bugler also decided to sound "charge," a call to which many of the attending students responded by "running wildly" through and out of the airport terminal.

The still-puzzled police observers initially mistook for rage and anger the welcoming cries of "Hail, Thallus," which rose spontaneously as the Thallus, waving to the crowd, alighted from the American Airlines plane. The Arabian head of state then made his first serious mistake by accepting proffered police protection, only to be driven directly to station headquarters. During the ride he committed a second fatal error by blurting out his real identity ("I'm only Artie Schein from Brooklyn"), so he soon found himself facing a disorderly conduct charge. He was accused under a section of the Penal Law which says that "a person is guilty of disorderly conduct when he 'by his actions' causes a crowd to collect, except when lawfully addressing a crowd."

Many of the ramifications of the stunt could certainly not have been anticipated either by the initiators or participating students. Despite consistent reports to the contrary by most of the news media, *all* of the demonstrators knew that a hoax was on. The *News* had been cleverly duped. Before the managing editor ran the item he had checked with the Lenox Hotel, where such visiting dignitaries usually stayed; when informed that the Thallus had indeed been booked for a two-day stay (apparently by some thoughtful student), he decided to print the story. The *News* was subsequently in no mood to check out the "facts" or verify the forthcoming irate statements from angry airport spokesmen after the hoax was discovered. The managing editor of the *News* was even less amused. He became more angry and chagrined upon learning that his arch rival, *The Courier-Express,* had not taken the bait when offered a chance to print the same item. No one reported what the publisher, no admirer of the university, thought about the matter.

In the Associated Press (1964) wire story, based on the original account in the *News,* students "broke windows, slashed seats, and frightened travelers." A "white-faced" airport manager claimed that "chairs and couches were ruined" and "table legs were broken" in the *Buffalo Evening News* (1964b). (The intimation was that knives had been used and furniture deliberately destroyed.) It was also charged that "some persons attempted to overturn the automobile of a radio-TV reporter."

"Bud" Wacker (1981), an "embarrassed city editor" of the *News* at the time, discussed the incident seventeen years later in "The Visit of the Liverwort King." "None of the travelers or passengers 'were bowled over' or reported any injuries, and not one student arrest—other than the Thallus— was made," he concedes. "The 'broken windows' turned out to be one window with a crack in it," and "the 'overturned or broken' ashtrays totaled four, valued at $15 each. Four airport employees did work 90 minutes overtime to clean up the mess, and the damage figure which started at $2,000 later shrank to $600."

Several national publications subsequently referred to the incident as a riot, uniformly and incorrectly noting that the students involved thought they were reacting against a real person rather than a fictitious one. The *National Observer* (1964) incorporated the affair into its December 28 story on "The Anatomy of Rising Revolt on the Campus," referring to "more than 2,000 students" and the "cutting of a trail of $2,000 damage." These errors were compounded by adding that "most of the students" were unaware of the hoax. Bill Ward (1965), writing about Syracuse student behavior in *The Nation* —and despite the geographical proximity of Buffalo to Syracuse —wrote that, "More seriously (next time) it may be violence as in Berkeley and at Buffalo," when any element of violence was nonexistent during the airport affair.

The Jamestown, N.Y. *Post Journal* (1964), in a strong December 19 editorial, referred to the hoax as an incident "that endangered the lives and limbs of many a traveler and damaged property extensively." Recommended, in all seriousness, was the imposition of different college entrance tests to reveal "maturity and good sense" prior to approving an applicant's admission to college. The *Post Journal* obviously had to rely on originally incomplete and biased reports, so its reaction was based on the locally reported "facts." A similar reading of the incident appeared in the *Utica Daily Press* (1964) of December 17 under a banner headline, "Buffalo U. Students Vandalize Airport."

The lighter touch provided by the *New York Herald Tribune* (1964) heightened the anger of the staff at the *News*. The *Herald Tribune*'s tongue-in-cheek report reproduced the item as it had originally appeared in the *News* under its headline "Thallus' Trip: Pranksters Even Fool Buffalo Police." The *Herald Tribune* reported that "Damage estimates varied considerably: Cheektowaga police said $200. Richard Rebadow, airport manager, said $2,000."

The Spectrum (1964), UB's student newspaper, jubilantly announced the "THALLUS HOAX SUCCESSFUL" in its headline of December 18. The *Spectrum* article included a revealing comment from a "bewildered" policeman, clearing the building, who said, "I know my son is in there somewhere, and when I catch him I'll break every bone in his body."

Several days later, just as things were quieting down, University President Clifford C. Furnas unfortunately observed to a *Courier-Express* reporter that the episode was a minor incident, blown into exaggeration by airport officials and the media. This reignited Rebadow, who informed Dr. Furnas through the media, that "airline personnel and passengers had been terrified by the mob, and that it was a miracle that persons knocked down were not trampled" (*Courier-Express* 1964a). (This exchange is noted to discourage college presidents from too quickly volunteering off-hand comments, even when they know they are true, that might turn dying embers back into flames.)

"If the students thought the hoax would be quickly forgotten, they misjudged the temper of the times," explains Wacker (1981). "Those were the days when curfews, close-clipped hair and clean-cut fifties style respectability were making their last stand on the nation's campuses. Student protest was a new (and frightening) thought, and students who created any kind of fuss were ranked by the general public just above the unwashed, pot-smoking beatnik types who were beginning to appear at Berkeley."

The "Morning Mail" and "Letters to the Editor" sections in both local newspapers were soon printing reactions from the general public, all of which deplored such student behavior. The following extracts from one self-explanatory letter, signed "DISGUSTED," in the December 18 *Courier-Express* (1964b) betray the deep-seated resentment of some members of the local community toward university youth:

> It is deplorable that the taxpayers of the State of New York should be forced to pay for the education of such rowdies. . . . At the very least they should be indefinitely suspended or better, they should be kicked out at once.

"DISGUSTED" goes on to describe UB students as he or she saw them during a recent plane trip to New York City, apparently forgetting that there are at least five other reputable institutions of higher learning in the immediate area. This includes the State University College at Buffalo, which also attracts many students from metropolitan New York.

> There were many "students" on board. It was hard to discover whether they were males or females, except that a couple wore beards. The women, with their lank and dirty hair, wore Russian short jackets and Nazi jack-boots and were a disgraceful spectacle. . . . Comments from other Buffalonians about these creatures were even more candid than mine, and certainly reflect what people think of the "students" at the University. . . . It is a case of too many worthless people having too much easy money, too much food, too much "fun," and too much time. The very least they can do is wash occasionally, and pretend to be human, even if they are not.

A few days later both local newspapers would extol the antics of another Buffalo crowd—several thousand rabid football fans who gathered at the airport to await the arrival of the Buffalo Bills football team, which had just won the AFL championship. Airport fences were torn down, and incoming planes had to be redirected to Rochester at considerable expense. This was somehow different, though, because the fans represented "community spirit."

My official role as Dean of Students dictated an early appearance at the airport the following morning. I was accompanied, at my request, by the Thallus himself. I wanted him to observe all the damage first-hand as an important object lesson. My investigation revealed a somewhat different picture of the reported destruction. Employees (including ticket sellers) uniformly volunteered that damages had been mininmal and that there had been no "riot"; most expressed genuine surprise at the extent of the ensuing publicity. No seats had been "slashed," nor had any furniture been destroyed. There were no broken windows.

On December 17, *The Courier-Express* (1964c), which admittedly could be more objective than a distraught *Buffalo Evening News,* reported that only 1,000 students had been involved and damages were now placed at around $1,000, instead of $2,000. The *Courier* also pointed out that "no advance story [about the Thallus] was published by the newspaper, when the facts could not be verified," which must have been received with mixed feelings by the people at the *News.*

On December 18, the *Courier* (1964d) clarified matters further. "Original reports of the student actions were exaggerated," according to the article, which also exonerated the students from charges about slashed seats and the alleged attempt "to overturn the auto of a radio-television reporter." Instead, "a photographer was on top of the truck and the students merely crowded around so they could be in the picture." In addition, a reporter perched on the top of the vehicle was exhorting the crowd to "do something" and "make more noise" for the benefit of the radio—TV audience.

I informed the press that we all regretted this had happened, and the students, I knew, regretted it most of all. Schein was placed on "indefinite suspension," an administrative maneuver that allows a student in circumstances like this to continue with classes until such time as the case is disposed of in outside courts. I could also truthfully tell reporters that students had voluntarily begun a fund-raising campaign to pay for any and all damages. Full restitution was made within a week, and no student government monies were involved.

Not one passenger had been deliberately pushed or injured; not one person at the airport filed a complaint to airport officials or disclosed any incident of violence or harassment to the media. Not one student was ever apprehended or charged with vandalism or malicious destruction, although more than fifty police, state troopers, and Erie County deputy sheriffs were originally reported by the *News* as having arrived almost immediately at the scene. This number also sharply contrasted with the *Courier*'s December 17 summary, which placed a dozen Cheektowaga patrolmen, ten state troopers, and six deputy sheriffs at the airport, where "order was restored in about 30 minutes" (*Courier-Express* 1964c).

The *News*'s December 17 report about the student drive to cover the alleged damages included the following four paragraphs about ongoing police investigative efforts to round up the ringleaders:

> Marchantia is the name of a moss type plant known more commonly as liverwort. Thallus is a biological term.
>
> Because of the use of the two words police are checking on students in biology classes.

"We have species of liverwort in our laboratory," said Dr. Joseph L. Hindman, a UB assistant biology professor, "and nearly all biology students have been exposed to it. It was part of lab exam about a week ago."

"We have the names of some students in biology courses," said Lt. Kostizewski, "and we're getting more." (*Buffalo Evening News* 1964b)

This incident illustrates the futility of trying to fight news clippings, since one cannot unprint previous reports. The first AP story naturally reached both coasts with all of its original implications intact. Since major elements of a news story are neatly encompassed in lead paragraphs and details of lesser importance are subordinated at the end of news articles, there would never be any appropriate follow-up or objective, adequate coverage of this relatively minor incident. Non-malicious aspects were never brought to light except in the *Herald Tribune* story. Real concern is justified if such distortion is possible when more serious matters are involved. It may be an axiom that the further from its origins a newspaper story appears, the more likely it is to be perceived incorrectly. This is especially true as time passes, since pertinent follow-up material is frequently not carried in distantly located newspapers. Such items also quickly outlive their original value as "news," but previous impressions live on.

Charges against the Thallus were ultimately dismissed, so he escaped the life sentence that had likely been secretly desired for him by both the editor of the *News* and the airport manager.

The continuation of the Thallus story helps to explain why college student personnel officers occasionally derive some small satisfaction from their roles, which are frequently misunderstood by students, faculty, other administrators, and the general public—to say nothing about the "Animal House" image of Deans of Men, a vanishing species.

I realized that both the university and the Thallus would be best served if I went down to the police department to see what I could do. I found a tired, confused, and repentant Arthur Schein, who clearly had not fully anticipated the predicament in which he now found himself. As he was entering the judge's chambers at 11:00 P.M., Schein asked me how he should plead. Former friends, who had pledged support and counsel, had disappeared. I advised the Thallus to plead "not guilty." (This is standard advice, since initial admission of guilt weakens the effect of subsequent appeals.)

The next problem was to find $200 in cash for bail before midnight, or Arthur would spend the rest of the night in jail. My wife, Lois, was surprised when a shabbily dressed youth, whom I commandeered for the assignment, turned up to relieve her of some money we had stashed away for Christmas presents.

Since I knew that returning the Thallas to the residence halls at an early morning hour would unnecessarily create further excitement, I brought him home with me. Lois had coffee and doughnuts for us, and two curious young sons, who had never seen a Thallus before, were still up. At my suggestion, Arthur called his parents ("Gee, Ma, I don't know why I did it"), and shortly after midnight he was safely ensconced in our guest bedroom.

Lois and I went to bed, but sleep would be elusive. Around 1:00 A.M. we received a telephone call from a young woman who identified herself as "Artie's girlfriend" and wanted to speak to him. I had no problem with that, but when I went to call him to the phone he was soundly asleep, apparently exhausted from the day's work. His friend agreed that we should not wake him up. (Had I been involved in a similar escapade in college I would have been lying there wide awake, staring at the ceiling and wondering how to put myself away—unable to close my eyes for at least a week.)

A half hour later we were again awakened, this time by the sound of several automobiles that stopped directly in front of the house. Car doors opened and closed, and a muffled discussion followed among what sounded like six or seven persons. My first impulse was to kill, since I immediately concluded that a delegation of UB students had arrived to hear the Thallus speak Arabic words of wisdom, or some such foolishness, from our front balcony in what had previously been considered a respectable neighborhood.

I was wrong. The little group, assembled directly beneath our bedroom window, sang softly (although not with great distinction) two Christmas carols and quietly drove away. I learned later from one caroler that the choirboys were Artie's Allenhurst Complex housemates, expressing appreciation for my having rescued him from an unpleasant, overnight stay in a cold jail cell.

"No one, other than Schein, was arrested or even identified as taking part in any wrongdoing," reports David M. Snyderman (1988) in *The Reporter*.

> He was charged with disorderly conduct and fined $50 by Cheektowaga Peace Justice Joseph E. Psyczynski on Jan. 18, 1965. . . . "The lower courts found him guilty and we went up on appeal to the County Court," said Paul Birzon, Schein's attorney and an adjunct faculty member of the Law School. "It was reversed on a technical ground," Birzon explains. "The specific provision on which he was charged was causing a crowd to gather. Our argument was that he himself did nothing to cause the crowd to gather. The crime required a form of intent which he did not have." According to Birzon, "the scope of the situation came as a complete surprise to Schein. He had no idea how the thing had mushroomed in 24 hours."

Our nation's print, radio, and television media may be a potentially greater educational force in our society than all of our schools and colleges put together. We are frequently reminded by the Fourth Estate itself that news accounts should be accurate as well as timely. We are fortunate that our press is free and unencumbered, and we would have it no other way. There are safeguards to unintentional distortion in the news and readers may occasionally find two versions of any given story in two different newspapers, as evidenced by *The Courier-Express* and *Buffalo Evening News* coverage of one simple incident. However, it was disconcerting to observe firsthand how the press influences public reactions. Incomplete reporting of such events to the detriment of college youth implies the possibility of similar carelessness in covering major and more complex situations. During the late sixties, no photographer in his right mind would think of taking a picture of a neatly dressed student on a picket line when he could capture for posterity a bearded or barefoot example. Such pictorial reporting may have been news, but was it objective?

Almost anything college youth do seems newsworthy when it happens, but the need remains for serious writing about what goes on in higher education. The press should consider carefully its traditional responsibility for accuracy, objectivity, and fair play—especially if we return to a milieu similar to that of the sixties. During quieter periods, institutions of higher education must engender effective relationships among and between students, faculty, and administrators, as well as with the media and outside community. If troublesome times overtake us, the media can either be a positive or an unnecessarily negative factor, depending on how various incidents are reported. If news accounts are sensationalized or superficially treated, the media will continue to impede progress and retard the resolution of campus problems.

How, then, should college administrators, or designated university spokespersons, relate to the media? Press calls should be returned as promptly as possible. Admit it when you don't know the answer, but try to find out. Never lie. "No comment" is preferable to filibustering. Do not hesitate to tell reporters they were wrong when you know with certainty that they filed an inaccurate or incomplete story.

"Guidelines for Dealing with the Press" appeared in the July issue of the *NASPA Journal* (1964):

1. Give factual answers—or say you do not know. If the question involves a matter under consideration, say so and assure reporters that you will give them the answer just as quickly as you have it. Do not be afraid to say you do not know if you honestly don't!

2. Keep yourself as the primary source of information. Remember, a good reporter covering a major story wants his facts from the principal person involved. That most likely would be you. However, if you do delegate this mission, be prepared to give the latitude and backing necessary to do the job. Always cooperate with the public information staff of your own institution.

3. Do not issue a blanket order forbidding anyone in your organization from talking to the press. In the first place, it is impossible to enforce. Second, it only spurs good reporters, convincing them there may be more to the situation than really exists. Third, it is not necessary.

4. Try to understand the job confronting the reporters and photographers. They are being paid to get the news. Some will be easier to talk with than others, but this is true in all walks of life.

5. Above all, do not lose your temper. When you are angry, you will unintentionally say things you do not really mean to say. A sense of humor is invaluable in a crisis. This does not mean you should make light of the situation or the question asked; neither does it mean you should try to substitute jokes for facts. But an understanding smile often quiets a stormy conversation.

6. Do not fight the clippings. You cannot unprint what has already appeared in the papers, so do not try. Often statements and even stories that infuriate you are not digested by the reading public. But the minute you attack the reporter or the paper through another medium, you will get public attention. Of course, there are exceptions. When you feel such an exception exists, when your honesty and integrity and that of your organization is jeopardized, you should emphasize your position. However, do it with dignity. Never allow your words to indicate animosity. This only makes little fires larger.

7. Out-of-town newspapermen rely heavily on the advice of local reporters. If word passes that you always have been cooperative and fair with the press, it will have far-reaching effect on the overall situation.

8. Be honest with the press. Never cover up adverse news.

If relationships with the commercial press seem difficult, involvements with the student press are extremely complicated, especially when student editors at public institutions are involved. Ideally, a college newspaper should be completely independent—such as *The Harvard Crimson, The Michigan Daily, The Wisconsin Daily Cardinal, The Cornell Daily Sun, The Daily Illini, The Daily Texan,* and *The Rutgers Daily Telegram*—existing off campus and subject to the same economic pressures as the outside commercial newspapers. This is rarely possible, because of publishing costs. Most colleges and universities almost invariably permit student newspapers to occupy institutional space and to utilize heat and light without charge. This practice should be reconsidered. Some reasonable charge for space and utilities would help to establish the desired independent status of the student press, removing any perception that the university is one of the several publishers.

As Roger Ebert (1964), now a movie critic on national television, expressed it in the *NASPA Journal,* when he was editor of the *Daily Illini,* "From both the Constitutional and practical point of view, it is impossible to have a truly free student paper unless a separate publishing corporation is established to free the university from legal responsibility." Ebert observes that "whenever I am asked to put down some thoughts about freedom of the student press, I am reminded of a wry statement by Neal Johnson after he completed two years as director of a National Student Association's academic freedom project. 'My job was not to defend freedom of the press,' he said, 'but to protect numbskull college editors from themselves.'

"There is no such creature as a Constitutional guarantee of freedom of the press which applies to editors," Ebert concludes. "The Constitution, instead, defends the rights of publishers, and if a campus newspaper is legally published (or subsidized) by an institution, then the 'freedoms' belong to the Administration, and the student editor does not have any inherent right." He clearly warns us that "the publisher is legally responsible for everything that is printed in his paper and a University can be sued if its student journalists libel someone."

In any event, universities are usually rewarded for being benign landlords by having the student press publish items that result in libel suits, border on the pornographic or obscene (however defined), or are in grossly bad taste. It seems that any worthwhile student newspaper cannot long refrain from occasionally expressing negative views (sometimes justified) about the president and his staff. Any administrator at a public university who begins to think seriously about reprimanding or otherwise disciplining the student press in some form, however, should spend a few minutes with legal advisors. He or she should be reminded that most colleges do not like to be in the position of "censoring" the student newspaper—it creates an unfavorable public image and breeds discontent in the student body. It is also axiomatic that the most radical student elements somehow end up influencing student press coverage when such incidents begin to polarize a campus. What attorneys tell the president will often inhibit immediate plans to remove an editor or deprive the newspaper of financial support. The editor immediately seeks an injunction to stop the punishment; worse yet, the president is likely to lose every time—legal theory drawn from the Fourteenth Amendment is that the state cannot abridge an editor's right to freedom of the press.

Until the United States Supreme Court rules differently, our nation's student editors at public universities and colleges may be among the most legally protected people in the world. Lower courts have consistently come down in favor of student editors, which complicates the lives of college presidents who often have sound reasons for trying to do something about editors who believe the Bill of Rights is within their sole domain.

Attorney-at-law Dennis Black (1989), who has worked closely as Dean of Students with the student press at UB, notes that legal counsel is likely to emphasize the following points to a concerned president:

> The right to free speech protects student publications from virtually all encroachments on editorial content by public institutions of higher education.

An institution can more easily be held for libelous statements when the student newspaper is sponsored by the school (for example, training purposes by the School of Journalism), or if the college employs the staff (or an advisor), or if a formal university committee is in place to review prior to publication.

The courts have held that "publication cannot be suppressed just because some college officials dislike the editorial comment. Censorship of constitutionally protected expression cannot be imposed by suspending the editors, suppressing circulation, requiring imprimatur of controversial articles, excising repugnant materials, withdrawing financial support, or asserting any other form of oversight based on the 'institution's power of the purse.' " (*Joyner* v. *Whiting* 477 F2d 456, 4th Or. 1973)

Free speech cannot be stopped because of any potential reaction to an article, such as "lack of taste." (*Bazaar* v. *Fortune* 476 F2d 570, 489 F2d 225, 5th Or. 1973)

Editors were fired at the Florida Atlantic University because of poor quality and violation of rules. Poor quality, even if it could embarrass, is not enough reason to limit free speech. The student editors (funded by fees under the control of the student government) were not seen as state employees, so they could not be relieved of their duties by the University because of poor quality. (*Schiff* v. *Williams* 519 F2d 257, 1975)

Regulations on sex-related help-wanted advertisements would likely be upheld in the courts; false or misleading advertisements —or ones promoting illegal activity—could also be regulated. (*Virginia State Board of Pharmacy* v. *Virginia Citizens Consumer Council* 425 U.S. 748, 1976)

Institutions may discipline students or organizations for publishing obscene material, but authority extends only to content that is actually obscene—and the nature of what constitutes obscenity has historically been extremely difficult to judge.

The staff of a university student organization can be prohibited from racial discrimination.

Although on treacherous ground, a university may, in special cases, *temporarily* regulate the press to prevent significant disruption of the campus or the educational process. (*Schiff* v. *Williams*).

Although an unlikely possibility—prior restraint is always tricky —the institution could halt publication of the material if it knew in advance that publication of libelous matter was imminent. This is subject to stringent procedural safeguards and administrations had better be certain that the pending statement was false and that nominal damage was involved (usually damage to reputation). There must also be a showing of actual malice if public figures are involved.

Although still subject to state laws on libel and obscenity, private institutions have a freer hand in regulating a student press, because the First Amendment does not similarly apply.

As if this were not enough, the attorney may refer to a 1983 case, *Stanley* v. *Magrath* (719 F.2d 279, 1983), which the University of Minnesota lost after a long, drawn-out lawsuit brought by the student newspaper. *The Minnesota Daily* had "satirized Jesus Christ, the Catholic Church, evangelical religion, public figures, and several ethnic groups" (Black 1989). The publication also contained "scatological language" and many explicit references to sexual acts. "There was, for example, a blasphemous 'interview' with Jesus on the Cross that would offend anyone of good taste, whether with or without religion." There was certainly much in the way of content to raise the blood pressure of even the most sanguine college administrator.

President C. Peter Magrath had been instructed by his board to develop a system by which students could receive a refund of that portion of their student fee that funded the student paper. The 8th Circuit Court, following precedents in lower federal courts, held that a public university may not constitutionally take adverse action against the student press simply because it disapproves of the newspaper's content. The nonrefundable fee was restored, Black says, and the university also paid over $180,000 in legal fees and contributed $5,000 to support a program on the campus about freedom of the press.

An editor's immunity from consequences will understandably continue to disturb many college presidents. Student newspapers will continue to humiliate administrators, provoke legislators into reducing appropriations, and negatively influence alumni loyalty drives. One can also anticipate some form of student outburst when major alumni giving programs are launched. Any university that tries to control or coercively influence content may expect many legal troubles and even more difficult times if prior restraint has been improperly imposed. Encouraging the student newspaper to seek private incorporation status and moving the press off campus, if at all possible, are among the best ways to insure that the university is not trapped into a controlling mode. Writing about "Censoring Campus News" in the *New York Times,* Dirk Johnson (1988) provides this warning from Louis E. Ingelhart, Professor Emeritus at Ball State University and author of *Freedom of the College Student Press:* "University officials commonly justify censorship on grounds of legal liability. But ironically, it is just such an effort to control newspaper content that can make the university legally responsible. The universities that try to control editorial policy get themselves into hot water on two counts. They are violating the First Amendment. And they are making themselves responsible for the content." At the very least, the student newspaper should not be permitted to identify itself on its masthead as the "official university publication." Paradoxically, chances for university liability appear to increase in proportion to the number of institutional regulations promulgated by the institution about the student press. At the very least, a good liability insurance policy is in order, no matter who appears to be in control of student operated media.

Black points to an important 1988 landmark free press case (U.S. Supreme Court, *Hazelwood* v. *Kuhlmeir,* 56 USLW 4079) that established new guidelines relating to the student press at the secondary school level. The high court ruled that the First Amendment does not protect high-school student newspapers published by a journalism class; instead, such publications were viewed as class materials—subject to educational controls of the school system—and not public forums for protected expression.

If the high-school press is no longer "free," should college students not also be concerned about the future status of their publications? Are their newspapers public forums for expression or are they class assignments subject to academic controls? Although a few are independently supported, college publications usually depend on university facilities, sometimes involve journalism students, and frequently offer academic credit for participating students.

In a footnote to the majority opinion, Black reports that Justice White went directly to the question of whether or not *Hazelwood* might influence the current freedom of college/university publications: "We need not now decide whether the same degree of deference is appropriate with respect to school-sponsored activities at the college and university level." Noting that the court "need not now decide" is far from concluding that *Hazelwood* would not be applied in the future at the college level. The Student Law Press Center, which filed a friend of the court brief on behalf of the high-school students, warned about this potential, pointing out that *Hazelwood* had little to do with the maturity of the intended audience. Instead, the ruling focused on *educational* rights and needs, at least suggesting the possibility that adequate protection to presently free college student publications could be in jeopardy.

"Advocates of the college press worry that the Hazelwood decision will embolden administrators in higher education to crack the whip too," suggests Johnson (1988). "Some college administrators contend that if the university finances a school paper, it has not only the right but the responsibility to guide that paper's editorial policy. 'As long as you take the king's shilling, you can't avoid doing some of the king's bidding,' said John R. Silber, president of Boston University. On the other hand, Dr. Silber believes that campus newspapers should remain financially independent of the university, and thus free to pursue an independent editorial direction."

Johnson quotes Mark Goodman, executive director of the Washington-based Student Press Center, which provides legal counsel to high-school and college newspapers: "Complaints of censorship have been rising in recent years from a new attitude among college administrators. School administrators today seem to have much more training in the corporate-management point of view. To them running a school is like running a business. These administrators might be very good at things like the bottom line, maintaining the quality of the physical plant and so forth. But they tend not to view free expression as quite as relevant as we think it should be in an educational environment."

Despite this, the collegiate press will likely retain its traditional freedom and protection. The following factors should be considered in assessing possible *Hazelwood* implications:

Is the newspaper sponsored by the institution?

Does the school provide space, advisors, and allow for academic credit?

Does the newspaper constitute a recognized public forum for free expression?

Is the intended readership more mature, and does the newspaper function within an environment of greater discretion?

While uneasy college editors contemplate the potential impact of *Hazelwood,* Black says that some states have begun to consider legislative steps designed to circumvent the decision. A recent Massachusetts law holds that "The right of students to freedom of expression in the public schools of the Commonwealth shall not be abridged, provided that such rights shall not cause any disruption or disorder in the schools" (Black 1989). The legislation, which also provides protection to school officials from liability in civil or criminal actions caused by protected free expression, is intended to return the student press to pre-*Hazelwood* standards.

Clarification will result when another case, more clearly focused on issues applicable to a college or university press, is brought before the Supreme Court. Problems of inaccurate reporting and manipulation of news by the press may never be resolved.

References

Associated Press. (1964). News release, December 16.
Black, Dennis R. (1989). "Report on Legal Cases and College Student Press," December 15.
Buffalo Evening News. (1964a). "Ruler Due Here From Marchantia," December 15.

Buffalo Evening News. (1964b). "UB Students Raising Money to Pay Airport Damage," December 17.

Courier-Express. (1964a). "Rebadow Attacks Furnas Statement," December 20.

————. (1964b). "Letters to the Editor" and "Morning Mail," December 18.

————. (1964c). December 17.

————. (1964d). "Students to Collect Funds for Damages," December 18.

Ebert, Roger. (1964). "Plain Talk on College Newspaper Freedom," *NASPA Journal,* July.

Johnson, Dirk. (1988). "Censoring Campus News," *Education Life, The New York Times,* November 6.

NASPA Journal. (1964). "Guidelines for Dealing with the Press," July.

National Observer. (1964). "The Anatomy of Rising Revolt on the Campus," December 28.

New York Herald Tribune. (1964). "Thallus' Trip: Pranksters Even Fool Buffalo Police," December 16.

The Post-Journal. (1964). Editorial, Jamestown, New York, December 18.

Siggelkow, Richard A. (1965). "Aveillugd Urubod, The Press, and Higher Education," *NASPA Journal,* October.

Snyderman, David M. (1988). "Ruler of Marchantia Caused Major Incident Here in '60s," *The Reporter,* December 8.

The Spectrum. (1964). "Thallus Hoax Successful," December 18.

Utica Daily Press. (1964). "Buffalo U. Students Vandalize Airport," December 17.

Wacker, Lewis (Bud). (1981). "The Visit of the Liverwort King," *The Buffalo News Magazine,* March 29.

Ward, Bill. (1965). "Campus Violence," *The Nation,* January 25.

CHAPTER III

Administrative Confusion and the Selective Service System

It is not that history repeats itself, but that statesmen and their people make the same mistakes.

—Historian Thomas A. Bailey

A major student protest, involving several hundred participants, occurred late in the spring term of UB's 1965–66 school year. The demonstrations tend to be overlooked because dissenters were "peaceful," in sharp contrast with activist tactics to come. Challenged by students and a few faculty was the university's agreement to administer the Selective Service Qualification Test, originally scheduled at UB for May 21 and June 3, 1966. Underlying concerns of protesters included higher education's commitment to federal policy and the unwillingness of administrators to understand the importance of involving students in educational decisions directly affecting their lives.

UB ignored preliminary warnings that appeared periodically in the press during the immediately preceding months about how other equally unprepared colleges and universities were confronting this issue. Similar rigidity, ineptitude, lack of foresight, and unwillingness to communicate with students would be repeated by different administrative players later in the decade.

"It was national policy—a government contract involving the Educational Testing Service and the University to determine the eligibility of draft age students with the lowest academic records for temporary exemption from military service—and Vietnam," explains Allen H. Kuntz (1991), then director of the university's Testing and Research Center and an assistant professor in Educational Psychology. "At that time the war was in its initial stages and had not yet assumed its divisive nature." In 1966 the great majority of our citizenry still believed in the nation's commitment and the need to defend what they thought was right; anti-war sentiments were generally considered misguided and unpatriotic. "The episode would set the pattern for the more serious protests that soon followed," maintains Dr. A. Westley Rowland (1988), then Assistant to the President. Kuntz also believes that the testing controversy "sparked the beginning of dissonance in the intellectual community that would continue throughout the Vietnam engagement."

While unprecedented numbers became involved, major differences existed between 1966 activism and the violence of later demonstrations. Despite the usual inability to find common ground when lines are drawn too firmly and too soon, protest movement leaders and administrators were still able to communicate in 1966. There were no physical confrontations and deliberate property damage. Orderly and well-disciplined hallway sit-ins sharply contrasted with later techniques of "trashing" and ransacking buildings. Most important, the 1966 demonstrators—although a vanguard openly opposed to the war effort—did not concentrate on Vietnam as the primary university issue.

In February *The Spectrum* (1966a) reported that a draft deferment test might be given college students to ascertain their continued eligibility for deferment. The March 4 *Spectrum* (1966b) verified that voluntary college student deferment tests would definitely be offered nationwide. Official dates and registration procedures were published, but there was no accompanying announcement that the exam would be held at UB. The campus atmosphere was soon permeated by uncertainty, as students conjectured about personal draft possibilities and the test content itself. The Selective Service project became a national issue, covered extensively by the media. Amid growing local and national controversy, an *ad hoc* student group—the Graduate Faculty Committee on the Selective Service (GFCSS)—was formed at UB on March 31.

Inflationary trends in grading first surfaced in 1966 with the development of the Selective Service academic deferment examination. Concerned during the sixties and early seventies that a poor grade might adversely influence a student's draft deferment status, some faculty began awarding inflated marks. "They had the power, by giving a failing grade to a student, to end his draft deferment and send him to possible death in Vietnam," Robert Reinhold (1989) explains in a *New York Times* article. Devaluating traditional standards may have been well meaning, but awarding grades higher than actually merited to maintain a student's draft exemption status translated into his being replaced by someone less fortunate, likely poorer, and more often a black—who would become part of a doomed war effort already being fought disproportionately by minorities and poor whites to the virtual exclusion of the middle class.

According to Sharon Edelman (1968) GFCSS argued that the entire student deferment process was discriminatory since the possibility of an individual attending college is greatly dependent on various factors, i.e. financial status and socio-economic background. "Student deferment permits members of certain 'classes' only to avoid military service. Not only is this undemocratic and unworthy of the theoretical American tradition, but it is also resented by many members of the nonacademic community, resulting in antiintellectualism." Also noted by Edelman was the possibility that principles of academic freedom would be violated, if UB decided to administer the examination on campus. The university would be in collusion with the "military-industrial complex," and turned into "an arm of the government." The military, through the Selective Service System, "would be undermining the autonomy of the University by establishing for the University the definitive qualities for intellectualism and intellectuals, using the coercive device of the II-S deferment."

We should have been listening closely or more carefully reading the student newspaper; some progress could have been made in developing appropriate and meaningful avenues for discussion and involvement before the decision. It might have been possible to establish procedures for considering future related problems.

A special Division of Student Affairs report chronologically covers what followed the April 8 announcement that the dreaded Selective Service Qualification Test would indeed be offered at UB on May 21 and June 3. As one of several administrators aware of such university commitments, I recall no particular concern being expressed by any staff member about the potential impact of the decision. Rowland (1988), closest to the president on this occasion, reports that there was no apparent reason to anticipate a response that would erupt into the "Movement of May." The Director of the Testing Center, who reported to me, assumed that it was just another ongoing university responsibility to convenience our own students who could now voluntarily take the examination on familiar ground. Reassuringly, the test was also scheduled simultaneously at State University College across town and Canisius College, a local, private Catholic institution. Kuntz (1991) was subsequently "stunned by the pervasiveness of feeling that surrounded the event."

Dr. Furnas, who served briefly as an Undersecretary in the Department of Defense under the Eisenhower administration, automatically sanctioned the use of university facilities for such purposes. GFCSS, by letter, invited President Furnas to enter into dialogue with students and faculty to consider reevaluating the policy decision, and they wanted to know the university's official policy concerning distribution of student grades and class standings to draft boards. No official statement would be forthcoming until some time elapsed. While university policy may have been unclear about revealing an individual's grades (these should always be sacrosanct, issued only with student approval) the administration could have been immediately reassuring about class rankings. No system existed then or now to retrieve that exact information.

Apparently reasoning that such action represented a waste of time, Furnas responded by memorandum (how easy it is, after the fact, to suggest taking a few hours to consult others and think such things over) that he did not intend to meet with GFCSS representatives or review the policy decision. He erred in not enlisting early input from key faculty groups, other administrators, and student government bodies. Although an intelligent administrator, he was not inclined to accept outside input on what he clearly viewed as solely presidential prerogative. The president was fond of pointing out to us that "the pilot of an airplane never leaves the cockpit to confer with passengers on how to fly his craft."

GFCSS viewed the prompt reply as an affront, but gave Furnas a second chance. He agreed this time to meet with GFCSS on Monday morning, May 2, apparently to insure that his original message had been completely understood. The August 5 special report of the Division of Student Affairs (1966) chronicles the sequence of events:

Monday, May 2:

Meeting with thirty-four students, Dr. Furnas stated that he couldn't even identify who made the original decision, adding, "All I know is what I read in the newspapers." He went on to repeat that it was a "routine" administrative action that merited no further discussion, and certainly not an open forum to reconsider the matter. Shortly after returning to Norton Union, two graduate students of the delegation spontaneously returned to the administrative suite in Hayes and sat down in the hallway leading into the president's office. They were joined shortly by thirty more students in a sit-in to force open discussions between the president and the academic community. Furnas repeated that the original decision would hold and that an open meeting was not warranted. Students and faculty, he explained, could participate in such decisions only insofar as the chief executive delegated authority permitted such involvement. He said the students could sit-in indefinitely, as long as the operations of his office were not impaired. He made arrangements to keep the main entrance to Hayes Hall open all night, so that demonstrators could enter and leave at will. Apparently concerned about setting a dangerous precedent, he added that he "would not be coerced by any unauthorized group."

Tuesday, May 3:

Jeremy Taylor (1966), the editor of *The Spectrum,* stressed the importance of the symbolic gesture—"a dramatic act of protest"—but did not realize that the next sit-in would attract two hundred participants. He editorially suggested that Furnas should resign for "administrative ineptitude and his inability to understand the problems," adding:

> He rejected the ridiculously reasonable proposals of the GFCSS and refused to even discuss the matter before the academic community on the grounds that the needs of the government for cannon fodder superseded

any responsibility the University might have for free discussion and debate. . . .

The administration has turned the university not only into a propaganda arm of the present government, but into a procurement agency for the military—and it has done so without a whisper of protest. . . .

Responding to GFCSS contacts, support was now publicly offered by the Young Socialist Alliance, The Viet Nam Committee at Berkeley, the Ripon Society, the Young Americans for Freedom, and free-lance representatives from the local chapter of Students for a Democratic Society. All were organizations tending to reinforce presidential intransigence. GFCSS began to get publicity from local news media.

The Student Senate, an authorized body and approved university channel, passed a resolution respectfully requesting the president to agree to an open meeting and discussion of the decision, with only one dissenting vote. That afternoon, Clinton Deveaux, the Undergraduate Student Association president [currently a city court justice in Atlanta], personally delivered the resolution to the president. Although he still declined to appear personally, Furnas promised to send Dr. Rowland and the Director of the Testing Center to explain the ruling at an open forum. He reportedly stated that he would "highly consider" any recommendations made by his two representatives after the meeting. After being informed by Deveaux about the compromise offer, GFCSS was still unwilling to participate without a guarantee of the president's personal appearance. The peaceful, relaxed sit-in continued through that night.

Wednesday, May 4:

By morning it was evident that GFCSS would be allowed to sit-in "indefinitely." Final exams were approaching, term papers were due, and there was no visible groundswell of faculty support or indications of major involvement by more students. At 9:30 A.M. the weary demonstrators voted to end the sit-in and requested that the open meeting be held Thursday evening, May 5. Their focus subtly changed to concentrate on a common concern among larger universities—lack of communication among and between students, faculty, and administrators. Emphasis on the test itself had evolved into determining what role students and faculty should play in setting university policy before unalterable administrative decisions are reached.

The Spectrum (1966c), in a special edition supporting GFCSS, significantly emphasized that the original concern about military absorption of institutional autonomy had shifted to reviewing the bureaucratic structure within which institutions like UB functioned.

Also reported was the adoption of a Student Senate resolution proposing that the University should not send grades to the Selective Service (unless requested by individual students) and not lend its facilities to the Selective Service for the administration of the Selective Service Exam. At the Senate meeting arguments were made in support of the administrative decision, and the overwhelming majority of faculty and students were still either uninterested or not sympathetic to activist demands.

Thursday, May 5:

At 7:55 P.M. the anticipated open meeting took place. The panel, moderated by Deveaux, included Rowland, Kuntz, the vice president of the Undergraduate Student Association, a GFCSS representative, and a faculty member. A surprising 1,000 students, faculty, and staff members crowded into Norton Hall's multipurpose room.

Without preliminary elaboration, Rowland immediately read the prepared statement. The Furnas paper began by forcefully noting that its purpose was not to defend a "routine administrative action," but "to define a problem and clarify issues." It was indicated that a copy had been sent to Martin Meyerson, who had just been appointed to succeed Furnas as president on September 1, 1966.

Furnas perceived the on-going sit-in, albeit orderly, as "throwing down the gauntlet" against the university's chief administrative officer, reminding the audience that he had categorically refused requests of the Graduate-Faculty Committee on the Selective Service for him to address a university-wide public meeting on the issue. The decision to give the examination, he added, "was similar to that made by hundreds of colleges and universities in the nation." Furnas (1966a), through Rowland, concluded with the following rationale:

> The State University by its public nature cooperates with a large number of State, Federal, and private agencies. In this particular case, Selective Service is the law of the land, and in this instance, a Federal Law. In giving this test on the campus, the University is cooperating with the Federal Government as it does in many other ways. In fact, many students are studying at this University today because of funds made available to them through the Federal Government. . . .
>
> The test is being given here and in many other locations in the United States, as a convenience for those students who wish to take it. No one has to take the test. It is not mandatory. But certainly this would be a gross infringement on the personal freedom of the individual. As a matter of fact, it would definitely be an infringement on the rights of those students who desire to take the test if they were to be denied the opportunity by the actions of another group of students. . . .
>
> The idea that a democratic coalition of students, faculty, and administration can manage the giant enterprise is an illusion. The idyllic image of the university as an autonomous and independent oasis—apart from society . . . is a mirage. . . . The burden of that leadership rests squarely on the university president.
>
> Obviously, I must be and am perfectly willing to give due consideration to honest and sincere opinions and requests which arise from either fac-

ulty or students through approved channels of the University as a whole. These recognized channels include the following bodies: The Faculty Senate, the Graduate-Senate Association, and the Student Senate.

. . . I believe that the administration of a university should be sensitive to sincere and well-considered concerns of the university faculty and students for changes which are legal and appropriate in our dynamic changing society.

Rowland and Kuntz had no room in which to maneuver. The president indicated at his last meeting with them and his cabinet that he would tolerate no significant changes in his original decision. The two messengers were reduced to emphasizing that the examination was held on campus to make life easier for students who had to deal with the draft question in some manner. "Furnas very unwisely gave us no room to wiggle," says Kuntz (1991). "We clearly understood that we were under orders to carry this out or look for another job." Rowland (1988) felt that he had to preclude the possibility of any dialogue at the outset of the meeting and repeatedly announced that the decision was not subject to change. He did not—or could not—acknowledge that suggestions from the audience might be taken under advisement. The hard-line approach of directly confronting all comers and repeating several times that extensive discussion would be meaningless aroused an initially passive audience. GFCSS began to enjoy support from previously neutral students and uncommitted faculty.

It is usually a mistake to allow no room for movement, especially if there is a little available space. The level of audience alienation rose in direct ratio with each of Rowland's statements that the issue was "irrevocably settled." The implication was that we were all wasting our time, and some members of the crowd began to ask a logical question: Why was this meeting held at all? Since nothing changed, GFCSS called for another rally at 10:00 A.M. the next morning, to determine the next step to change the administration's "rigid, condescending, and unimaginative" stance.

The meeting had not been held without incident as far as Kuntz, by now a well-known campus figure, was concerned. "Although I didn't request it, I was being escorted around campus by two Buffalo plainclothesmen; I tried to dismiss them at the rally, but they had orders to stay with me," Kuntz says. "Some students spat at me when I walked out of the lounge that night, and I instinctively clenched my fists; one of the policemen put his arm around me and said, 'Not here, Doc—across the street.' "

Friday, May 6:

A morning meeting was attended by around three hundred students. Many seemed ready to demonstrate because of their impression that the administration completely disregarded their existence as potentially meaningful members of the academic community. A confused two-hour debate ended with a decision to picket Hayes Hall. All proposals to close the administration down and physically block entrances were soundly rejected, and approximately 150 students joined the picket line.

The local AAUP chapter passed resolutions that university facilities should not be used, and that the university should not disclose grades or quartile standings unless specifically authorized to release such records by each student involved.

Another open meeting in the multipurpose room at 7:00 P.M. was attended by over one thousand students and some faculty members. While everyone in the audience was not fully sympathetic, the GFCSS had gained adherents. The first open meeting exposed the absence of proper channels through which student issues could be presented effectively. It also appeared to many observers that less than clear channels of communication existed between the president and his chief spokespersons, since the president's alleged promise that room for discussion existed had clearly been negated by Rowland's unyielding posture at the open forum. Some student leaders claimed that the entire exercise was an administrative "diversionary tactic." Empty promises of open forums and meaningful discussions, they argued, were really designed to inhibit action until the semester ended.

Leaders now demanded satisfaction (the era of "nonnegotiable" demands was not yet upon us) by Sunday, May 8 at 6:00 P.M.; otherwise, there would be another sit-in at Hayes, starting at 7:45 A.M., Monday, May 9.

Saturday, May 7:

Furnas, aware of his role as a lame duck, and hoping not to jeopardize Meyerson's arrival as president in the fall, held an emergency session with the executive committees of the Faculty Senate, the Graduate Student Association, the Student Senate, and the president's cabinet. Furnas consistently refused to invite GFCSS members to the meeting.

Deveaux suggested that the president appoint a committee of faculty, students, and administrators to study the situation and make recommendations for improving interactions among campus constituencies. According to Edelman (1968) the president agreed to establish a Special Task Force to: "(1) inquire into and make proposals with respect to establishing an open and continuous dialogue among such groups, and (2) make such proposals as they deem appropriate regarding organizational means for participation by these groups in the formulation of educational policy in the University." This closely paralleled similar actions by Martin Meyerson when he became acting president after the Berkeley uprising, "after the riots had occurred" there, Edelman adds.

Sunday, May 8:

Mr. Deveaux convened a special meeting of the Student Senate to brief that body about the events of the weekend. A resolution was passed calling for the election of task force representatives from the Senate, thereby legitimatizing the special committee structure agreed upon Saturday morning.

Monday, May 9:

The GFCSS sit-in was postponed, pending the outcome of a meeting scheduled for Thursday, May 12, at which the president was to announce his "final" decision about whether or not the test would be held on campus. (Dr. Furnas would be in California until then.)

Wednesday, May 11:

In the last issue of *The Spectrum* (1966d) for the current semester, it was reported that 250–300 students at a May 9 meeting agreed that Hayes Hall should be picketed and closed off by physically blocking all entrances. Taylor editorially discussed "The Problems of Victory." Marching demonstrators were drenched with water when they ventured too close to the men's high-rise dormitory. Throwing plastic bags filled with water from the ten-story hall was a favorite pastime for bored male resident students; now they had live targets.

Thursday, May 12:

After lengthy discussions and time-consuming meetings, UB came full circle. Arguments presented at this special morning meeting would determine the fate of the Selective Service Test. Attending, in addition to the usual administrative personnel, were the executive committees of the Faculty Senate, the Student Senate, the Graduate Student Association—and, yes, the executive committee of GFCSS. Furnas said that he was holding the meeting with an open mind, he would listen carefully to all arguments, and his final decision would be in the best interests of the university as a whole. The meeting was to demonstrate to the academic community that such discussions could be held and that the president was willing to listen to opinions of the academic community. It is unlikely that anyone really thought he would revise his earlier decision, but the session satisfied an overdue need for dialogue.

Friday, May 13:

"After due consideration and listening to all inputs," the president announced through the Office of Public Relations, "it would still be in the best interests of the university as a whole if the test were given as scheduled" (Furnas (1966b).

It was over. The issue vanished immediately. The "Movement of May" disappeared overnight, and there were no further demonstrations as the shadow of the examination period enveloped the campus. Even the previously most involved students now redirected their attention to achieving passing grades to keep their draft deferment status alive and well. "The tests were administered at three different locations on a Saturday morning and went off without a hitch," reports Kuntz (1991). "In retrospect, I would have felt better had there been open discussions with faculty and students earlier on; I don't believe in conciliation, but there could and should have been discussions *vis à vis* the moral correctness of a device called a test to provide exemptions from military duty for some, but not for others." The final Task Force report, not issued until April 1967, was generally ignored and rests in the university archives.

The incident reveals what happens when politically influenced administrative decisions are made too quickly and without anticipating ensuing developments. It also represents an isolated instance of student government effectiveness when undergraduate leadership did not quickly disintegrate under pressure, as it would several years later.

A remarkable lack of administrative insight unnecessarily complicated and prolonged the controversy. The Selective Service issue was debated in major universities from coast to coast, but each institution appears to have approached the question unilaterally.

For the president to reiterate cavalierly that it was a routine decision reflected lack of understanding about what was going on in Buffalo and throughout the nation. Not listening to views and opinions over an issue affecting students resulted in unnecessary confusion, considerable financial cost, and hours of student, faculty, and administrative time. The question might have been resolved much earlier had prior efforts been made to feel the collective student pulse.

Originally simple issues become increasingly complicated when too much time elapses without closure. It did not dawn on the demonstrators until an avoidable second day of a sit-in that larger questions were involved. Negative conclusions were understandably reached about the unmovable bureaucracy when there was no way to talk seriously with an inaccessible president.

When college administrators don't know what to do, they often form a task force after the fact to decide how to respond to unforeseen developments. They seem no more inclined today than they were twenty-five years ago to anticipate potential problems; it is not surprising that university personnel are so frequently caught off balance, even when there are clear warning signals. Presidents might profit by establishing—and using—standing committees of faculty, students, and staff whose special role would be to review periodically internal and external events that might impact on academic life in the immediate future. This would allow for advance planning to deal more effectively with troublesome situations.

Our nation may consider reinstituting the draft to adjust to an anticipated reduction in the number of young men and women of military age and to better match personnel needs with more sophisticated and computerized military forces. Studying potentially charged issues, such as university involvement in classified research projects, would constitute the proper role of a special committee.

In 1966 students had valid concerns about the Selective Service test. Time was not taken to acquaint them with the positive aspects for conducting the examination on campus. When an informal poll was finally conducted toward the end of the controversy, fifteen hundred students favored giving the test in university facilities by a 2 to 1 margin. What might the climate have been—and how much time and money saved—if a similar measure had been taken before the initial decision? Periodic surveys, if only for advisory purposes, might well constitute standard fare when issues clearly relate to student interests.

"Such events will happen again, because we fail to learn from experience," predicts Kuntz (1991). "UB [along with most colleges and universities] still lacks a clear statement of what a university is, and what it should represent. We have become a technical school on the shores of Lake Erie, still short-changing undergraduate education for students who, when they realize this, may again try to tear the place down."

References

Division of Student Affairs. (1966). Special Report, SUNY/Buffalo, August 5.

Edelman, Sharon. (1968). Unpublished report on unrest at UB, prepared for University Archives, August.

Furnas, Clifford C. (1966a). Prepared statement, May 5.

——. (1966b). Statement issued by Office of Public Relations, May 13.

Kuntz, Allen H. (1991). Interview and Questionnaire.

Reinhold, Robert. (1989). "The Past Examined, the 60's Legacy," *Education Life; The New York Times,* January 8.

Rowland, A. Westley. (1988). Interview and Questionnaire.

The Spectrum. (1966a). February 4.

——. (1966b). March 4.

——. (1966c). May 4.

——. (1966d). "The Problems of Victory," May 11.

Taylor, Jeremy. (1966). Editorial, *The Spectrum,* May 3.

CHAPTER IV

Dow Chemical: The "Open Campus"

It took a decade to acknowledge that we were wrong and the system worked.

—Tom Hayden, a founder of SDS

Early 1967 polls revealed that 57 percent of Americans, albeit for different reasons, disapproved of LBJ's war policy. Johnson was caught between a majority who wanted the war escalated into complete victory and others who demanded an immediate cessation of U.S. involvement. Secretary of Defense Robert S. McNamara, losing confidence in body counts of enemy dead as reported by his own military sources, now recommended curtailing the air war and limiting troop increases. "McNamara parted paths not only with his president, but with his own department and his days were numbered," Jeremy Barnes (1988) points out. "In November 1967 LBJ eased out his Secretary of Defense with the resignation to become effective in February 1968. However, his replacement, Clark Clifford, would prove to be far from the vigorous manager Johnson had hoped for."

Beginning in September 1967, approximately fifty to seventy-five members of UB's loosely organized chapter of Students for a Democratic Society shuffled daily around the Norton Union fountain to protest the war. Most remained overnight, bedding down in sleeping bags. Their ceaseless vigil failed to attract additional participants but the silent little group drew peer attention. They endured daytime taunts from students between classes and evening threats of physical assault when a few athletes, occasionally armed with raw eggs, were looking for something to do after football practice. For their perseverance, if not their cause, the demonstrators slowly gained grudging respect from fellow students.

Norton Hall, our student union, had opened during the 1959–1960 school year; life in and around that building at the Main Street campus during the turbulent sixties defies description. Student Personnel officers are generally viewed by students as hired help to restrict their freedoms and inhibit activists, but I frequently visited the marching SDS contingent. Sometimes I remained at work after midnight, especially when rumors persisted that outsiders, strongly opposed to any form of student protest, intended to teach the "hippies" a lesson and remove them physically from the campus. Despite lack of enthusiasm by campus security for the assignment, I arranged for a nightly periodic presence of an officer in a police vehicle to safeguard the demonstrators and protect their right of dissent. On particularly brisk fall nights, when Buffalo weather matched its reputation, some marchers would suggest breaking ranks to share with me the light and warmth of my second-floor office, which overlooked the fountain. I discouraged this and reminded them about commitment ("What are you, summer soldiers?"), while respecting their symbolic—and courageous—peaceful protest.

SDS leadership was gradually shifting to a hard-core radical segment, not all of whom were officially enrolled UB students. They functioned effectively within the larger group, but their methods and rhetoric were not always supported, at least initially, by the full SDS membership of approximately 250 persons. Disagreements were common among the free spirits comprising SDS, but they were united in opposing the Dow Chemical Company, scheduled to interview UB chemistry and engineering seniors on October 31. Dow, among less controversial endeavors, manufactured napalm that was used in the Vietnam War.

SDS warned us that the recruitment visit would be physically disrupted, if necessary. Conveniently overlooking other companies equally involved in the war effort, activists argued that Dow, a "nonacademic" organization, should be barred from campus. By condoning Dow's presence, they maintained, the university institutionally approved the war. (This suggests some relationship with the Selective Service Test issue.)

Not in favor of restricting Dow or anyone else, an overwhelming majority of students did not then support the SDS antiwar position. Graduating seniors were especially concerned about threats to bar potential employers, and public opinion still favored the Vietnam involvement. The *National Observer* (1967) describes an incident on another campus where "a half-dozen students clambered over sit-in demonstrators protesting on-campus Marine recruiters waiting indoors. One student who made it through the pile of bodies . . . delivered a 2,500-signature petition supporting U.S. forces in Vietnam."

Months would pass before the conflict became so unpopular that Americans could accept the never previously considered option of military defeat to escape an increasingly untenable situation. I was already learning about U.S. military miscalculations in Vietnam through my involvement as a military reserve officer in a five-year course with the Command and General Staff College which included a two-week summer session at Fort Leavenworth.

We were warned about difficulties that resulted when reasons for armed intervention are not clearly understood by the citizenry, supply lines are too long, and civilians in warring nations do not automaticaly welcome an outside military presence. Most important, our statesmen overestimated American patience.

Richard Reeves (1988) pointed out that there is still no American consensus about what happened, much less what Vietnam means. He concluded, after reading a study reported in *American Heritage* of June 1988 that many of our leaders and respected observers were far less insightful than they are today—and future generations may have to re-learn lessons from past history.

"The man who probably was most influential in prosecuting the war, former Secretary of Defense Robert McNamara, offered only 25 words, but they constituted a sweeping answer that almost seemed to concede that he had been wrong from the start," according to Reeves.

" 'The United States,' McNamara said, 'must be careful not to interpret events occurring in a different land in terms of its own history, politics, culture, and morals.' "

Arthur Goldberg, U.S. Ambassador to the United Nations from 1965 to 1968, acknowledged in the same report that " 'Vital national interests were not at stake.' " Reeves includes comments by Clark Clifford (Secretary of Defense in 1968 and 1969) that, " 'the original calculation was erroneous. . . . It seems clear now that the national security of the United States was not involved in the war in Vietnam.' " Reeves adds the reactions of Marvin Kalb, who covered the war for CBS and has written about U.S. involvement in Asia: " 'No American must ever be called upon to sacrifice his life for the cause that is poorly understood, blurred, or deceptively explained by the administration.' "

For several weeks prior to the scheduled Dow visit we were following, perhaps too closely, reports about serious student demonstrations against Dow at Harvard, Illinois, and Michigan. At Wisconsin, my *alma mater,* many persons were reported injured when police wielding riot clubs and tear gas tried to break up a sit-in—employing such tactics as deliberately shoving unsuspecting spectators into a cordon of police to trigger physical confrontations. Ralph Hanson (1990), then director of the University of Wisconsin police and security, recalls the 1967 Dow confrontation in Madison. "We had no model; we were unrehearsed and unprepared for what followed, not only here, but at Columbia, Berkeley, and other places." Two days of confrontation between students and police on the Wisconsin campus resulted in seventy arrests as well as injuries to thirteen campus police officers and nineteen students, Hanson recalls.

"The Dow protest was our grand-daddy—whatever mistakes there are, you'll find them there," Hanson said as he was retiring after twenty-five years. "If we were to go through that again, I would have got the Dow recruiter out of there and let the protestors leave the building. We learned that 40 to 50 willful and determined young people could bring a university down by consistently disrupting its functions. By tactics like this (blocking entrances to the building and trying to occupy it) you forced the administration to use force, and in this instance force means the police officers," who at one point had to cope "with 5,000 kids and all the cameras and newsreels." The end of the sixties came none too soon for him.

"You had a lot of hostility," Hanson explains. "We became a surrogate for the Pentagon, the Government, and all the other agencies of social control. They (the students) couldn't go to the Pentagon or Washington, but by God, they could strike out right here at the university." The culmination of on-campus tensions at Wisconsin was the bombing of the Army Math Research Center in Sterling Hall, killing a graduate student in physics. "Now the campus is politically more sedate," Hanson said. "It isn't that young people are not politically involved; if we did something misdirected in Central America or the Middle East I'm sure that they would react."

After intense discussions with SDS representatives, it was clear that the Dow recruitment effort at UB would be seriously jeopardized. Activists maintained that the "open campus" principle avoided the real issue of universal aid to the "military-industrial complex" and the war effort; furthermore, they argued, Dow was not contributing to anyone's education. Any input from university governing bodies and university-wide referenda to determine campus opinion was disdained by them as "administrative tricks" and "underhanded devices." Beginning in 1959 when he was national chairman of the Student Peace Union—the forerunner of SDS—UB Professor Philip G. Altbach (1990) has studied campus unrest. He has written extensively about student movements here and in other countries. "The radical movement contained strong moral and political elements," he says. "Activists could not understand how any right-thinking person could oppose their cause or fail to understand their reasoning."

The SDS position was crystal clear. Violence in some form appeared inevitable. Radical hardliners wanted to determine which groups or industries could speak or recruit on campus—a privilege no person in a university should be able to assume unilaterally. English Professor Lionel Abel (1968) explains the SDS approach in a *New York Times Magazine* article through his interview with a leading member:

> Student: "Do you know why the demonstrations and protests succeeded? Because we didn't play the rules of the game. Our movement wasn't organized democratically. We kicked the Dow people off the campus although they had every right to be there.
> "It was our unrepressed intolerance and thorough anti-permissiveness that brought our actions success."

We needed planning time and an educational opportunity to discuss the open campus principle with student and faculty involvement; closing a campus selectively denies opportunities to students that are rightly theirs as members of the academic community. Believing that an essential element of academic freedom is an "open campus," I recommended to President Meyerson (1966–70) that we postpone, temporarily, the October Dow visit pending a review of UB's career recruitment policies.

The incident suggests what might be accomplished when there is time to discuss vital questions surrounding a given issue. Avoidance and procrastination may afford temporary intervals of relief, but the real value of any interlude as an educational opportunity is lost if an administration falls into the trap of exclusively addressing tactical and operational concerns.

Negative reactions from the academic community and the general public were inevitable and immediate. The media charged that the university's integrity was destroyed by an administration that so weakly capitulated to a handful of student radicals. UB should have forged ahead, it was maintained, holding the interviews as originally scheduled. (I should have called both newspapers when we announced the postponement to explain our position, an example of failure to educate the press.) *The Buffalo Evening News* (1967a) lead editorial on Monday, October 10 established the tone:

> The State University of Buffalo has timidly bowed to threatened demonstrations in withdrawing invitations to the Dow Chemical Company. . . .
> Richard A. Siggelkow, Vice President of Student Affairs, says the invitations are being withdrawn for the time being because "the entire academic community has not had sufficient opportunity to resolve this matter through full and open discussion." But it is obvious to all that the UB administration is fearful of the antiwar demonstrations which the UB branch of Students for a Democratic Society says it will hold if Dow recruiters appear on campus.
> UB officials understandably are concerned about the ugly clashes that have erupted over similar issues on other American campuses in recent days. But their present action comes close to capitulating to mob rule. . . .
> UB should simply have let the interviews proceed, permitting dissident students to exercise their right of peaceful protest, but making it clear that the university will not tolerate violence or lawlessness by any student, or any faculty member, at any time and for any reason.
> A great university cannot be built on the quicksand foundation of fearing controversy and appeasing would-be demonstrators.

Under the heading, "Students Rap UB Plan," *The Courier-Express* of Tuesday, October 31, carried an account of the formation of a Committee for Concerned Students:

> Posters announcing the right to free speech for everyone and voices over loudspeakers asking that "all have the right to be heard" filled the lobby of Norton Hall Monday in a "backlash" demonstration.
> Students are protesting . . . "intimidation of the administration by minority groups" . . . and "suppressing freedom of speech by banning the representatives."

The article included comments by two CSS student leaders (one was David Wachtel, who later became an undercover deputy in the Erie County Sheriff's Department) that " 'a lot of American students are tired of activist groups' " and " 'students are sick of people thinking all UB students are leftists.' "

The University News Service (1967) issued a press release on October 31:

> The decision to withhold interviews by the Central Intelligence Agency and the Dow Chemical Company on the campus of the State Univeristy of New York at Buffalo was explained today by Richard A. Siggelkow, Vice President for Student Affairs. . . .
>
> All members of the university community must continue to share responsibility for maintaining a climate in which diverse views can be expressed freely and without harassment. Intelligent controversy remains essential to the educational mission of higher education, and it would be most unfortunate if thoughtless actions and emotionally inspired conflict among persons holding opposing points of view physically disrupted the educational program of the university.
>
> The general welfare of all must be considered when situations could develop in which potential danger is present. . . . No university should allow itself to become a battleground for conflicting opinions that could too easily disrupt its basic educational functions and subject individuals to possible physical harm. It is well recognized that serious divergencies of opinion among faculty, students, and administrators exist as to appropriate use of university placement resources. . . . In view of the fact that the entire academic community has not had sufficient opportunity to resolve this matter through full and open discussion, campus interviewing facilities are being withheld from the Dow Chemical Company for the time being. . . .
>
> It is important both to preserve the rights of those who desire to arrange such interviews through the Placement Office and still not ignore the deeply felt concerns of other students relative to current use of on-campus facilities.

The October 31 *Spectrum* (1967a) ran a front page editorial, "So This Is Victory":

> Someone hung a sign in the Union Friday: "The University has withdrawn its invitation to Dow Chemical Co. to recruit on campus. Victory!"
>
> Victory?
>
> Victory for whom?
>
> Victory for what cause?
>
> Success by a minority who threatened violence is no success.
>
> Satisfaction in having prevented any group from coming on a university campus is perverted satisfaction.
>
> Triumph of the cause of a few which potentially denies the rights of many is no triumph. The University chose to postpone the interviews in an effort to avoid violence. When universities must bend to the will of minorities which apparently threaten violence, they are no longer universities.
>
> In the present situation, the decision by the University was a good one. Any effort to avoid turning the campus into a battlefield should be commended. Any group that would turn this campus into a battleground

because of a difference of opinion should be condemned.

Those who gloat over their "victory" have done the greater harm. No matter how strong their beliefs, no matter how valid their beliefs, they have no privilege to deny the rights of others. There are others who have opinions and beliefs that are just as strong.

Those self-appointed designators of what is or is not acceptable for the University community are no better than bigots. Their self-righteous attitudes are dangerous for the university community. No one has challenged the right of anyone to dissent, but when dissent emerges as a threat of violence, it is no longer of any value. Proponents of that course have no place in a university.

Their minds are closed and narrow. Their actions are tainted with deleterious overtones. The value of their views is substantially decreased. They are, in fact, worthless in any constructive search for valid answers to real problems.

Your victory is not so sweet, victors, you have so very little of which to be proud.

On October 30, President Meyerson issued a major declaration to faculty, colleagues, and students, emphasizing points he repeated at special Faculty Senate meetings called later. The statement also appeared in the November 10 issue of *The Gazette* (1967a), a bi-weekly in-house University Relations publication directed primarily at faculty and staff.

Meyerson emphasized that UB had maintained an "open campus" concept for decades "in accord with a long history of academic freedom." The action to postpone the Dow visit provided time to discuss the matter with care and explore the issue with reasoned deliberation. The president scheduled a special meeting of the newly enlarged Faculty Senate on November 13 to review the traditional open campus concept and consider measures to protect this approach and prevent the disruption of our academic life and freedom.

At the spirited Faculty Senate meeting, called to discuss only this issue, resolutions ranged from reaffirmation of the open campus principle to discontinuing campus recruiting altogether, creation of a faculty-student body to study and resolve the entire recruitment system, and an early call to end the Vietnam War. Meyerson reported his earlier concerns and discussed the role of the placement office for the November 13 *Gazette* (1967b):

In the call for the meeting, I suggested that the issue was relevant to academic freedom. Some of you deny this on the ground that career recruiting is not a primary educational responsibility of the University. I would agree that career recruiting is a secondary responsibility but would point out it has a large educational component. . . .

Many, and perhaps most, of the questions of academic freedom arise not from the primary educational mission of the University but from secondary activities, particularly those of a political nature. Paradoxically, some who have been trying to extend the concept of academic freedom to include aspects of action as well as speech, are, on this recruiting issue, seeking to narrow the concept.

Academic freedom must protect more than literal speech. Thus, as you no doubt know, the national Council of American Association of University Professors and civil liberties spokesmen have maintained that the question is one of academic freedom and civil liberty. . . .

I should also point out that suggestions to restrict or prohibit public speech are usually made from outside the University. It is no less a question of freedom when these suggestions to restrict come from within the University; nor is the danger to liberty less when the target of restrictive pressures is private discussion between a recruiter and individual students who choose to converse with him.

Academic freedom in a university cannot be limited to a few specified rights. It goes further and imposes an obligation on us not only to protect unpopular ideas but to preserve the broadest range of expression and activity in the university communty. This we must do with a most sensitive regard for fairness and equality, regardless of popularity or power. . . .

Once we in the University begin to discriminate among employers or students, do we not open a Pandora's box? If we bar some recruiters, shall we not bar all? And if we impose such a bar in placement activities, may it not be extended in the name of conscience to many other academic activities as well?

We should be reminded, too, that universities have resisted the pressures of political powers and various public and private groups through the successful enunciation and defense of the "open campus" principle. We should be aware that any erosion of this principle may erode this defense. . . .

As the official who initiated the postponement, I was asked about my actions. My comments followed:

We had been informed by individuals intending to demonstrate that peaceful behavior was most unlikely by some of those involved despite our presently defined procedures for peaceful protest that have been traditionally upheld and respected. . . .

I did not feel either then or now that postponement represented "appeasement." The immediate alternative of physical conflict without fully considering all implications is one route by which everyone may ultimately be deprived of liberty and freedom. Any effort to limit either the freedom or the openness of the academic community must be of grave concern for all who would hope to continue to share in the benefits of that community. There were other issues, such as whether or not a majority or minority is entitled to forcibly deprive others of their rights, a need to consider the far reaching implications of violence that was surely about to occur on this campus, and academic freedom. For these reasons, the interviews were temporarily postponed. . . .

Meanwhile, no university can tolerate or condone violence; however, we know equally well that serious incidents have and are continuing to erupt on other campuses. Some students and some faculty are apparently willing to risk violence to make their point. The presence of police elsewhere did not serve effectively as either a deterrent or as an effective solution. The use of civil authority often tended to move discussion even further from related issues, creating additional strife, confusion, and mutual distrust. These actions also made it increasingly difficult to consider the matter rationally rather than emotionally. . . . It is to the credit of this institution that we have not previously had to resort to outside authority, but situations can alter radically when emotion overpowers reason.

If a major concern is whether or not the academic community is to remain free and open, what sanctions should be applied? It would be necessary to inform in real terms what will happen to those who deliberately decide to infringe upon the rights of others. We need, then, to be alerted to the harmful effects the University and its members are likely to sustain if force and counter-force represent the vehicle through which freedom and order are either to be violated or maintained.

Each member of the academic community has a commitment to preserve the rights of all others. "A free university in a free society," (the slogan of one of the dissident groups) should mean freedom for all. Self-restraint, and even greater sacrifice, may be required by any protesting group if freedom is to endure.

There are few positive conclusions to draw from what must be generally considered a deplorable state of affairs—one may only hope that such controversy still represents that all too rare occasion to learn, and to renew or apply fundamental facts and principles.

The November 24 *Gazette* (1967c) carried the results of the November 13 Senate meeting:

Following "spirited" and "intense" debate, the Faculty Senate on November 13 endorsed the "open campus" principle. After the vote, Dr. Richard A. Siggelkow, Vice President for Student Affairs, indicated that an invitation to the Dow Chemical Company to recruit on campus would be reissued almost immediately. . . .

The Senate PASSED unanimously a resolution submitted by the Executive Committee pro tem:

"RESOLVED that the Faculty Senate supports the action taken by the Vice President for Student Affairs, as approved by the President, in postponing campus recruiting by Dow Chemical Company . . . pending further consideration of the issue by the Faculty and student body."

In the action which upheld the "open campus" idea, the Senate PASSED by a vote of 197 for and 72 against a second resolution submitted by the Executive Committee pro tem:

"RESOLVED that the maintenance of the opportunity for all legal groups to partake in recruiting on the campus is in keeping with the responsibility of the University to its students and to society, as is the freedom of the Faculty and students to express, in a peaceful manner, opposition to the ideas or actions of the recruiter. . . ."

In a separate action the previous week, the Student Senate passed a resolution that the Student Senate cannot condone the threat of violence by any student group and supports the rights . . . to recruit on campus.

Undeterred, the radicals welcomed the additional time to firm up their strategies. The November 15 *Courier-Express* (1967b) reported that "The Students for a Democratic Society, a minority group on the UB campus, has vowed it will continue to interfere with recruiting at the university, even to the point . . . 'of asserting our right to remove them (recruiters) from the university.' "

On December 13 President Meyerson again wrote to students and faculty colleagues. His warnings preceded by one day a reconvened Faculty Senate meeting called because the previous session had been abruptly adjourned after an unauthorized entry of several hundred demonstrating students:

> Internal threats to the University through disorders can easily result in our losing control of our own affairs. Recent events in Wisconsin, California, other parts of New York State and elsewhere in the country, indicate that disorder breeds further disorder, that the use of force (even "nonviolent") breeds counterforce. The use of force more often than not is beyond the control of university authorities. The fabric of a university, even the strongest, is a fragile thing.
>
> The open campus policy, which has the support of the Faculty and Student Senates, as well as organizations devoted to academic freedom and civil liberties, is a policy designed to protect against a tyranny of either majorities or minorities. It is a policy which preserves the opportunity for dissent at the university . . . and provides the one best hope that the university can become a bulwark against repression and coercion. If the universities are not these bulwarks already, we ought to aspire to that end. What we must face and fear is that those who break up meetings today may be unable to hold their own meetings tomorrow. Admonitions for peace and order are easy enough to make. The difficult task is to understand what the consequences of disorder are likely to be.
>
> To preserve the university, not merely for what it is but for what it can become, will require from all of us understanding and respect for others. (Meyerson 1967)

The spotlight of an unmarked Buffalo police car picked out my house number just before daybreak on Dow Day, December 18. I had not requested police protection, but others insisted on it. At my first opportunity I assigned one of the two plainclothesmen to accompany Professor Robert H. Rossberg, the official Faculty Senate observer.

Our spotters were stationed at key campus locations to relay information, logged by two secretaries, about the mood and exact location of the protesters. We carried bullhorns, automobiles were strategically located to move interviewees and recruiters if necessary, and code words were designed for emergencies. Our central planning group included Robert O'Neil, who had been recently imported by President Meyerson from Berkeley as a special presidential staff assistant (who later became president of the University of Virginia and chancellor of the University of Wisconsin system). Other key administrators were Laurence Smith, currently Vice President for Student Affairs and Director of Marketing Services at Eastern Michigan University; Ronald H. Stein, now one of UB's top vice presidents; and Anthony F. Lorenzetti, then Associate Vice President for Student Affairs.

When a third of the twenty-one students who originally signed up for interviews expressed concern over physical assault, we decided on two different interview sites. The placement office did not have adequate interviewing facilities and conferences were traditionally held wherever space could be found on the overextended campus, including the Union, the chemistry building, and the engineering complex. What differed was my decision not to disclose the location of a second site, which would become an alternative for completing the interviews if the primary area were closed down. The publicized primary location was the Alumni suite, a well-appointed set of small offices—a maze of narrow hallways with doors all over the place that resembled a rabbit warren. Although we had innocently selected the location because there was sufficient outdoor space to accommodate picketing and demonstrations, the odd room pattern unintentionally helped our cause. When one radical contingent later invaded the hallways in search of the elusive quarry they must have thought themselves trapped in a carnival-like fun house.

I prepared in advance four different press releases that ranged from the best to the worst scenario. Spontaneous reactions under stress turn out to be exactly that. Statements outlined beforehand help to avoid misunderstandings that can result when harried administrators are tracked down by reporters. Calling a journalist back after a five-minute delay also occasionally enables you to make better sense when reacting to unforeseen developments and is preferable to "no comment," or an immediate "I don't know what is going on." Interviewees under certain conditions may wish to have another staff member present when answering questions posed by reporters, and there is nothing wrong with recording a phone conversation to protect against misquotes or being quoted out of context.

We photographed interviewees as they arrived at the alumni site. Movies were taken to illustrate that the demonstrators had the broadest possible latitude for peaceful dissent. We also believed it important to establish that we actually used the identified entryway and building. A statement was read twice at the placement office between 8:00 and 9:00 A.M. and three times during a Student Senate informational open forum with another Dow representative between 9:00 and 10:00 A.M.: "A Dow Chemical recruiter is located on campus in the Alumni office at 2530 Winspear Avenue. The building is bounded by the football field, Winspear Avneue, and the nuclear reactor. No interviews will be held in Norton Union, Schoellkopf Hall, Hayes Hall, or the annexes. The entrance to the recruitment office is located at the rear of the building adjacent to the warehouse receiving area."

Stein and Lorenzetti escorted the first two candidates without incident from my Harriman office to the designated site shortly after 8:00 A.M., passing directly by a preliminary SDS rally in progress at the fountain area. We had witnesses identify the candidates as they left our office on schedule at twenty-minute intervals. We did not smuggle interviewees into the building in advance and lock the door, and we continued to send them over to the Alumni office after the demonstrators arrived there *en masse* at 9:20 A.M. One SDS member, a chemistry student, requested and was given a conference time although he was clearly not interested in working for Dow. We scheduled him for the last interview during which he and six fellow protesters harangued Dow's Dr. Robert Bumbe for over an hour. We finally spirited the recruiter away in a car strategically parked nearby.

Valuable time (for them) was lost by the demonstrators when they paused to recruit additional supporters before coming to the clearly designated area. A December 19 *Spectrum* (1976b) report follows their progress:

> The demonstrators had marched two abreast around the Norton Hall fountain to pick up additional supporters and at 9:15 they finally marched two abreast to the Winspear facility. There were about 300 of them. Shortly before 10 A.M., 30 marchers linked arms and encircled one of the entrances.
>
> Forty minutes later a student at the front end of the building broke a glass door panel with a motorcycle helmet, reached in, and opened the door.
>
> A score of students poured in. They searched the offices but did not find the recruiters. Dean Siggelkow appeared and told the crowd this was where interviews were now taking place.

When the group went in one door and ran out another I was waiting for them. I was surrounded and accused of lying about the site. ("Why are you hiding war criminals?" and "Whose side are you on, anyway, Siggelkow?")

I was almost as confused as they since I had assumed the demonstrators would find the recruiter in the Alumni suite, forcing us into the alternate site. I was truthful—and fortunate. When the interviewer heard the demonstrators running through the hallways in hot pursuit, he calmly switched off the office light; the conference resumed after the search party noisily passed by. It is no wonder that I was charged with prevarication.

A related incident is worth noting. Former *Spectrum* editor Jeremy Taylor, who became a Unitarian minister, was committed to peaceful methods of protest. Although one of the original members of UB's SDS chapter, he refused to join those pledged to physically preventing job candidates from entering buildings, choosing instead to document the day's events with movie film. Jeremy was camera ready when I called him aside to inform him that the demonstrators were erroneously picketing the wrong entrance. I pointed to a well-dressed student entering the correct door (unlocked) for his appointment.

"Should I let them know about their error?", I asked.

Jeremy shook his head, which was enough for me. We both returned to watching the picketers mull around in the wrong area. I would have pointed them in a proper direction had they inquired, but they probably would not have believed me.

I later announced from the Harriman Hall stairwell through a bullhorn (which I cheerfully shared intermittently with a radical spokesman) that the recruiters had left and the interviewing was completed. SDS flooded the campus the next several days with mimeographed flyers. One titled "SiggelDOW, Is This an Open Campus?" charged that I had deliberately misdirected the demonstrators, announcing that recruits had left the campus while they were still interviewing, lying about and not holding *any* interviews at the announced location, and generally acting in bad faith by leading protesters on a wild goose chase. Major radical strategy was to undermine administrative credibility and make the open campus concept so difficult that staff and faculty would begin to wonder if it was worth the price.

The Courier-Express (1967c) reported on December 19 that three hundred had protested while "an estimated 10,000 other students went about their classes as usual." *The Buffalo Evening News* (1967b) on Monday, December 18, noted that "Dow recruiters Ron Haughton and Dr. Robert Bumbe completed their interviews and left the campus without incident." The articles also noted that the demonstrators "carried anti-war placards," and "some of the young men wore beards, long hair, and clothing (khaki green dungarees) associated with the hippie movement." (Ironically in an earlier *Buffalo Evening News* photograph taken during the SDS protest march at the fountain area, the only two participants with beards were later proudly identified as undercover sheriff's deputies who had infiltrated SDS—and one of them would soon be serving time as a convicted drug dealer.)

A *Courier-Express* (1967d) December 18 lead editorial noted:

> The question of whether or not representatives of Dow Chemical Co. and of the Central Intelligence Agency should be allowed to conduct recruiting on the campus of the University of Buffalo seems to have been answered quite decisively by UB students. . . .
> And we agree with UB President Martin Meyerson, who held that the open campus policy "is a policy designed to protect against a tyranny of either majorities or minorities. . . . It is a policy which provides the one best hope that the university can become a bulwark against repression and coercion."
> That is what the university should be striving for. That is what everyone—the dissenting minority most of all—should be hoping for. Without such bulwarks, the freedom of all of us is endangered.

A December 20 *Buffalo Evening News* (1967c) commentary lauded the university equally for its handling of the situation without resorting to outside force, but the final paragraph of *The Spectrum's* front page editorial of December 19 was in closer touch with future reality:

> While also complimenting the leaders of the demonstration for handling the crowd as they did, the campus police (unarmed) must be commended for their patience.
> The administration must be complimented for its strategies. The plan

was masterful, extremely well engineered, and carried out with no visible flaws.

All involved must be commended for the restraint which was displayed. . . .

But while we all can claim victory, all might just as well claim defeat. The administration proved that it could bring bubonic plague on campus unmolested—a dangerous precedent to set. . . . The fact that no direct confrontation evolved this time does not preclude the fact that it might have happened or that it will happen next time. (*The Spectrum* 1976b)

After Dow I assumed a loss of whatever previous rapport I had with the less militant SDS membership, so I was surprised two weeks later to be invited to meet Tom Hayden, the primary author of the *Port Huron Statement,* a fifty-four-page manifesto promulgated during the founding of SDS.

Contending that the American political system had failed to achieve social or international peace or end poverty and exploitation, the statement called for "participatory democracy" in which individuals could share in social decisions affecting their lives. Advocated was activism governed by basic principles of human and social value.

As editor of the *NASPA Journal* I had mentioned to SDS member Rick Salter (now an attorney in Canada) that I wanted to solicit an article from Hayden, if he visited the UB chapter. I hoped to balance the generally bland content of the Student Personnel publication and acquaint the conservative membership with different viewpoints.

Although paranoid enough to believe that local police had staked out the location, I accepted the unanticipated invitation to meet Hayden. (I was right about being noticed, but it was the FBI.) Distinctly out of place as the only person in a suitcoat and necktie, I mused about Lawrence of Arabia and mingled uncomfortably among forty to fifty SDS members (all men) while cautiously sampling the *hors d'oeuvres*. No one—including the student who broke a window with his motorcycle helmet at the Alumni office area during the Dow episode—was unpleasant or referred to the recent confrontation.

The contact with Hayden was disappointing. Clearly unimpressed with me, he was not about to share his thoughts with a Student Personnel journal editor, let alone a Vice President for Student Affairs. Had I clairvoyantly predicted Hayden's future relationships with Jane Fonda and his current role as a respected member of California's political establishment he might now recall our chance encounter.

In an April 23, 1968 letter Irwin Shaw, a top Dow executive, complained about how his recruiters had been mistreated during their UB visit. I reacted, perhaps too hastily, and sent my response without discussing its contents with another staff member. A colleague's reaction to first drafts is often desirable, especially when some parts of a communication composed in anger might better be consigned to a wastepaper basket. I don't know what Dow expected, but my warm reply included the following comment:

I would also be most surprised, judging from what I have learned from other campuses, if your recruiters had a more difficult time here than they experienced elsewhere. We will do the best we can to carry through the interviews next fall, and while I may be reading too much into your comments, the arbitrary and cavalier attitude of recruiters and their employers may only serve to increase lack of support from the placement function in universities, a tragic aftermath and sad commentary of our time.

I would still remind you that all interviews took place without disruption, including one with a demonstrator, also a qualified candidate, who contacted Dr. Bumbe as his final interviewee. . . . I am further constrained to note that the recruiters were well protected, whereas members of my staff had to directly face a potentially volatile situation throughout the entire period.

We can also say all we like about using the police and outside force, but it is certainly appropriate to point out that the various recruiters have an equal obligation to consider the terrific pressure their own limited attitudes may place upon institutions of higher education in admittedly difficult times.

Universities are not yet well equipped to deal with those who wish to disrupt, since a relatively small number of demonstrators often capitalized on psychological advantages, and vacillatory sympathies of uncommitted students and faculty. There is questionable value in the deliberate use of force to contain the situation, and there is no victory for anyone in these matters. . . .

Fortunately, demonstrators did not take advantage of their opportunities to disrupt or block entrance ways for those candidates who were, therefore, able to enter the building without incident. Since our present policy is to the effect that we are, indeed, an open campus, our procedures will continue to be forthright. I am assuming that we understand each other clearly and do not expect a response to this letter. (Siggelkow 1967)

We had survived the Dow crisis only to face new ones.

References

Abel, Lionel. (1968). "Seven Heroes of the New Left," *The New York Times Magazine,* May 5.

Altbach, Philip G. (1986). "The New Wave of Student Activism: Why Now?" *The Chronicle of Higher Education,* May 15.

———. Interview and Questionnaire, April 1990.

Barnes, Jeremy. (1988). *The Pictorial History of the Vietnam War* (New York: Gallery Books).

Buffalo Evening News. (1967a). "UB Knuckles Under," Editorial, October 10.

———. (1967b). December 18.

———. (1967c). "UB Passes Test," December 20.

Courier-Express. (1967a). "Students Rap UB Plan," October 31.

———. (1967b). November 15.

———. (1967c). December 19.

———. (1967d). "Open Campus Policy Strengthened," December 18.

The Gazette. (1967a). November 10.

———. (1967b). November 13.

———. (1967c). November 24.

Hanson, Ralph. (1990). Quoted in the "Campus Life" section of *The New York Times,* "Chief of Security Recalls Old Days, Good and Bad," May 20.

Meyerson, Martin. (1967). Open letter to university community, December 13.

Morris, Earl F. (1970). "Bar President Defines Differences in Dissent and Civil Disobedience." *Newsletter, Higher Education and National Affairs,* American Council on Education, April 19.

National Observer. (1967). "A Campus Counter-Protest," November 6.

Reeves, Richard. (1988). "What Was Vietnam Really All About?" *The Buffalo Evening News,* Op-Ed, June 22.

Siggelkow, Richard A. (1967). Letter to Dow Chemical Company (Irwin Shaw), April 30.

The Spectrum. (1967a). "So This Is Victory," October 31.

———. (1967b). December 19.

University News Service. (1967). Press release, October 31.

CHAPTER V

Administrative Change and "Educational Reform"

I learned politics in the early part of my life as a member of the faculty of Princeton University. The second half of my career I practiced among the amateurs in Washington.

—Woodrow Wilson

Whereas only the elite attended college a hundred years earlier, between 1955 and 1965 enrollment at American universities increased from 2.7 to 5.7 million; in 1969, almost 8 million attended college, Peterson reported (1968). Since the end of World War II, "the proportion of the college-age population (18–21) attending college doubled, from 22 percent in 1946 to 45 percent in 1965. In the fall of 1967 approximately six million students were attending about 2,300 colleges and universities. Something over one-third of these are public, tax-supported institutions; given their typically large size and equalitarian admissions policies, however, the public institutions presently enroll two-thirds of the total student population" (p. 55).

Universities "boomed even faster than the college-age population," adds Gitlen (1987). "By 1960 the United States was the first society in the history of the world with more college students than farmers. (By 1969 the number of students had nearly doubled, to three times the number of farmers.) The number of degrees granted, undergraduate and graduate combined, doubled between 1956 and 1967. The proportion enrolled in public institutions rose especially fast" (p. 299).

The relative prevalence of organized student activism concerning off-campus political and social issues in the large institutions is probably less the result of university-induced alienation than it is a reflection of the gross numbers of individuals brought together at one time and place, Peterson maintained (1968). "Even if only two percent were vocal (as often estimated) 100,000 students on a national scale represented a real force to consider. The larger the student body is, the greater the likelihood of there being some student who wishes to start something—an SDS chapter, a speech walkout, a student strike—and of his being able to find others who will sympathize" (p. 55).

After his arrival in fall 1966, President Meyerson had enjoyed a brief honeymoon period, although his new staff appointments (while necessary) increased tensions and anxieties that invariably accompany major administrative change. Established faculty, whose opinions had been clearly more valued by previous administrations, felt ignored. New faculty, with their own ideas about academic change, were being recruited at a record pace. During this period of extremely rapid growth incoming young faculty were independent operators with little time to develop loyalty to their department, the institution, or the community. A more rigorous tenure review system had also been adopted, adding pressure on newcomers to produce; they had little time to consider institutional concerns.

To effect change, the president apparently decided to breach such traditional barriers as the Graduate School (generally a powerful influence at most large, multi-purpose research-oriented universities) a strong, entrenched Faculty Senate, and rigid departmental structures.

Although the new administration did not initially realize the depth of feelings at the time, Warren G. Bennis (1972) acknowledged the omission after he left UB:

> Many old-guard professors took the administration's neglect as a personal snub. They were not asked for advice; they were not invited to social affairs. They suspected that we acted coolly toward them because we considered them to be second-rate academics who lacked intellectual chic and who could not cut it in Cambridge or New York. Ironically, some of the old-guard academic administrators who kept their positions were notoriously second rate. . . . We succeeded in infusing new blood into Buffalo, but we failed to recirculate the old blood. We lost an opportunity to build loyalty among respected members of the veteran faculty. If veteran faculty members had been made to feel that they, too, had a future in the transformed university, they might have embraced the academic reorganization with some enthusiasm; instead the veteran faculty were hurt, indignant, and—finally—angry (p. 119).

G. Lester Anderson (1989), Academic Vice President under Furnas, had voluntarily returned to the faculty just before Meyerson's arrival. A distinguished SUNY Professor and an acknowledged expert on higher education, Anderson reports that "Meyerson and his newly appointed administrative personnel seemed to ignore the importance of operating with faculty cooperation in decision making. His administration chose not to involve senior faculty in the development and ongoing affairs of the university they knew so well."

"Change is most successful when those who are affected are involved in the planning," wrote Bennis (1972). "Nothing makes persons as resistant to new ideas or approaches as the feeling that change is being imposed upon them. The members of a university are unusually sensitive to individual prerogatives and to the administration's utter dependence on their support. Buffalo's academic plan was not generated popularly. Students and faculty did not contribute to its formulation. People resist change, even of a kind they basically agree with, if they are not significantly involved in the planning. A clumsier, slower, but more egalitarian approach to changing the university would have resulted in more permanent reform" (p. 120).

Meyerson failed to inform, involve, and educate campus constituencies about changes directly affecting them. He may also have been incorrect in believing that his proposed academic reorganization and educational ideals always matched those of most faculty and students. He established his own goals, which may have been what UB needed, but he did not indicate clearly why or how the new practices would be integrated into the existing organization. He failed to create awareness about the need for change or gain support for his proposals, which would have created a sense of joint ownership. By spring 1968 the college system had taken shape; by fall 1969 the four-course load, the pass-fail system, and departmental reorganization were in place. Meyerson knew what a university was about, but he did not foresee how his well-intentioned—but not necessarily new—reforms, first proposed to and adopted by the Faculty Senate without debate on November 28, 1966, would ultimately impact negatively on UB. He forced us to face up to an uncomfortable adjustment to rapid change, but tried to reach his own goals too quickly. We often seemed to move in new directions without knowing why. Meyerson was sometimes compared to a lost airline pilot who reported that while he didn't know where he was going, he and the crew were making record time. The influential *Los Angeles Times* carried an item written by veteran educational staff writer William Trombley (1968) under the heading "Buffalo's Old Campus Pulsates with Change, Top New Administrators, Swift Actions Aim for Excellence—Despite Resistance." What UB senior faculty read included the following paragraphs:

> A rather average private university is being fashioned swiftly into a state university of quality, with highly unusual arrangements. Many Old Guard faculty members regard the "boy deans" with dismay, if not contempt.
>
> "The main thing I set out to do was to change the tone at Buffalo," said Martin Meyerson, former acting chancellor and dean of the College of Environmental Design at UC/Berkeley, who is completing his second year as president of the New York institution. . . .
>
> Academically Meyerson had reorganized the university into seven fac-

ulties, in an effort to establish more meaningful ties between the basic disciplines and the professional training that stems from these disciplines. . . . Meyerson deplored the separation of graduate and undergraduate studies, and especially the isolation of professional schools and research institutes from contact with all but a handful of the most advanced graduate students. . . . "We want each faculty to establish general education courses for both undergraduates and graduate students." . . .

On the new Amherst campus Meyerson plans to organize colleges of no more than 1,000 enrollment which will be "centers of identification" for both graduate and undergraduate students. . . . "Each college will develop its own intellectual or professional interest."

One of the boldest and initially most promising organizational and curricular changes centered around establishing centers of identification, or radically new colleges, each rotating upon the axis of its own interest. The original plan had been for groups of students and instructors with similar interests to come together in a social/academic environment in numbers possibly up to a thousand, which would provide identity, concern, and belonging to a university world otherwise so large as to swallow up all individuality.

" 'This whole effort at Buffalo is really a bootstrap operation in an underdeveloped country,' said Bennis in the *Los Angeles Times* article. " 'We are trying to change a sleepy, drowsy university with a very mixed faculty, into a first-rate institution. The question is whether we will be kept from doing so by deadwood, by organizational dry rot, or by people who fear the future and hope the whole effort will collapse.' An 'optimistic' Meyerson acknowledged that 'opposition from faculty members who resist change is sometimes a problem, but . . . the university is changing rapidly and a large proportion of the faculty is new. I think the new faculty are just very ready for change' " (Trombley 1968).

Claude E. Welch (1989), then Dean of Undergraduate Education, confirms that academic reforms were proposed by the administration in accordance with the president's belief that the system needed change. "Meyerson came into office proposing to open up the university and he did with his educational reforms for students." Professor Fred N. Snell (1989), Biophysical Sciences, arguably the foremost faculty leader for radical experimentation in learning and most closely identified with the new collegiate system, agrees: "Like the four-course load, the creation of the colleges" (perhaps most important to the protesters) "did not involve student participation." Snell remains angry today because students were bypassed in the planning.

"Meyerson and others believed that academia was stale, that it needed some innovations," adds Shapiro (1979), but the colleges never worked out the way Meyerson envisioned. "Their identification with radical activism— and the sometimes huge enrollments they were able to draw in 1968–70— made the colleges a threat to traditional academics."

What followed after the president selected Robert L. Ketter, Dean of the Graduate School, to become Vice President for Facilities Planning and oversee developments on the new Amherst campus heightened concern and suspicion among senior faculty. Over protests from the Graduate School Executive Committee, Snell was appointed to the vacated deanship. Although holding an MD from Harvard and a PhD from MIT, it is unlikely that the biochemist would have been ultimately selected had the president—at his own peril—not short-circuited normal search procedures already in progress. Despite pleas by key faculty that other potential candidates should be considered who were at least as well, if not better qualified, presidential pressure insured Snell's appointment. The search process was abruptly terminated by the president on grounds that Snell was about to embark on an overseas sabbatical and would become unavailable.

Many believed the appointment was deliberately engineered to gain control of the Graduate School. Attributing Machiavellian intent to Meyerson is unfair; he could only have wanted to ameliorate the strong influence of existing administrative structures. Still, senior faculty anxieties were not reduced when Snell's first order (without discussion) to Assistant Dean Andrew Holt was to transfer immediately half of the Graduate School staff to other campus units. Within the week an Associate Dean of the Graduate School was not speaking to his new superior and Snell chose not to schedule any meetings with the formerly closely involved campus-wide representative executive committee or with any other previously established policy-making groups. Threats of a no-confidence vote at an upcoming Graduate School faculty meeting in June 1968 if Snell's deanship continued into the next academic term convinced the president to reassess his earlier decision, maintains Holt (1989). Meyerson created new problems by appointing Snell Master of College A, the first unit of the newly established "colleges." Overnight Snell changed his conservative professorial image and became a folk hero of radical students, marching with them and supporting attacks against educational traditionalists.

The first two colleges, A and F (Tolstoy College), aspired to educate students through alternative courses emphasizing the need for social change in America. Large enrollments in 1968–70 "made the colleges a threat to traditional services," and they "became a haven for students involved in radical activism," reports Shapiro (1979). College A in particular concentrated on "learning experiments" in which credit was awarded for unsupervised non-classroom activities. "Alternative methods of learning became the sole academic threat of the activist portion of the student body," according to Cacavas (1979). "Thousands of students flocked to courses in College A which was quartered in a Main Street storefront and stressed an unstructured self-styled approach to education. Cynics saw it as a way to grab credit for political activism while supporters saw the College as one of the few relevant and responsive methods of learning that the university could muster." Some who still believe in the early college overlook the insular radical concept of education that included silencing anyone espousing counter positions.

College A students literally established their own academic policies and elevated grade inflation to an art form. They were granted the power to protect themselves from the draft, albeit at the expense of their peers who were subjected to less benign standards elsewhere. "There were no traditional courses, no examinations, no requirements, no distinctions between professors and students," Paul Kurtz (1971) complained about the aptly named college. "Students were permitted to grade themselves—with the result that 94 percent received 'A' grades," still on their permanent academic record. The Master of College A quipped that "a student could take a course in tying shoe laces if that was what he wanted; students received academic credit for studying projects conceived by themselves" (p. 233). Attendance at rallies and involvement in student protests were considered academically legitimate for credits. Participants evaluated themselves with self-assigned grades and were not obliged to submit written accounts about their activities.

Myths and misperceptions live well beyond their inception. *Reach* (1987), a student-published guide to UB, issued to incoming freshmen and transfer students, sets the tone historically: "It is only since the sixties, which spawned the civil rights, student rights, anti-war and women's movements, that student history takes center stage at UB and nationally. Although there have been some strong student movements in the past, in foreign countries and in the U.S. during the thirties, it has only been in the last twenty years that students have been able to find, and use their power to influence policy at their individual schools and nationwide, bringing about exciting innovations in education." Student activists of the era erroneously believed that educational reforms initiated at UB in the 1960s—doing away with General Education by restructuring the undergraduate division (one remaining vestige of Meyerson's reforms) establishing the colleges, bulletin board courses, the four-course load, the pass-fail grading system—resulted from "demands and pressures" they placed on the administration.

At UB "the administration and faculty, led by the liberal ideals of then President Meyerson, devised the changes and implemented them, often without significant student participation," explains Shapiro (1979). "For the most part, the student role in formulating the academic reforms (including the colleges) was limited to mere acceptance of Meyerson's plans." Instead of producing positive or lasting educational reforms, UB activists destroyed whatever promise initially existed in the structure introduced by the Meyerson presidency.

One man's dead wood is another's art object. Meyerson's proposals "soon inveighed opposition from members of the old administration and faculty, who were not dazzled by the innovations," wrote Kurtz (1971). "Many of the faculty so bitterly condemned as 'reactionaries' or 'dead wood' . . . were themselves progressive in education, innovators before, during, and after the Meyerson regime; they merely insisted upon the careful evaluation of programs. To claim that one believes in experimental education means nothing, unless one is prepared to develop parameters for testing new methods of learning" (p. 233). Significantly, the president's reorganization plan was implemented, even though the graduate school faculty—albeit by a one-vote margin—voted not to accept the orignal proposal.

On October 31, 1968, Governor Rockefeller ceremonially broke ground for the planned $650,000,000 construction of the new UB campus, which, after much discussion, was to be located in Amherst instead of downtown Buffalo. "The Governor was later reported to have said that he 'struck water with the first shovel,' " Ketter, a member of the Engineering Faculty since 1958, who became president in 1970, writes (1971). "That embarrassment, if it occurred, was only an omen toward difficulties which long prevented a second shovelful being turned. Emphatic objections arose immediately among the black community to their being excluded, in terms both of jobs and self-respect, by the construction companies and building trade unions of the area."

Many observers periodically deplore the decision to build UB on its present Amherst site instead of a downtown Buffalo waterfront area, but there were serious problems with the alternative site. A 1,500-acre campus contrasts sharply with an uncertain, limited acreage of a potential 500 acres, not all of which was even then available. Certain advantages would have accrued to the city, but UB would likely have become a high-rise, constricted urban institution, flawed by serious transportation and security problems and lacking adequate space for future growth.

Buffalo News reporter Louise Continelli (1989) erroneously agrees with other uninformed observers who maintain that it was the specter of campus unrest "that accelerated the drive to send some students to the wilds of Amherst" and literally influenced the choice of the site on which UB is located. That decision, reached during Meyerson's presidency after considerable study, was made only to accommodate, on the best real estate available, a then predicted but never realized, enrollment of 40,000 students.

Another persistent belief, shared by faculty and students, is that the present UB campus was deliberately designed to be riot-proof. "Every year I am asked the same question and give the same answer," complains Harbans S. Grover (1990), director of UB's Office of Architectural Services. "Prisons are meant to be riot-proof, but inmates find ways to riot. It is impossible, even if we had wanted to do it, to construct buildings that could be protected from demonstrators.

"Each building on the new campus," Grover continues, "was designed by a different person. No one was instructed to consider a 'riot-proof' campus. Those who contend that smaller windows on some buildings were deliberately installed do not realize that this campus was built during the energy crisis. Small windows were favored because glass wastes heat, and the driving factor was to conserve energy."

While UB's urban campus was physically compact, like Berkeley, the fifth-floor presidential complex in Capen Hall on the new campus is far more vulnerable than former executive offices in Hayes Hall—a building with over one hundred first-floor windows and eight entrances. It was literally impossible for two hundred activists to effectively deny access to anyone persistent enough and sufficiently motivated to get into, or escape from, the Main Street adminsitration building. Today a determined band of demonstrators could easily commandeer the three elevators rising to the fifth floor of the presidential suite, block the only back stairs fire exit, and sit-in effectively. Campus security would encounter real problems coming to the rescue. So much for "riot-proof" buildings, especially modern ones not connected by extensive underground heating system tunnels.

"Rumors began to circulate that course cards for College A—the unit devoted to independent study and self-evaluation—were being sold, snatched up by students who did little or nothing and rewarded themselves with A's at the end of the semester," acknowledged Bennis (1972). " 'Why do you think they call it College A?' one cynical student asked. There were tales of credit trips to Europe and the building of bird cages." Farr (1990) recalls that a "folk art" mentality prevailed, and one course was devoted solely to making wooden spoons. Bennis was concerned about this academic rogue elephant, but his explanation in 1972 for administrative inaction accompanying the preceding evaluation is difficult to understand. "The master of College A regarded any impugning of its grading system as an anti-revolutionary tactic. No one in the Meyerson administration, including myself, wanted to take a harsh public stand against this nonsense, particularly after College A and its master became the target of vicious community attack," Bennis writes. College A continued on, unchecked.

Many faculty and administrators may have preferred a conciliatory view, perhaps vainly hoping to fuse the past with the unforeseeable future, but too often voices were effectively muted by ideological intimidation and fear of the radicals. The university unintentionally provided the activists with a private theater for radical courses and protests—a haven for students seeking independent study credit for organizing and carrying out political activism.

UB's academic reputation was damaged. Bewildered high-school counselors called the Admissions Office to find out how some of their former students managed to achieve straight-A averages after compiling secondary school records predictive of a far less intellectual promise, Holt remembers (1989). Employers who hired UB graduates on the basis of academic performance should have been warned against taking seriously the transcripts of any job applicants who were awarded credits by College A. The experimental self-grading policy was not explained by any appropriate footnote on transcripts of students who elected these courses.

College A is reverently identified periodically by current generations of nostalgic students as but one of a series of significant educational reforms destroyed by a "reactionary, conservative Ketter administration," that removed all traces of the 1960s and dragged UB back to the nineteenth century. *Reach* (1988) reports that College A was phased out because it was "too progressive" for those "who feared threats to traditional academics and experimentation." Details are overlooked by uninformed observers who do not probe deeply enough to find out what "experimentation" and "innovation" involved.

Snell (1989) gave up his title as Master of College A in 1972. Student interest in reform had diminished and "College A disappeared, killed by the administration," he recalls. Snell notes that the 1970s brought about the loss of the educational reforms introduced under Meyerson. "Besides a different breed of student, educational reforms here were taken back simply because they were gifts from above, not clamored for from below. At the time reforms were more of what Meyerson sensed that this is what should be."

By the late 1980s the collegiate structure virtually disappeared. Predicting the success or failure of any experimental program is impossible, but it is unfortunate that the other colleges never received a fair trial because of negative initial impressions and unforesen influences.

Education Professor Charles R. Fall (1990) is one faculty member who wanted to alter the university. "The reformists were not wrong, because UB needed changing," he maintains. "The majority of student activists with whom I interacted were sincerely committed to what they thought they were trying to do, but their operational pattern was too radical to be assimilated into the existing structure. As far as education is concerned today, we are back behind where we were in the sixties when there was some hope for changing UB's stagnated educational structure." Fall believes that College A failed in large part "because Snell didn't know anything about educational theory. What is worth remembering about the newly established colleges is that they attempted to do something different. Their boldness encouraged others to think differently about the sytem and try new things—even if they didn't always work."

In mid-December 1969, I was visited by an older, handicapped (close to being legally blind) female student, registered in College A. Tearfully, she told me she had used personal finances to travel to Little Rock, Arkansas, to study the integration movement. She had worked hard, completing an extensive report that matched in size the university's telephone directory. Her complaint? When she proudly submitted her project to the store-front college, she was informed that there would be no formal review, discussion, or evaluation by anyone at College A. She was told to assign herself whatever grade she thought her work merited for the official transcript and deposit the report—along with a large stack of other apparently never-to-be-read papers—in a corner of the room. My futile efforts to arrange some form of faculty (or peer) review through College A were resented. I was forcefully reminded (at the highest levels) that such "academic matters" were outside the purview of my office.

In early February, Paula Brookmire (now with *The Milwaukee Jour-*

nal), then editor of *Ethos,* one of the few student publications never intimidated by the radicals, invited me and several other faculty and administrators to evaluate the progress of the colleges. Concerned about grading policies and how independent study was being destroyed as a viable educational option, I wrote the following critique which appeared on the front page of the issue:

> On the Colleges: What is noted here does not refer to all of the colleges, but it certainly needs to be stated. Up to this point at least, the colleges have been a great disappointment, although I realize that I speak for myself.
>
> It is important that the colleges have allowed for broad experimentation, presenting opportunities for student growth that otherwise would not have existed. Still, there seems to be a headlong rush to reach the lowest common denominator. Some students, who have abdicated their right to have their work evaluated—regardless of the grading system—are being cheated academically. When credit is awarded for doing nothing, and when an experience is not related to a theoretical base, the individual concerned might better drop out of school, since it is doubtful if he should receive academic credit. Indeed, certain credits may not apply toward any final objective. We somehow have become involved in being party to a transaction in which neither the student nor the institution achieves anything.
>
> When a student conducts an independent study project without supervision and appropriate faculty contact to insure a relationship between theory and practice, it is like trying to assemble a jigsaw puzzle with half the pieces missing. Unless the exposed individual can consider that experience with a psychologist, political scientist, social worker, sociologist, or some other qualified faculty member, the increasingly nebulous concept of independent study on this campus will become a mockery.
>
> The so-called college concept, that had so much hope initially, is deteriorating through lack of responsible leadership and direction, and fear of what radical elements might or might not do to the institution. When a college turns into a haven for irresponsible elements, hiding behind claims that all other curricula is "worthless and irrelevant" something is seriously wrong with the entire system. The inevitable result, if this trend continues, will be to destroy the marvelous concept of independent study, as well as what remains of the colleges themselves. (Siggelkow 1970)

References

Anderson, G. Lester. (1989). Interview and Questionnaire.

Bennis, Warren G. (1972). "The Sociology of Institutions, Or Who Sank the Yellow Submarine?", *Psychology Today,* November.

Cacavas, Elena. (1979). "The Split Campus," in "Through and Through the Looking Glass: The Shattering of a University 1968–72," *The Spectrum,* May 11.

Continelli, Louise. (1989). "The Riot Squad," *The Buffalo News,* March 21.

Fall, Charles R. (1990). Interview and Questionnaire.

Farr, S. David. (1990). Interview and Questionnaire.

Gitlen, Todd. (1987). *The Sixties—Years of Hope, Days of Rage.* (New York: Bantam Books).

Grover, Harbens S. (1990). Interview.

Holt, Andrew W. (1989). Interview and Questionnaire.

Ketter, Robert L. (1971). "Report of the President," SUNY/Buffalo, *The Reporter,* February 11.

Kurtz, Paul. (1971). "Inside the Buffalo Commune: Or, How to Destroy a University," *In Defense of Academic Freedom,* Sidney Hook, ed. (New York: Pegasus Press), pp. 220–244.

Peterson, Richard E. (1968). "The Student Left in American Higher Education," *Daedalus,* Winter.

Reach: User's Guide to UB 1987–88, (1987). September.

Reach: User's Guide to UB 1988–89, (1988). September.

Shapiro, Harvey. (1979). "The Rise of Academic Reform . . . Students Play an Observer's Role, in "Through and Through the Looking GLass: The Shattering of a University, 1968–1972," a special issue of *The Spectrum,* May 11.

Siggelkow, Richard A. (1970). "On the Colleges," *Ethos,* February 10.

Snell, Fred N. (1989). Interview and Questionnaire.

Trombley, William. (1968). "Buffalo's Old Campus Pulsates with Change, Top New Administrators, Swift Actions Aim for Excellence—Despite Resistance," *The Los Angeles Times,* July 6.

Welch, Claude E., Jr. (1989). Interview and Questionnaire.

CHAPTER VI

The 1968–69 Academic Year: Still Holding On

Nineteen sixty-eight was more than a densely compacted parade of events, more than the accidental alignment of planets. It was a tragedy of change, a struggle between generations, to some extent a war between the past and the future, and even, for an entire society, a violent struggle to grow up.

—Lance Morrow, *Time* magazine (January 11, 1988)

On January 30, 1968, Vietcong and North Vietnamese forces had attacked Da Nang, the second largest city in South Vietnam, and seven other major towns. "Almost 24 hours later, they mounted a wave of near simultaneous attacks throughout Vietnam," writes Morrow (1988).

"All this was the work of an enemy that the Johnson administration had reported to be 'struggling to stave off military defeat.' The Communists had hoped to use their Tet offensive to provoke a general uprising in the countryside. In that, they failed. They also suffered disastrous casualties. Yet Tet was for them an enormous victory. It turned American opinion decisively against the war. . . . Tet broke whatever residual spell was left in America's cold war calls to arms in the name of defending freedom around the globe" (p. 21), at least until the Persian Gulf era.

Tet proved to be the turning point of the war, explains Barnes (1988). "The sublime irony was that it turned the war in favor of the communists. If wars were fought entirely on the battlefield, that would not have been the case, but they are inescapably political as well, and it was on the political stage that America lost the Tet battle and the war.

"The American people had been stunned by televised images of the fighting," Barnes continues. "Walter Cronkite reacted like millions of Americans: 'What the hell is going on? I thought we were winning the war.' Political satirist

Art Buchwald produced a column headed 'We have the enemy on the run, says General Custer at Little Big Horn' " (p. 136). Opinion polls reflected a sharp upturn in those dissatisfied with the war, and for the first time the doves and hawks in Congress were almost equal. Between 1965 and 1968, 30,000 troops had died in Vietnam; after Tet the ranks of disenchanted Americans who had tired of the seemingly endless conflict increased steadily.

On April 17, 1965, Gitlen (1987) reports "when 25,000 students marched in Washington against the Vietnam war, there were about 25,000 American troops in Vietnam. At the end of 1965 there were 184,000 troops; at the end of 1966, 385,000. By the end of 1967, the number was 486,000, and 15,000 had been killed, 60 percent of them in the single year 1967. These were the prominent figures, numbers of Americans" (p. 242). Congress still passed war appropriations by huge majorities.

"By the beginning of 1968, almost 16,000 Americans had been killed in Vietnam and more than 100,000 wounded," Morrow (1988) points out. "During that time the war in Vietnam had become a gathering presence in American life. History obeyed Newton's Third Law of Motion: for every U.S. action in Vietnam, there came a (seemingly) equal and opposite reaction back home. America internalized the war as if it had swallowed fire" (p. 21).

The match that kindled the radical student movement was the open aggression in Vietnam and the draft. "Everything about this conflict irritated the sensitive among activist students: its secretive nature, its pompous oratory, its napalm stories to create fear, panic, and a scorched earth, its conflicting reports covering the motives of the war, and the credibility gap about American successes in both North and South Vietnam," explains Philosophy Professor Dale Riepe (1971).

According to Gitlen (1987), Tom Hayden warned the National Commission on the Causes and Prevention of Violence, in October 1968, that the leadership of the New Left was moving toward confrontation because they were not being heard by the establishment. The turning point, in Hayden's opinion, "was October, 1967, when resistance became the official watchword of the antiwar movement" (p. 285).

Lyndon B. Johnson campaigned in 1964 by promising not to send Americans 10,000 miles "to do what Asian boys should be doing for themselves" (p. 20). By treating the war as a crusade for freedom his own presidency was to be among the casualties. More than any other force, the war alienated American youth from their elders and, in equally tragic ways, from one another. "Many of the young," explains Morrow (1988), "cherished (almost autoerotically) the illusion that they were part of 'the Revolution,' a force of history that would overthrow the power structure of the U.S. And illusion was an indispensable instrument of the war effort: the 'body count,' for example, or 'the light at the end of the tunnel,' the longed-for illumination, never seen, that would indicate that victory and salvation were near. At the close of 1967, the official invocation of the light at the end of the tunnel was still ritual. The *New York Times,* influenced by government briefings, reported in late December that 'military indicators in Vietnam present the most dramatic and clear-cut evidence of progress in the war since the dark days of 1965' " (p. 24).

An isolated draft incident in August 1968 would impact significantly on UB, although the primary figure was not—and never had been—a university student. Seventeen-year-old Bruce Beyer and another man publicly burned federal court orders citing them for draft evasion. Granted political sanctuary in a Unitarian church on August 7, their originally stated intent was to dramatize antiwar sentiment by waiting out the period until arrested. When FBI agents, reinforced by a large number of Buffalo police, tried to arrest the two men fistfights erupted between the agents and Beyer sympathizers. Nine persons, including Beyer, were charged with assault. Individually released on $5,000 bail, they became known as the Buffalo Nine.

It was initially too easy for us to view Beyer, an acknowledged leader of the group, as a minor concern. We would become increasingly aware of his influence during his trial, especially when sentencing triggered a major campus demonstration.

After Mark Rudd appeared before a large, orderly crowd in Norton on November 27, 1968, we expected to survive the first semester without incident—only to be surprised in December. A provocatively titled "Police Brutality" forum was scheduled for Monday, December 9 in Norton by six students as their Speech and Communication term project. Fifty black students arrived *en masse* just as the exercise began, increasing the racially mixed audience to approximately 150 persons. Ten minutes later a false fire alarm abruptly ended the program. During the ensuing confusion an indeterminate number of eggs were hurled, with some success, at two primary targets.

"As the audience and speakers prepared to leave in view of the alarm sounded at 3:17 P.M.," *The Buffalo Evening News* (1968a) reported, "the eggs started to fly." According to the *Courier-Express* (1968a) the apparent targets for an estimated five to seven dozen eggs "were Lovejoy Councilman Raymond Lewandowski . . . and Donald Jackson, a Negro panel member who espouses right-wing causes." Lewandowski was a frequent critic of college-youth lifestyles and Jackson was representing an organization called "Negroes for Wallace." Roosevelt Rhodes (1990), a black student activist, now on the UB staff, maintains that Buffalo's black community applauded the incident. Jackson was the primary target of the Black Student Union, but Rhodes explains that the fire alarm was not a signal for the egg-throwing exercise. "The people who threw the eggs were rushed into it and hadn't planned on doing it right then."

A *News* (1968b) editorial described the incident as "a disgraceful debasement of civilized behavior deserving the sternest rebuke by every element at the State University of Buffalo and the metropolitan community." President Meyerson apologized to all aggrieved parties by telephone, and the university expressed its regrets over "the rudely hostile treatment of the speakers. . . . No measure of redress after the fact can undo the harm to the university and its respect and tolerance for the broadest range of views and opinions. . . . If one speaker whose ideas may be unpopular to many on campus can be silenced today, similar tactics may silence tomorrow the very speaker those persons most want to hear" (*Buffalo Evening News* 1968a).

The December 11 *News* (1968c) reported a Buffalo Common Council call for a state investigation of the incident, and Lewandowski demanded "some kind of review board to pass upon the fitness of students." I was appointed to investigate the matter, and the media kept the issue alive. We could find no witness willing to identify any of the participants, and no one would testify that eggs hit anybody. The general confusion was reflected in a December 16 follow-up article in the *News* (1968d):

> Estimates by those present of the number of eggs thrown varied from one to seven dozen and the number of persons involved reportedly ranged from 8 to 25, depending on who was making the statement. . . . Many white students report an inability to identify black students because these two groups do not have sufficient interaction with each other. . . . When asked what sort of mark the seminar students could expect on the forum Siggelkow observed that "they probably failed the course."

I refrained from responding to another reporter's question about whether Grade A or Grade B eggs had been identified. I explained that the class members were among the most aggrieved "since their academic meeting had been disrupted. . . . The reaction by our students has consistently been one of dismay and concern." Looking ahead, I added that "the university has an extremely difficult and important educational task to acquaint students of diverse backgrounds with the significance of freedom of speech and academic freedom. If universities are to survive as places of free speech and inquiry, it will be necessary to play a more effective educational role. . . . The greatest danger presently capable of eroding academic freedom throughout the country is the trend toward ever increasing violence" (*Courier-Express* 1968b).

I was eventually forced to acknowledge that, especially since the panelists had been bombarded from the rear of the room, we were unable to identify any student actually in the act of throwing anything. The names of several suspects had been obtained, but the case, like the Thallus episode, remains unsolved.

Shortly after the beginning of the second semester, thirty draft cards were reportedly burned at the first of two on-campus rallies stemming from Beyer's conviction in Federal Court on two of three counts of assault. A February 27 gathering attended by over 2,000 led to the formation of CTUB (The Committee to Transform UB). Widely circulated throughout the campus and presented to the administration for immediate compliance, *The Spectrum* (1969a) printed the "non-negotiable" demands that were jointly adopted by a self-appointed coalition of student government members and CTUB:

1) the immediate establishment of a people's university; open admission to working and poor families—especially to blacks, Third World peoples, and Vietnam veterans.

2) . . . the immediate establishment of Black and Third World colleges and a Worker's College controlled entirely by the students in the respective colleges. These colleges will be open to those working class youth who have been screwed by their education and will address itself to the needs, culture, and history of working class people.

3) . . . state funds for the implementation of a new Student-Faculty Congress in which students control 50% of the voting power and membership on all departmental and University decision-making bodies, especially in matters concerning curriculum, degree regulations and the hiring and firing of faculty and staff . . .

4) an end to all contracting of defense research, the abolition of University ROTC, construction of a large hall to accommodate deeply felt student needs as a first step to a total architectural restructuring of this University, and the end of commercialized athletics which degrade athletes and deprive the students of sports.

5) We support the idea of a bicameral legislature in this university in which students have veto power over the faculty. . . . The Congress will replace the powerless Student Association Polity and Advisory Committees.

Rick Schwab (1988), then president of the Undergraduate Student Association and now editor of *The Ligenier Echo* in Pennsylvania, explains in his weekly column, "Generally Speaking," why the radicals opposed legitimate student government groups. "What I do recall were our elaborate efforts aimed at keeping the SDS-type radicals from calling the shots. We did this by packing mass meetings with moderates. One SDSer threatened to kill me if I didn't stop getting in the way." In November 1968 the radicals had failed to remove Schwab from office with a recall petition.

Other demands that didn't exactly fall into President Meyerson's realm included the firing of Buffalo Police Commissioner Frank Felicetta, support for the Buffalo Nine, "justice" for Martin Sostre (convicted in a 1968 narcotics case), and the clearing of Bruce Beyer. Since some demands related to campus matters, there was of an air of expectancy as the adminstration drew up its response. It was a situation that had led to violence and disruption on many campuses across the country.

Meyerson scheduled a general university convocation for Monday, March 3, to present counterdemands. We held our final preparatory meeting March 2 at the president's home. I suggested that the radicals—as they had done elsewhere—might try to commandeer the stage and advised Meyerson and the platform party to arrive early to insure seating and minimize last-minute confusion. My warning was cavalierly dismissed.

Clark Hall gymnasium was the only large on-campus meeting space available. Satisfactory in earlier days, it was clearly too small for an estimated audience of 4,000, which would include all the staff and faculty we could muster along with moderate students, who would be encouraged to attend by responsible student leaders. The basketball court of the venerable sports arena, located on the second story, would sustain more weight than it had ever been previously subjected to in its long history. (I visualized the floor disintegrating and caving down into the swimming pool below and wondered what would happen as the crowd panicked and fought to escape through one of the inadequate three exits.)

Arriving two hours early, I was not surprised to find two of the dozen reserved chairs on the platform already occupied by grim-faced activists with placards that read "Free Martin Sostre" and "Make Room for the Masses." It is generally assumed that interloping protesters can be forcibly removed, but we were still relying on understaffed, untrained, and ineffective campus security personnel, who had not yet appeared.

I plucked five trustworthy students from their prime seats on the floor (which they voluntarily lost forever) to occupy chairs directly behind the speaker's table on the makeshift platform that already seemed close to collapse. They promised not to move until the royal party (the president, the executive vice president, the academic vice president, the chair of the Faculty Senate, and the student association president) arrived.

When the tardiest of the originally designated platform party finally got there, they were probably surprised to find substitutes permanently installed in their assigned places. An unlikely platform group, most of the faculty who ended up there had not anticipated the honor. In packing the stage, the composition of the originally all-white-male component was appropriately altered. An early arrival, Berkley Eddins, a black philosophy professor, was comfortably seated in the front row until I asked him to consider moving to the stage. He understood. Another cooperative surrogate was my dentist, Dr. Ronald Jarvis, also a faculty member. At my urging he found himself on the platform. (Why he arrived early is still a mystery; as his frequent patient, I always waited at length for him.) None of the imposters rejected the honor so suddenly thrust upon them.

Media coverage was complete. Cameras from three local television stations focused on the podium. Print reporters were hoping for either a successful disruption or the spectatular collapse of an overstressed gymnasium floor.

Anticipating the inevitably unpredictable question-and-answer period, I insisted on control of the two microphones customarily located on each side of the main floor. We learned that the activists planned to enter the arena and try to shout down the president fifteen or twenty minutes after he began his presentation. The student operators were to watch my hand signals, which would indicate when the sound should be turned up or off, in midsentence if necessary. Such precautions circumvent hecklers, individuals desiring to substitute lengthy speeches for questions, and occasional lunatics who publicly explode with profanities and obscenities.

Right on schedule about 150 activists burst through a rear entrance and marched down the two side aisles. Two leaders shouted into dead microphones; without electronic reinforcement their words were effectively muffled and unheard by the large crowd. Unfazed by the arrival of the radical contingent, the president neither acknowledged their arrival nor paused in delivering his prepared remarks. Effectively overpowered by the public address system, the two columns of activists fell helplessly silent and could only wait impatiently for a live microphone during the question-and-answer period.

As reported in the *Buffalo Evening News,* the president's counterdemands boiled down to a plea to reason together and find ways to make the university more relevant to its time and functions. He received suggestions for popular reform enthusiastically, but deplored excesses and "the authoritarianism and mindless obscenity we have witnessed" (Allan 1969). He emphasized curriculum review, the openness of sponsored research, and some form of participatory bicameral legislature for the university. I recall his identifying values of obedience to law and his concern about racism. Calling attention to the absence of black faces in the crowd, he emphasized the need to increase minority enrollment. Faculties and departments were advised to expedite interdisciplinary contacts and develop methodologically sound procedures for evaluating courses and teaching effectiveness. Administrators holding faculty rank, including the president, should teach a class regularly and serve no more than five years, with terms renewable only after faculty/student evaluations, Meyerson proposed. The March 5 *Spectrum* emphasized his desire for smaller classes, undergraduate seminars, and more problem-centered and cross-disciplinary courses.

We were ready when questions were invited from the floor. One microphone was activated, and I signaled to cut the sound after the semblance of a question could be distilled from angry rhetoric. The president, in full command, responded effectively. It was his audience. It did not matter if the speaker from the floor was still expounding on his theme; the impression was that a question was being answered forcefully. Although I had to remain standing in one corner of the platform to convey my hopefully unobtrusive hand signals, no one ever asked me about my peculiar role. Nor did members of the original platform party berate me for reassigning their seats, but they may not have known how they lost their places. At one point the president called on Dr. Eddins to respond from the stage to an allegation about racial discrimination.

The session appeared orderly and well mannered to the audience (with the possible exception of persons in close proximity to the floor microphones), a forum worthy of any academic setting. Meyerson's performance enhanced his reputation for dealing with campus unrest and disruption. The only criticism I received was from the president who asked me why the activists had been allowed to monopolize questions from the floor. He would, he said, have welcomed participation from other students. I thought he was lucky to have had a reserved seat, since it still pays to arrive early for some events.

UB emulated other universities nationwide by attempting to diffuse campus unrest by encouraging (but not officially mandating faculty involvement) a series of teach-ins and "rap" (rapport) sessions. In early March loosely organized forums, symposiums, and meetings were held. *The Spectrum* erroneously maintained that "most regular classes were abandoned" for such "relevant" subjects as "The Sociology of Anarchism" and "Decision Making as a Process." Participants included students, community members, some faculty, and a few staff.

While the experiment held possibilities for dialogue, the effort was not uniformly supported. Activist leaders claimed "unofficial" administrative agreement to cancel all regular classes, but most faculty, including my own department, continued meeting regular classes. Graduate and professional programs, especially in such disciplines as engineering, were never visibly affected; a majority of the humanities faculty routinely followed normal schedules, but often devoted some discussion time to accommodate the prevailing mood. *The Spectrum* was reduced to asking students to help compile a list of faculty members who refused to take part.

During these years sorrows came in platoons for college administrators. A week-long "New World Drug Symposium" (February 27–March 5, 1969) kept the pot boiling. Invited and uninvited celebrities from the world of drugs and revolution—including Timothy Leary, Allen Ginsberg, Abbie Hoffman, and several bewildered guest speakers from the Federal Narcotics Bureau—converged on campus. "The open and unimpeded use of all sorts of illegal drugs infuriated both the Buffalo and University communities, already upset by the political activities," explains Sharon Edelman (1969), a student employee at the University Archives.

Almost immediately after the successful convocation, however, disappointed CTUB members, apparently seeking increasing radical leadership, formed a more extreme group, CRC (the Community for Real Change). Further plans to demonstrate in support of Beyer at his sentencing March 19 were developed by the CRC and the Buffalo Defense Committee. Other non-students, like Beyer, posed as legitimate members of the university community. Leon Phipps, a black, twenty-year-old fifth-grade dropout from the

Chicago public schools, also somehow found his way to UB. His powerful build and a scar reaching from his forehead to below his chin caused some students to fear him.

Phipps first turned up among the protesters who marched faithfully around the fountain during the earlier, peaceful protests against the war. He always carried school books under his arm, but knew I was aware of his non-student status. Most students, generally non-judgmental and trusting, gradually accepted Phipps as one of their own after becoming better acquainted with him. He expressed himself well, and faculty members were invariably surprised to learn that Phipps was not a student.

When Beyer received two concurrent three-year terms on March 19, an estimated three hundred protesters burned the judge in effigy and paraded around Lafayette Square in downtown Buffalo. After several arrests, the aborted demonstration was wisely adjourned to safer confines on the UB campus. The rioters torched two construction shacks—in full view of campus security—at the site of the Department of Defense Project Themis. Ketter (1971), explains:

> Actually a reputable scientific study of one aspect of human physiology, [Themis] would once have been welcomed from the promise it gave of widening the horizons of knowledge. In a raw and overheated atmosphere, however, all that could be distinguished about it was the Office of Naval Research supported it. The Pentagon, the Vietnam war, and militarism, imperialism, fascism, colonialism, napalming of babies and the drafting of young men billowed upward in the smoke and flame which destroyed the construction shacks, and thereafter a rational examination of Themis was as impossible as a rational examination of the Reserve Officers Training Corps.

During the previous month Meyerson had moved me from my Harriman office to a Hayes Hall office that was just around the corner from the presidential suite. Around 500 persons, including many non-students, marched to Hayes Hall in what would become an overnight occupation. One enterprising individual broke into the Hayes Hall clock tower and the long-silent bells began ringing incessantly to herald the newly named (Beyer Hall) building's "liberation." Even though the police had been turned back, the *Spectrum*'s next day's editorial, "Ring Dem Bells," acknowledged their presence: "The clock remained stuck at twelve, bells ringing uncontrollably, unable to move its hands, not knowing whether it was noon or midnight, darkness or day. That's how we feel, like that big weatherbeaten clockface, looking with the same blank inscrutability in all four directions. . . .

"The cops finally came. We knew if we pushed hard enough, the blue-shirts would eventually appear. The response to the 'demands' never came. We knew it most likely never would. . ." (*The Spectrum* 1969b).

Meyerson, who was out of town during the takeover, had informed me that outside police would (reluctantly) be called if offices in Hayes were literally occupied and protesters refused to leave, so when I heard glass breaking at the president's door shortly after 5:00 P.M., I assumed the imminent arrival of Buffalo police. Most office personnel had left before the demonstrators arrived and the few staff members still there saw no reason to remain. Since altercations were likely between demonstrators and the police I decided to remain in Hayes as an observer; my presence might inhibit an overzealous policeman. I also perceived my office as my home away from home and was determined not to leave unless forcibly removed. I knew how demonstrators treated office files and equipment and was unwilling to host some indeterminate number of uninvited guests who would—based on past performances elsewhere—convert wastepaper baskets into urinals and destroy the contents of office files.

I did not have long to wait. A large delegation—all strangers to me—invaded my office and demanded that I leave. One man suggested that I might "get hurt," to which I replied, "I don't think so." When another threatened to drag me out, I responded, "You can't, I'm overweight," but levity is lost on dedicated demonstrators. A news item by Jack Quinn (1969) of *The Buffalo Evening News* picks up the story. His account is important because of his conclusions about reactions among and between various student/activist factions.

A handful of UB administrators and students took a symbolic stand in Hayes Hall Wednesday despite ultimatums and threats from dissident students who swarmed through the building.

The handful accomplished something valuable for this community as did some of the dissident students.

I was with the handful for the four hours the group stayed in Dr. Richard A. Siggelkow's office.

At UB on a routine assignment I was in Hayes when the first rush of students pushed into the office complex near University President Martin Meyerson's office.

Initially free to leave the building, I decided to stay inside—to try to get both sides of the story, the administration's and the students'.

Ordered Regan Out

Each side has a story to tell and both sides Wednesday proved a point —a point which may be lost in the public clamor for a crackdown on campus troublemakers.

These points were in evidence Wednesday evening when 100 to 200 of the almost 500 students "occupying" Hayes Hall crowded at the door of Dr. Siggelkow's office.

Aroused, intent on stating their demands and having them met, the group ordered Dr. Peter Regan, Acting University President, to get out of the building.

Thus the students "symbolically liberated" Hayes Hall to dramatize their demands. Now they stood in confrontation with the administration.

"A Matter of Principle"

Dr. Siggelkow, University Vice President for Student Affairs, made his decision and began proving his point:

"Anyone who wants to leave can," he said, "but I'm staying. I'm not being chased out of my office. I'm not leaving unless I'm carried out.

"It's simply a matter of principle," Dr. Siggelkow explained. "I'm staying."

From 5:46 to 9:45, the time the last of the group left Dr. Siggelkow's office, the tactics of the students outside his door changed completely.

They began demanding the office and building be cleared. It was implied, strongly, that those in the office would be carried out bodily.

Then we were told by a student representative allowed into Dr. Siggelkow's office, we were not to be allowed to leave at all. . . .

The group in the office was told later that the refusal to leave angered several of the unnamed "leaders" of the students at the door.

These "leaders" tried to convince the students to storm the locked door and carry us out. The students voted it down, arguing against any violence toward the group in the office.

For me it proved this point that is largely ignored by the community in general:

Dissidents Can't Be Lumped

From outside the building it looked as if all the dissident students were of one mind, ready and willing to take over the building—violently, if necessary.

From the inside, however, it could be seen that "dissidents" can't be lumped together. They're still individuals and this time the individuals, despite harangues from the leaders, opted against hauling us out of there.

Out of the total University population—roughly 23,000—at most only 500 were involved in the Hayes Hall takeover. Of the 500, only a very few wanted to clear us out of the building with force. . . .

Before the violent approach was voted down, the group in the office met with two student representatives who explained we were taking a risk by staying there.

One student in the crowd at the door yelled loudly: "One way or another, we take their bodies out of the building ." . . .

Why Not Leave?

Dr. Siggelkow suggested that the rest of us leave. By now Buffalo police had arrived at the Main Street campus.

A police-student confrontation was imminent. We could leave. Why shouldn't we?

Dr. Siggelkow, at the university 10 years, repeated his earlier decision: "I'm staying. I'll leave when I'm ready."

When ordered out by the students, the office group refused to leave. Now free to leave, the office group decided it was not leaving just because of the tacit approval of the students. . . .

With Dr. Siggelkow through most of the office stand were: Larry Smith, Assistant Vice President for Student Affairs, James Magavern, Assistant to the President, Robert Dombrowski, Associate Director of Student Affairs, and four students, one of whom explained, "We're here to show that there are students who care about the university." . . .

What did the office stand amount to? Maybe it was the whole point, crystallized.

The students have a right to protest. They took their stand and moved in on Hayes Hall.

Dr. Siggelkow and his group had the right to remain in their offices. They took their stand. . . .

I think the Siggelkow group proved something by staying and the students—by voting down the forced entry to the office—also proved something.

It was no draw. Each side won something. A small something, sure. Probably it'll be lost entirely in the over-all story of what goes on at UB from now on.

I hope not.

Wardlow (1969) concludes the story in a May 31 article he wrote to summarize the events of the 1968–69 school year:

"President Meyerson returned home from out of town during the evening and immediately plunged into the task of restoring order. He did so in an atmosphere of high tension, for scores of police had lined up along Main Street, and were ready to move onto the campus and clear the hall. Meyerson spent two hours in direct confrontation with about 200 of the occupiers—and failed to budge them." (Almost resigned to resorting to police force that evening, he heeded, instead, Associate Vice President Anthony Lorenzetti, who pointed out how some aroused and unsympathetic police might, under cover of darkness, welcome an opportunity to teach demonstrators a lesson.)

"By morning the president had been granted a court order for students to leave the building. Faced with imminent police enforcement, the demonstrators withdrew."

Injunctions generate a favorable public reaction, persuade moderates to refrain from participating in disruptions, and may cause students to obey a court order when they would ignore orders from a university official. Disadvantages include the necessity to utilize local law enforcement officers to serve process and enforcement of an injunction through court proceedings may involve some of the same problems that result when police are used to quell a disturbance. A university unprepared to enforce the injunction through contempt proceedings should not seek one, the American Bar Association (1969) warned in *Campus Government and Student Dissent*. "To obtain an injunction in such a situation might permit a court decree to be flouted by students with immunity. There may also be substantial problems of identification when large numbers of students are involved. . . . Certainly no institution should depend upon the injunction relief as the sole remedy to assist it in dealing with disruptions or threats of disruptions."

Injunctions were attacked by activists for exerting a chilling effect on the right to dissent and as attempts to intimidate demonstrators. Although not supportive of radical goals, Schwab (1988) reflects the ambivalence toward the administration by responsible students: "Our university administration pulled some fast ones during those times," he writes. "It was one of the first in the country to seek a court injunction to end a sit-in. That meant the students had to leave or face a contempt of court charge. It was a clever move, but some of us questioned it at the time and turning fellow students over to the Buffalo police didn't seem right." Student government officials will continue, on most campuses, to oppose trustees and administrators to maintain credibility with the student body.

Student leaders almost invariably see themselves as compromised by ties with university officials—a paradox, since they are elected as representatives of the student body to communicate with key administrators.

Some faculty colleagues were surprisingly jovial about the Hayes Hall takeover. During lunch I received unsolicited advice for several days on how to overcome protesters who were determined to storm the administration building. Among the most imaginative suggestions, intended (I think) to boost my morale, were these:

Spread manure at all entranceways just before obscuring the building with a dense smoke screen.

Drop itching/sneezing powder from the second floor on the crowd below.

Construct a special moat around the administration building with trapdoors just inside the main entranceways.

Install a large belt that can be switched to fast reverse when demonstrators try to storm the building.

Issue large fish nets to all administrators so that they can entrap activist ringleaders as quickly as they can be identified.

Evacuate the building with false fire alarms and bomb scares; administrators would remain inside and take control of the vacated area before students realized they had been duped by their own tactics.

Meyerson, now under constant attack from the aroused local community, was blamed personally for unrest, drugs, and student demonstrations in any form. Letters to him—usually carboned to the local press, area legislators, and the governor—were often referred to me for response. I contacted those who identified themselves, took them to lunch on campus, and tried to explain what was going on. Most of the letters were from a dulled public that was unable to differentiate between fact and fiction. A few were thoughtful, even sympathetic, and invariably advised a firmer hand; the worst were anonymous—often signed "A Taxpayer"—and there was an anti-Semitic flavor ("What do you expect from a man with a name like Meyerson?")

"Housewife" wrote on March 22: "After following the reports of the activities taking place at 'OUR UNIVERSITY' in the past few days, I find it necessary to write to you. . . . I AM ASHAMED of the generation. . . . I understand that you are a so-called 'HIPPIE.' I AM NOT. I am just one of many taxpayers from whom you benefit. . . . right now I have a petition circulating to replace you IMMEDIATELY with an ADULT with a BACKBONE. Please do us TAXPAYERS a favor and resign. Enclosed you will find a copy of the petition, which has many signatures on it already, and I am sending this to Albany."

"Mother of Two" said: "God help our children—our whole society of people like you. . . . What are you afraid of? What in God's name are you thinking of? . . . Why don't you use your authority? 'People' like these belong in mental institutions and you let them dictate to you? This must be stopped—assert yourself!" A "Mother and Taxpayer" noted: "I sincerely hope my thoughts are shared by many. . . . I wonder what would happen if all the taxpayers refused to pay taxes . . . deep down I wonder just how much the university wants to preserve democracy?"

Another writer advised, "If you do not have the courage to manage our university, please resign. It is positively unthinkable to allow a couple hundred young, wet nosed communist punks to dictate the operative policies at any institution owned by the people of the state. Maybe an even exchange can be arranged: you, Rockefeller, and one million dollars to California in exchange for Hiwkawa [sic] and Regan [sic]."

My personal favorite was from a gentleman from Elma, whose letter appeared in the "Morning Mail" of *The Courier-Express,* and was copied to the governor:

> There should be immediate proceedings to re-evaluate Meyerson's qualifications and fitness to continue as president. . . .
> Gutlessly he acquiesces to vocal pseudo-intellects and smugly recites "academic freedom" as though it were holy writ subject to no questioning and a license to exceed the bounds of good morals, manners, drugs, and conduct. How naive or stupid does Meyerson believe the citizens of New York are?
> I don't appreciate my hard earned tax dollars contributing to the support of an institution harboring the likes of Meyerson or crumby, tee-shirted, bearded, bushy-haired, kooky pseudo-intellectuals who consider drug addiction, bad manners, immorality, smut and filth, and a lack of respect for authority and discipline an inherent right. . . .
> P.S. I've asked my wife to read this letter at her next League of Women Voters meeting.

Members of the Buffalo Common Council demanded the president's resignation, and a resolution was filed denouncing the weakness of administrative actions to control the students. The Faculty Senate responded to the council at a special March 23 meeting by voting unanimously to support the president's actions during the crisis. The Senate also passed a resolution saying that it was a matter of personal choice whether or not any faculty member conducted research involving military defense contracts. Current commitments to all research projects were reaffirmed. The undergraduate student government, under Schwab's leadership, voted not to oppose Themis or ROTC and courageously refused to express support for those who burned construction shacks and invaded Hayes.

The president issued a memorandum on March 24 explaining and supporting Themis. Referring to the injunction and the Hayes Hall trespassers, he openly declared his intention to turn to outside authority if faced with "personal injury, property damage, threat, theft, sit-downs, lie-downs, and attempted intimidation of teachers of students."

"Major targets of the radicals were those felt to be manifestations of the Vietnam War: the draft, Project Themis (a University research effort developed by the Department of Physiology and the U.S. Navy), the ROTC training program, and the apparent compliance of the University with the government in such military matters," summarizes Edelman (1969). As the protests continued other issues evolved. Demands increased for a construction moratorium on the (newly designed) Amherst campus (until blacks would be included in the union work force) and the perennial call for a re-definition of the students' role in the actual decision-making processes, (including tenure and curriculum policies) at the University.

"Emphatic objections arose among the black community to their being excluded, in terms both of jobs and self-respect, by the construction companies and building trades unions of the area," reports Ketter (1971). "The protest won such a rapidly widening and sympathetic hearing at the University that it produced the closing and climactic event of the 1968-69 school year: the moratorium, or work stoppage. Proposed by student petition, endorsed in the faculty, urged by President Meyerson, and finally consented to by Governor Rockefeller, all work and work negotiation ceased late in the spring of 1969 under what was considered a temporary suspension. Neither the moratorium nor the formation of a Minority Coalition to help arbitrate it, was achieved without threat of violence on the part of student activists who now—definitively—had emerged. The threat ramified into dramatic scenes."

UB was still standing as the semester ended. Degrees were awarded at an uneventful 123rd Commencement, and we welcomed the end of the 1968-69 academic year. A feature article by Woodrow Wardlow (1969), in the May 31 *Buffalo Evening News Magazine* sympathetically defended UB and gave Meyerson high praise. Barring unforeseen actions by "zealous revolutionaries," Wardlow maintained, "new ways of working and learning together" could solve the university's problems and set educational patterns that will be occupied throughout higher education.

The faculty is "joining in the spirit of the quest for better ways of educating," he wrote, and most students remain genuinely concerned about their school, "not about to let a small band of radicals lead them into an orgy of disruption and destruction." The administration, he added, "has done an intelligent job of responding to provocations and pressures."

During the two preceding academic years "the only group that seems to be moving in the other direction is the community at large," Wardlow asserted. Public concentration has been largely on nonacademic matters, he noted, such as long hair, dirty clothes, four-letter words, political unorthodoxy, and impertinence. Community disenchantment centered on *The Spectrum,* the Leslie Fielder case (a bogus charge that his home was a marijuana den for children), the "raucous voices" of radicals and "student power people," the egg-throwing incident, Project Themis, the one night takeover of Hayes Hall, and the integrated work-force controversy.

Wardlow identified the March 19 sentencing of Bruce Beyer, "a nonstudent," as the most dramatic event of the period, since it triggered the destruction of construction shacks at the Themis site and the overnight stand in Hayes Hall. The influential newspaperman concluded with commendation for Meyerson's adroit handling of that volatile situation and added this endorsement from the May 6 issue of the *Modesto Bee* (California):

> "President Meyerson for three years has withstood all efforts to intrude politics or rash police action onto the campus. At the same time he pacified disruptive elements within.
>
> "Above all, he displayed creative approaches, which brought reforms without capitulating to violence or to punitive pressures from outside. . . ."
>
> If things come off at their hopeful best, Buffalo can have one of the great schools in the land, the finest new plant in the world." (Wardlow (1969).

Despite his friendly assessment, activism at UB would escalate dramatically during the forthcoming 1969–70 term.

References

Allan, Jerry. (1969). "Meyerson Presents Demands of His Own on Faculty, Students, for a Better UB," *Buffalo Evening News,* March 3.

American Bar Association. (1969). *Report of Commission on Campus Government and Student Dissent* (Chicago, Ill).

Barnes, Jeremy. (1988). *The Pictorial History of the Vietnam War* (New York: Gallery Books).

Buffalo Evening News. (1968a). "UB Hunts Egg Tossers and Sends Apologies to Spattered Panelists," December 10.

———. (1968b). Editorial, December 10.

———. (1968c). "Council Members Ask State Probe UB Egg Throwing," December 11.

———. (1968d). "UB Inquiry Board Still Seeks Identity of Forum Egg Tossers," December 16.

Courier-Express. (1968a). "UB Students Throw Eggs at Speakers," December 10.

———. (1968b). "Egg Incident Called Peril to Freedom," December 17.

———. (1969). "Morning Mail," March 22.

Edelman, Sharon. (1969). "Crisis at SUNYAB—Spring, 1969." Unpublished summary report, UB Archives, June.

Gitlen, Todd. (1987). *The Sixties—Years of Hope, Days of Rage.* (New York: Bantam Books).

Ketter, Robert L. (1971). "Report of the President," SUNY/Buffalo, *The Reporter,* February 11.

Morrow, Lance. (1988). "1968: The Year That Shaped a Generation," *Time Magazine,* January 11.

Quinn, Jack. (1969). "Inside View, UB Confrontation: How Both Sides Proved a Point," *The Buffalo Evening News,* March 20.

Rhodes, Roosevelt. (1990). Interview and Questionnaire.

Riepe, Dale. (1971). "The Radical Student Movement," *The Colleague,* SUNY/Buffalo, October 28.

The Spectrum. (1969a). March 5.

———. (1969b). "Ring Dem Bells," March 20.

Schwab, Rick. (1988). "Generally Speaking," *The Ligenier Echo,* November 22.

Wardlow, Woodrow. (1969). "At University of Buffalo, It's the Forward Look," *Buffalo Evening News Magazine,* May 31.

CHAPTER VII

Fall 1969: The Beginning of the End

A single spark can start a forest fire. —Mao Tse-tung

Meyerson's announcement on September 8 that he would be on leave for the 1969–70 term to serve as Director of the Assembly on University Goals and Governance added to the sense of general unease. He would still receive one-third of his salary for important presidential duties; otherwise, Executive Vice President Peter F. Regan would be "in full command" during the president's part-time absence. Some faculty and staff grumbled about Meyerson's timing and worried that he was abdicating when strong and continued leadership would be required. Although promising to return, Meyerson was soon denying persistent rumors that he was being considered for other presidencies. He virtually disappeared during the 1969–70 academic year but remained the subject of consistently favorable press reports elsewhere, if not at home.

There was no hint of rampaging disruption at UB in September 1969. The academic year opened with 23,567 students enrolled and a full-time professorial faculty of 1,308. The library had reached a million volumes; the Law Library had doubled its holdings; and the Science and Engineering Library subscribed to the astonishing sum of 3,000 scientific and technical journals. The university administered $14,600,000 in sponsored research programs during 1968–69. Expenditures for the year came to $62,169,739.

For the third consecutive year routine problems included severe overcrowding in the residence halls, an invariably tight off-campus housing market, and the perennially insoluble shortage of adequate on-campus parking space. Despite the size of its new campus, UB is currently identified as the only four-million-acre place in the world where you can't find a parking spot. Some things never change.

Inspired by SDS, a dozen tents were pitched in front of Hayes Hall to dramatize the housing situation. Only three occupants were students; the rest were non-students, transients, and one Buffalo resident. "The director of University Housing, realizing the students' predicament, offered temporary rooms in the dorms to a few of the tent dwellers," *Ethos* (1969) reported. "The offer was refused in lieu of the fact that this could only satiate a minority of the homeless students. . . . There are also rumors that there are a number of empty beds available in the dorms." Unresolved parking and housing concerns increase uncertainty and reinforce lack of confidence in administrative efficiency.

By registration time the main issues were defined. Some were real, deserving respectful consideration. Others were spurious. Among the real issues were: open admission, attention to the neglected or disfavored parts of the taxpaying community, especially to the blacks; the sources and extent of subvention for research (and athletics); the level of toleration for military studies; re-evaluation of the whole course of study or any part of it; apportionment of shares in the University's government among students, faculty, administrative staff, and the general public; the formation, style, goals, and standards of the proposed new colleges; freedom of opinion and discussion, especially of the unwelcome kinds; grading; and clear definition of exisitng laws on hard and soft drugs. "All of these sober thoughts moved into the second, spurious group when they were blurred and heated under such terms as repression, fascism (in this arena almost always spelled 'facism') and vengeance," writes Ketter (1971). "A third group straddled the first two, being both real and fictitious. It comprised the great, sad, continuing urgencies of life: hunger, injustice, the profanation of nature—all real, terribly real, but not more likely to yield to an academic community's insistence that they disappear than they had to religion, philospohy, or statesmanship."

Some of the same issues in American colleges and universities—curricular reform, institutional racism, the nature of research grants, university governance, and the historically unrecognized need for improved teaching methodology—exist today. Another unresolved problem concerns how universities intend to fulfill major responsibilities of teaching, learning, and research if faced again by interruption, interference, or outright disruption by militant activists.

Viewed as an interregnum caretaker from the outset, Regan had no time to establish himself or build firm faculty relationships. He was also suspect in some faculty circles because his academic roots were in the Medical School with the Department of Psychiatry.

Troubles surfaced immediately after school opened in fall 1969. Major concerns included long overdue minority pressure on Medical School admissions (no blacks had graduated in over a quarter century), attacks on ROTC, and the premature lifting of the construction moratorium by the governor. By November, the Dean of the Medical School—following a series of protests by 150–175 blacks, who made sure no whites were involved—received a vote of full confidence from the Medical School student body for "meeting the call for more responsible admissions policies" and developing plans to increase minority enrollment.

Sincere and soundly based challenges to traditional curricula are necessary, but it is difficult to understand how any responsible educational institution could have permitted the existence of the amorphous and educationally vacuous College A, without insisting on academic accountability. In September, pressure was belatedly exerted on this most unstructured and experimental of the colleges, to limit enrollment, tighten grading policies, move from its store-front location, and force more faculty contact, but Vice President Bennis was "eventually persuaded to support College A's unique status," reported *The Spectrum* (1969a).

The governor ended the construction moratorium without complete reconciliation of protesting minorities. "A controversy over who had asked for the Amherst work stoppage in the first place cropped up and became disagreeably contentious," recalls Ketter (1971). "Curiously enough, the University failed to advance its strongest point of defense, which was the belief that fair employment and labor practices were essential to a public enterprise in a democracy."

The *National Observer* (1969) would not help UB's image. A nine-paragraph front-page article, "The Return to Campus: Once Again, It's a Time for Anger," established the tone:

> A graduate student at the State University of New York at Buffalo, between sips of coffee in the Student Union, reports: "You can feel the tension. Kids are being busted for narcotics, and all kinds of groups are going around the campus collecting money to hire lawyers. The students are worried about the draft, the war, and a lot of other things. There's definitely going to be demonstrations." . . . It's the Buffalo campus that seems much closer now to some kind of explosion. Dan Bentivogli, a senior and leader of Youth Against War and Fascism, may have the explanation: "This campus per capita has more issues than any other in the country—racism, Defense Department Projects, ROTC, all of it."

The one-sided account called for a (never printed) response, which I wrote and sent Air Mail Special Delivery:

> Heavy reliance was placed on quotations from a student spokesman whose leadership is not representaive or generally accepted by more than a handful of his own followers. . . . The reporter's hopeful anticipation of "some kind of explosion" reflects questionable reporting, especially since his reactions were based on limited contacts. It would have been appropriate to talk to other students, including recognized student leaders. . . . If racism exists here, it does so to a much lesser extent than in most institutions. There are fewer schools in the nation that exceed the 22–24 percent

minority group representation within the incoming freshman class, and the institution has made a bold commitment to support programs for the economically disadavantaged. . . . If the radical fascist left succeeds in its efforts, the news media should receive credit for the lack of public support and understanding so necessary for the survival of higher education during this crucial period.

This University has been noted for encouraging legitimate forms of dissent, and a distinction must be made between dissent and disruption. In any event, we do not deserve to be "at the combustion point," although this may come because circumstances sometimes trigger such events. Serious upheaval may occur just for the sake of disruption rather than because of *bona fide* issues. . . . In short, radicals may temporarily gain support from moderates in whose hands the hope for stability of any institution really rests.

ROTC, one of 174 such Air Force units in the nation, was a uniquely pathetic casualty. Sustained chanting and "Revolutionary Dance" sessions by co-eds wearing false masks—including the liberal use of red paint by "Women Against ROTC" (WAR)—thwarted on-campus drills. A hit-and-run raid on October 15, when 100 demonstrators ransacked four ROTC offices in Clark Hall, resulted in damages estimated at $10,000. Charges (later dropped) were brought against only a few of the always elusive offenders. "There was a cautious feeling that many among the students and faculty were vehemently opposed to any prosecution, and in any event identification which would stand up in court was not abundant," explains Ketter (1971). "ROTC was probably as defenseless a first target as could have been chosen. It attracted fewer than a hundred earnest and forlorn young men, and apart from them had no constituency whatever. Most elements of the University were massively scornful or indifferent to it."

During the Faculty Senate hearing on ROTC it was soon clear that the program would not survive. Concerns were raised about the "academic inappropriateness" of course content and the qualifications of ROTC instructional staff. No one challenged the highly subjective content of credit-bearing courses offered in the colleges or openly expressed concern about the lack of academic qualifications of unsupervised instructors in Colleges A and F.

(ROTC was eliminated on many campuses during the Vietnam era. Few cadets wore uniforms to class, and enrollees were constantly harassed by anti-war factions. Today, "ROTC is riding high again at over 1,000 campuses across the nation," according to the *American Legion Magazine* (1988). "Enrollment in Army, Air Force, and Navy ROTC units has doubled since the 1973–74 school year. For example, enrollment in Army ROTC climbed from 13,200 in the 1973–74 school year to 61,587 in 1985–86," and "there are now as many as five applicants for every eligible ROTC scholarship.")

No one seemed to take seriously the strongly worded warnings—unaccompanied by efforts to consult faculty and seek out their reactions and support—that the acting president issued periodically after the ROTC episode:

> *October 16:* The university cannot permit itself to be corroded by this type of roving barbarism. If violence and the threat of violence go unchecked, faculty, students, and staff alike will live in fear, and those standards of rational inquiry and action which are a university's hallmark will be destroyed. (Regan 1969a)

> *November 11:* If classrooms are invaded again, the police will be on campus. There are vigilante faculty members who are ready to use clubs . . . . We cannot live long as a community when threats are received by members of that community. We've come this far, and the whole system is on the verge of something great, yet the threat of real anarchy is there. (Regan 1969b)

> *November 15:* We cannot and will not tolerate interference with regular functions of the university as they are conducted in the university's classrooms, laboratories, clinics, and offices. We cannot and will not tolerate harassment or intimdation of individual members of our community in the pursuit of their own chosen inquiries or accepted duties. (Regan 1969c)

> *November 18:* A trend has begun to take shape on our campus—the resort to violence, harassment, and intimidation as a political tactic. . . . No university can tolerate the proliferation of acts of intimidation and violence . . . it means a clear danger to continued freedom of speech and freedom from bodly harm because violence and fear permit those who claim the rights of free expression for themselves to deny those same rights for others. (Regan 1969d)

> *November 21:* Let it also be clearly understood that unauthorized intrusions into the functioning classrooms, laboratories, clinics, offices, and construction projects of this university are prohibited. If plans for intrusion into any of these areas become known in advance, I intend to call upon such internal or external security forces as may be necessary to bring the illegal activity to an end. (Regan 1969e)

The administration's inability to match rhetoric with action was clearly exposed, and Regan's repeated threats to use "the power of administrative suspension" were ineffective. The gun wasn't loaded.

Finding ROTC an easy victory, the student dissenters (all too apparently induced, too evidently insignificant in numbers, too clearly propagandized in the student press) moved on to a much more important target: the Colleges. Bennis prepared a *Prospectus on the College Plan,* which he placed before the academic community for scrutiny, modification, and ultimate approval or rejection in December. The *Prospectus* was liberal, enlightened and true to Meyerson's original concept of centers of identification. "Moving swiftly to fill a vacuum, two embryo colleges, A and F, presented themselves as matured and ongoing operations," explains Ketter (1971). "They claimed huge enrollments, a full staff of instructors, rich and varied courses of study, and locations just off campus. The most elementary probing showed them to have little substance—except for the off-campus locations, and these became a running sore which the community could not forebear scratching. Hated, picketed (by community groups), and raided as unsanitary, the first two colleges not unsurprisingly turned into casual lobbies for flouting everything that invited flouting."

Traditional town-gown relationships were abruptly altered by this inexplicable administrative decision to locate the controversial College A off campus. Students affiliated with the college soon made it clear that Buffalo was an ideal laboratory from which academic credit could be generated for projects designed to investigate the shortcomings of society. The combination of an influx of unsupervised activist students gathering in an unattractive and inadequate educational setting doomed the experimental unit at the outset. College A had become a magnet for many high-school youth in the area, and concerned residents readily believed any reports about sexual promiscuity and drug usage at the Main Street facility. Locating the college in an office building, symbolically facing the main campus and Hayes Hall from across Main Street, ranks among the most foolish and dangerous of UB administrative decisions.

References

American Legion Magazine. (1988). "Update," January.
Ethos. (1969). September 10.
Ketter, Robert L. (1971). "Report of the President, SUNY/Buffalo," *The Reporter,* February 11.
National Observer. (1969). "The Return to Campus: Once Again It's a Time for Anger," September 29.
Regan, Peter F. (1969a). Statement in *Ethos,* October 16.
———. (1969b). Statement in *Ethos,* November 11.
———. (1969c). Statement in *Ethos,* November 15.
———. (1969d). Statement in *Ethos,* November 18.
———. (1969e). As quoted in "Dr. Regan Rebukes Campus Harassment and Intimidation," *The Gazette,* November 21.
The Spectrum. (1969). September 15.

CHAPTER VIII

A Campus Sub-Divided: 1969–70

Actually the only real source of danger to America lies within ourselves. Whenever any group or agency among us gives way to panic or partisanship and seeks to deny to any citizen—even the most despicable, even the most disloyal citizen—the right of opposition, the right to his own opinion, the full protection of the law, America is weakened. By such acts America descends to the level of its enemies. By such acts democracy's claim to men's devotion is betrayed.

—Samuel P. Capen, Baccalaureate Address,
The University of Buffalo, May 29, 1949

While Seymour Axelrod (1989), a psychologist with the Department of Psychiatry in UB's Medical School, did not always subscribe to the behavior patterns of the most committed student activists, he was impressed with their determination and unshakable faith. He equates their zeal with that of a moth drawn to a deadly flame and refers to a fable written by archy, the philosopher-cockroach.

Painfully, archy learned how to typewrite (in lower case) by throwing himself onto the keys. Overnight, when the newspaper office was closed, the cockroach wrote philosophical essays, which author Don Marquis (1950) found in his typewriter the next morning. In "the lesson of the moth" archy relates how he repeatedly warned a moth not to fly too close to a flame and turn into "a small unsightly cinder." The insect acknowledged the danger, but replied:

> fire is beautiful
> and we know that if we get
> too close it will kill us
> but what does that matter
> it is better to be happy

> for a moment
> and be burned up with beauty
> than to live a long time
> and be bored all the while. . . .

Before archy could argue the moth out of this view, it "went and immolated himself." archy concludes:

> myself i would rather have
> half the happiness and twice
> the longevity
>
> but at the same time i wish
> there was something i wanted
> as badly as he wanted to fry himself
>   (p. 95)

A persistent myth of the sixties is that the majority of university students, if not radical militants, were activists who participated frequently in campus protest movements. Nationally, as at UB, students who massed to protest any given issue rarely exceeded 5 to 10 percent of a student body. Student activists comprised the majority of a student body, although they did merit considerable concern, analysis, and observation.

"Dissent is by no means the dominant mood of American college students," wrote Kenneth Keniston (1967), a close observer of student behavior in the sixties. Overt dissent, relatively infrequent, tended to be concentrated at more selective "progressive" and "academic" colleges and universities.

And even at these colleges, the vast majority of students—generally well over 95 percent—remain interested onlookers or opponents rather than active dissenters. . . . Whatever we say about student dissenters is said about a very small minority of America's six million college students. Yet this minority of student dissenters of all types arouses deep and ambivalent feelings in non-dissenting students and adults—envy, resentment, admiration, repulsion, nostalgia, and guilt. There has developed through the mass media and the imaginings of adults a more or less stereotyped—and generally incorrect—image of the student dissenter. (pp. 183–84)

Thomas T. Frantz (1968), a UB faculty member who wrote the "Research Review" column for the *NASPA Journal,* reported that between 4 and 8 percent of the nation's colleges had been sites of protests, in which about 1 percent of the students participated. Activists tended to come from affluent middle- and upper-class homes of liberal, well-educated parents who encouraged criticism and intellectual discussion. "It is easy to deprecate the activist because he is often brighter than we are, richer than we are, above religion, outspoken, and occasionally obnoxious," Frantz explains (p. 92).

He is intelligent and genuinely concerned with man and human suffering. Moreover he has not yet been strapped into the establishment and hence can give a quasi-objective evaluation of the institution. . . . Student protests tend to occur at large institutions with nonliberal administrations, many teaching assistants, large classes, and insufficient on-campus housing. However, the activist is lured to campus by the university's strong academic reputation and emphasis on the social sciences. Part of the trouble results from the discrepancy between the student's expectations of college life and what he actually encounters once on campus. The bright student, attracted by the institution's good reputation, is unaware that the reputation is based on the graduate schools and instead of finding a community of scholars, he finds large classes, I.D. numbers, mass registration, teaching assistants, and an impersonal administration and faculty. Is it any wonder he protests? (p. 93)

Rufus E. Miles (1969) observed in an insightful *Journal of Higher Education* article that "the disillusionment of students about monster, impersonal institutions and the kind of people who make them and are made by them is a major contributing factor in the process of alienation." Students

not only feel atomized but they see these impersonal institutions as the beginning of the end of their freedom. They had thought that higher education was going to be an emancipating experience, but it turns out to be a grave disappointment. They get little or no opportunity to deal with faculty as whole people, only as narrow and remote specialists. If the university is a prototype of the big organization into which they must move and become a cog, they don't like it. . . . The question is: If institutions of higher learning cannot organize themselves to be humane to all their members, and help one another in moving toward rather than away from a more humane society, who is going to do it? (p. 365)

Studies reveal remarkably consistent profiles of protest-prone individuals, who are generally outstanding students. (The average student arrested in Berkeley in 1965 was in the top 8 percent of his class.) Campus activists may be closer to their parents' values than nonactivists, and disproportionate numbers report that their parents held views essentially similar to their own, and that they accepted or supported their son's and daughter's political activities. Concepts of "generational conflict" or "rebellion against parental authority" are oversimplified as applied to the motivations of most protesters, explains Keniston (1967).

In brief, activists were not drawn from disadvantaged, status-anxious, underprivileged or undereducated groups; on the contrary, they are selectively recruited from among those young Americans who have had the most socially fortunate upbringings. The basic values of the activist are academic, idealistic, and nonvocational. Such students are rarely found among engineers, future teachers at teachers' colleges, or at schools of business administration. . . . Disproportionate numbers receive a B.A. within four years and continue on to graduate school, preparing themselves for academic careers. Many will be tomorrow's younger faculty members. (p. 187)

Idealistic and secure enough in their social position to take up causes of freedom, justice, rational public policy, and equal rights for all, descriptions of their personality traits include "altruistic," "highly motivated," "intellectually oriented," "unconventional," "curious," "impulsive," "nonauthoritarian," "flexible," and "liberal," Banning and McKinley (1988) conclude twenty years later.

Another distinct group of students, characterized by their alienation from society, also found an outlet through student protests, Banning and McKinley point out. "While there is, no doubt, some overlap between the two groups of students it is probably the 'alienated' group who most contributed to the labels 'hippies,' 'commies,' 'dirty beatniks,' 'conspirators,' 'politicos' and other less favorable descriptions applied to the person variable of the times," (p. 44). True hippies and political activists did not work hand-in-hand because there were different players and dissimilar agendas. The counterculture turned its back on and was not deeply interested in antiwar activism, seeking instead unrestrained freedom without responsibility.

For organized protest to occur there must be a sufficient number of protest-prone students to form a group, they must have an opportunity for interaction, and there must be leaders to initiate and mount the protest. Protests are associated with institutional size, particularly where large numbers of protest-prone students are in close proximity. More important than size alone, however, was the "image" of the university. A reputation for academic excellence and freedom, coupled with highly selective admissions policies, tended to congregate large numbers of potential activists on one campus. Certain institutions were magnets more because of their reputations of academic excellence than for being identified as havens for political activism.

While human beings are too complex to be neatly categorized, the demography of UB's student body during this period can be visualized by a series of concentric circles. Robert H. Rossberg (1968), professor of education, suggested "Student protests were fluid, changing entities consisting of a hard core of revolutionaries and militant radicals surrounded by successive concentric circles of students" (p. 63-4). His analysis generally matches reports about students at other large, public universities. "The smallest, innermost, and most identifiable sphere encompasses a group of 45–50 anarchists, nihilists, and others of uncertain ideology . . . dedicated to the total destruction of the social order," which they considered "intolerable, dehumanizing, and completely obsolete. Included in this group are others with a more orderly revolutionary orientation including neo-communists with a Maoist orientation. The latter are the cynical professionals of world revolution whose goal is to disrupt and destroy social institutions whenever feasible. For this group confrontation means power. Their cynicism is reflected in the fact that in the long run there is no loyalty to any issue, merely to the goal of destruction of the order. Their organization varies from campus to campus and frequent short term associations are characteristic. The membership in this group is probably less than one percent" (p. 64).

Professor Paul Kurtz (1971) concurred that UB faced a fanatical hard core of students who wished to destroy the system. "The views of the liberal, that he could reason out solutions with the revolutionaries—or isolate them—failed. For the aim of the revolutionaries was to demoralize the university by constant assault, whether epithets or threats of force—and thus compel capitulation and a new escalation of demands" (p. 232). He agrees with Rossberg that UB's "revolutionary militants were relatively small in number—possibly 40 to 50 hard-core students—yet they were able to capture 200 to 300 students and 100 faculty on crucial issues. Their main interest was not in reforming the university, but in revolutionizing society" (p. 236). Bentivogli (1989) agrees with the concentric-circle approach but believes the hard core, with which he associated, at one point may have encompassed as many as sixty persons.

The "hard core" deserves detailed treatment, if only because its members are often erroneously perceived as representing the norm. Bettelheim (1969) related this group and its closest followers to the Nazi movement.

> While history does not repeat itself and while the present situation in the United States is radically different from that of pre-war Germany, some similarities between the present student rebellion in this country and what happened in the German universities to spearhead Hitler's rise to power are nevertheless striking. Politically, of course, the German student rebels embraced the extreme right, but what is parallel is the determination to bring down the establishment. . . . Then, as now, these youthful followers of the extremists were anti-intellectual, resting their case on convictions based on their emotions. Their favorite technique was to disrupt meetings, not because they were not to their liking, but more as a demonstration of their power; they created disorder which then was claimed to demonstrate that the establishment was unable to function and hence had to be replaced by one based on their creed. (p. 18)

The hard core relied on intolerance, disruption, and physical intimidation. Labeling all who disagreed with their narrow perspective "fascist pigs," they employed totalitarian techniques to silence and intimidate opposition, but never offered a clear platform of their own ideas. Their goal was disruption, not reform. A few members of this segment equated arson and fire bombing—even if people got hurt—as appropriate forms of dissent. *New York Times* reporter Katherine Bishop (1989) asked Todd Gitlen how he explains to today's students that radicals from upper-middle-class families were involved in constructing bombs in their parents' townhouses. He responded with a quotation from *The Great Gatsby:* "They were careless people, Tom and Daisy —they smashed up things and creatures, and let other people clean up the mess they had made." Dedicated to discrediting administrative integrity and provoking violent clashes with authorities, radical activists often pursued the cult of power for its own sake, operating according to their own rules in complete disregard for the rights of others.

The "hard core" seemed to believe in the ancient Arabic fable about the Phoenix, a mythical bird of stunning beauty, the only one of its kind. After being burned on a funeral pyre that destroyed everything in its proximity, the Phoenix arises from the ashes in the freshness of youth, in even more beautiful form, to live through another periodic life cycle of 500 to 600 years.

"Perhaps the most vicious component of the New Left," former radical Barry Rubin admits (1989), "was its hysterical denunciations and slanders against anyone who disagreed with it. People also turned hatred on themselves, believing—as is common in many cults—that their doubts or deviations were only signs of individual weaknesses. And those who left were portrayed as opportunists. One talked less and less to anyone not sharing the faith. Again, the analogies to religious cults are compelling" (p. 50).

While the hard core may appear too small to be effective, Miles (1969) reminds us,

> under conditions of low or declining morale of a large organization a very small number of intensely alienated individuals may jeopardize its fundamental stability. It has long been assumed that almost any organization can control by appropriate means, a small number of alienated individuals, i.e., they can be contained or expelled. Recent experiences now indicate that a much smaller proportion of the total group than had previously been supposed, can thoroughly disrupt an organization. The capacity of a small group to disrupt the orgainzation becomes greatly magnified when there is a great deal of low level alienation which can be suddenly activated by the smaller more intense group and the authority structure seems to the majority of the organization to be remote, intransigent, and uncomprehending of the causes of the alienation. (p. 367)

Furthermore, student movements are marked not only by a reluctance to compromise, but also by impatience, explains Altbach (1990). "Student utopianism wants results quickly. Student generations last only a short time and the emphasis is on obtaining quick results. Student politics almost never have a long-term perspective. On campus, there is no such thing as a 'long march.' "

Bettelheim (1969) goes further:

> The inability of students to wait and work hard for long range goals marks them as emotionally disturbed. . . . Indeed, it is their hatred of society that makes it so easy for the militant student leaders to make common cause with another small group that provide temporary leadership for some of

the rebellious, outright paranoid individuals. The proportion of paranoids among students is no greater than in any comparable group of the population. But they are more dangerous because of their intelligence, which permits them to conceal more successfully the degrees of their disturbance. (p. 24)

Miles (1969) provides important balance. "Responsible members of the administration who may look for the cause of the alienation in too limited a context may delude themselves into thinking that the alienation is primarily related to psychological maladjustment and personal backgrounds of the highly alienated individuals," he warns. "Though this may in some cases be true"—and there were some certifiable "crazies" among the hard core at UB —"it is a dangerous conclusion to reach if the number of alienated individuals approach or exceed one percent of the organization, especially if there is similar, but low-level alienation among a much larger group. Only after the most thoroughgoing search for causes—those which are articulated and those which are subconscious—will a sufficiently large body of truth emerge to pave the way for essential institutional adjustments to changing times and circumstances" (pp. 367–8).

One reason universities were targets of leftist extremists, explains Rossberg (1968), "is that the majority of university professors may be classed as political liberals, and one of the basic goals of the radical left is to destroy this 'liberal' group." Radicals perceived the liberals "as the source of the ideology that maintained the current establishment in power since the days of Franklin D. Roosevelt. The liberals provided the spirit, the intellectual leadership, and the basic brainpower that enabled the 'power structure' to alter in form and change its substructures without a significant shift in its substance. The liberals are viewed as having prostituted themselves and their types to deceive the public and preserve an essentially corrupt political order" (p. 61).

Rossberg's second circle (an estimated 150 to 200 persons at UB) encompassed "militant activists" who were closely related to the hard core, frequently sharing their goals and methodology. Unlike the hard core, Rossberg contends, this group tends to be organized into groups of more or less permanent status. Left-wing radical organizations like SDS and others would be included here.

They represented approximately two percent of the total student population, if that. The leadership of their echelon of protest is generally more selective in the issue identified for protest and confrontation. The organizations they represent are identifiable, out in the open, and tend to communicate with each other from campus to campus. The leadership of these groups, though militant and hostile to the university as a critical institution in a rich social order, tends to be more rational than the shifting leaders of the hard core. Mediation and conciliation with respect to short run goals are recognized by this leadership as desirable if only to preserve the integrity of their organizations. (pp. 64–5)

Student movements tend to be focused on specific issues or crises. While the leadership may have sophisticated ideological perspective, the rank-and-file demonstrators have less commitment and little understanding that political change requires a long struggle, Altbach (1990) points out. "Student leaders have a tendency toward factionalism and confusion, which cripples the movement and confuses the issues. The rhythm of campus life also does not lend itself to sustained activism. Even on Tiananmen Square students were concerned about impending examination."

Surrounding these two groups at UB was another layer of 250 to 300 "active sympathizers." While carefully distanced from the hard core and unaffiliated with SDS or any activist organization, this third grouping frequently shares the goals of the hard core and the militant activists and may even participate in the early phases of active protest. According to Rossberg they are "most likely to be left liberals, concerned with reform and very willing to deescalate any confrontation if a reasonable share of their goals may be achieved by negotiation and compromise. They are not likely to desire direct confrontation with the police" (p. 64–5). The combined size of these three groups approximated 4 to 5 percent of the total college population at UB, which meant that attendance at rallies could reach a respectable 450 to 500 participants.

Mark Huddleston was president of the Undergraduate Student Association during the 1970–71 school year. In 1979 as an assistant professor in UB's Political Science Department, he reported to *Spectrum* interviewer Brad Bermudez (1979) that "a lot of people represented varying shades of Marxists . . . and there were the Yippies—anarchists interested in general hell-raising to point out the stupidity of things that were happening." Huddleston tried to "run a thin line" between "the astounding number of apathetics" and the leftist radicals. "I, and most others, were in the middle; all opposed the war, but were less interested in utopia."

Surrounding the first three spheres at UB was "a variable reserve," whom Rossberg labels "latent sympathizers" (p. 65). The size of this group was unpredictable and its involvement was determined by the issues and the response by authority. Although Columbia in 1968 was unique in light of the large percent of student involvement, *New York Times* reporter Edward Burke points out (1968) that "at Columbia estimates of 'sympathizers' climbed to as high as 25 percent of the total student population after the police intervention." Not to be overlooked are "pseudo-liberals," who did not march in cold and stormy weather, but want to tell their grandchildren how their involvement helped to bring about the end of the war.

Geography and associated climate may inhibit large outdoor gatherings. "In the 1960's major protests did not occur at times or in locations associated with cold weather patterns," explain Banning and McKinley (1988), but Buffalo's notorious reputation for bad weather did not always have a chilling effect on protests.

> Weather has always been an intervention tool for student affairs, or at least a "wished-for" tool. During the demonstrations of the late 1960's and early 1970's . . . rain is usually wished for in the hope that the momentum of the crowd will be dampened. . . . Few in the student affairs field can deny having had the "let's hope for rain" experience. . . . There is no reason to expect weather to play a different role in future activism because there have been no major shifts in either the location of campuses or in climate. (p. 48)

Even if the limited and erratic involvement of "latent sympathizers" is considered, the overwhelming majority of students recoiled from the far left, and never became activists. A gigantic circle, generally representing 90 percent of the student body, overwhelms the other spheres. Some of them watched and perhaps mildly sympathized during some protest demonstrations, but serious students wanted only to continue their education without interruption. Anyone who disagreed with protesters was labeled "apathetic," but the uninvolved also understood that arguing with closed minds was an exercise in futility. Others felt that no amount of university posturing would influence the war effort. Besides deploring the large numbers of apathetic students, Bermudez (1979) notes that Huddleston also observed that many segments of the university community "still adhered to lower middle class views of the community," and "Engineering was way off to the other side of the campus and could be isolated if it wanted to."

While rallies, teach-ins, demonstrations, convocations, and the Hayes Hall takeover were impacting on educational routine in spring 1969, interviews were being held with a random sample of junior-year students to trace ongoing reactions as undergraduates to "The University Experience" at UB. The longitudinal research study included verbatim responses by interviewees who had been encouraged since their freshman year to discuss whatever topics concerned them. Researcher Glen Ryba (1970) analyzed some of the views of students from among the 90 percent who did not wish to become involved, were unsympathetic with the strikers, and were disenchanted with radical tactics.

Ryba was struck by a sense of frustration by interviewees who were not actively protesting, but who felt that specific issues could have been more fairly and satisfactorily resolved if students had a greater voice in policy formulation. Some respondents reflected basic distrust of UB administrators, while others reacted favorably to their efforts. Students located at the Ridge Lea complex several miles from the Main Street campus reported that they were untouched by the movement. Faculty were occasionally praised, but more students reported that their instructors seemed unresponsive, uninspired, and unaffected by ongoing events, including teach-ins. Each interviewee was identified as to sex (M or F) and residence (R for residents, C for commuters). Preceded by Ryba's observations, selected responses follow:

"Some students were not strongly convinced about the need for change, the ability of students to make capable decisions, and their right to any significant voice in University policy-making:

> I don't see that it's our life work to make the University such-and-such. We're just going to finish and get out and we're not really as involved in it as we are in our own lives. It's just four years of our time, so why should we feel that we can mold it around our specifications? (FC #17)

> Why all of a sudden do the students want to run part of the school or have a voice in how it's running? I was home two weeks ago and I was talking with my mother, who went to college, and she said she couldn't understand, she says, how the change has come about. She says, 'When I went to school, we did our homework and we learned, we did the material in the books and that was it.' And she said, 'We never even thought about trying to run the school.' (MR #18)

"Some students could not understand why others would want to rebel against a society that seemed to be offering them so much:

> I try to understand why they would be so hostile. I don't know. I don't like it. It's stifling other people and making you feel that you are the one who is strange and different and not them. (FC #17)

"A few wished only to complete requirements for their degrees:

> I just intend to get through here with my BA with my high index and go on to graduate school and I care about as much about making decisions in this university as I did in high school: not at all. (MR #19)

> I can't get involved in some of these movements that say that this place is so oppressive and everything, because I think that the administration goes out of the way to make an effort to make it good. In a lot of ways I suppose I should have been involved in more activities, but for some reason I just couldn't. So I think perhaps I'm missing something along these lines. Maybe I should have been pushed into it, but I just didn't. But all in all, as long as I get into graduate school, then I'll be happy. (MC #10)

"Others doubted either the sincerity or intelligence of the students who were challenging the *status quo*.

> I just feel that this whole business is very, very immature—especially with the kids trying to act like hippies and play the part. (FR #20)

You can demand the world, you can demand the sky and the moon, you're always confined to reality and—they're in the wrong country if they think they can get things done by revolution, because this country is not one to do things by revolution. (MC #21)

Two years ago it was different. Now it's gone into revolutionary rebels, like leftists, communists. Well, they're not communists . . . they're leftists because they want such radical change and I just don't—I don't even like walking across campus. I'm going to find myself a nice, quiet, country-like school where I can learn what I'm looking for and have it nice and peaceful. I don't like all this ruckus and I don't think it does any good. (FR #22)

They're fighting for things they already have. They just pick up these nine ridiculous demands out of the air and some of them do have relevance, but I think the way they went about it was wrong, and it was immature and they're trying to show how smart they are and how mature they are. (FR #20)

Kids come to school to learn. We should come here and take our courses and learn and not run, not administer. That's what President Meyerson and Dean Siggelkow, people like this, this is their job, I mean they know what they're doing—at least, they should know if they've gotten the position. I just don't see where the kids want to do everything. (MR #18)

"Some students felt that there were real problems to be dealt with, but felt that those presently in power were generally the most capable people to work for those changes. Tampering with the present system would, for them, involve more dangers than present inequities:

I guess I'll be called old-fashioned, but the administration and the teachers—most of them—have just a little bit more knowledge and experience, especially the administration. They're supposed to be trained in some way for a manner of handling the situation, but I don't think they should be oblivious to student needs. If there was cooperation, I think this is the way it should be, but I'm deadly against violence and I'm deadly against another student interrupting my right to go ahead and study if I want to and not take part in the demonstrations. (FR #23)

Although it's not perfect—not a perfect place—and perhaps some of the motives of some of the people here aren't perfect, but it's still a lot better than other places. That's really what I think of it. (MC #24)

"Some students felt that questioning the administration was a good and necessary thing, but were quite disturbed by the extreme actions of the more violent radicals.

I think it's fine that they should demonstrate if they want. They have a right to be heard. But when they go around destroying property like the construction shacks and that, it's going too far. I kind of resent them doing this sort of thing because it's the kind of thing that makes the headlines and would tend to give the university as a whole a bad picture in some people's minds. (MC #25)

I refused to go because I thought, granted, it would have been a worthwhile thing if they had talked about things that were relevant, really relevant to the school, rather than firing the police commissioner. (MR #18)

You can't talk about something to somebody without their temper flaring. Nobody will listen to anybody else's viewpoint. It's a loss, as far as I'm concerned, for a learning experience. My idea of a learning experience is to talk to somebody and support his viewpoints and my own, and then later, at leisure, evaluate. It isn't to be shouted at. (MR #26)

"Obviously, there was a difference of opinion among students about the urgency of the problems under discussion. Even if they agreed wholeheartedly with the radicals on the basic issues, some students were distressed by the loud and obstreperous manner of some of the radicals:

I'm concerned about the way people are trying to get things done through the use of violence when they keep yelling 'peace, peace, peace in Vietnam,' and right away here they have violence, trying to knock down Themis and take over Hayes Hall. The majority . . . do not agree with the way these people go about it, even though they may agree with their ideas, or some of their ideas. (MR #27)

What I've seen is incompetence and mayhem and lack of objectivism, excessive emotion, to the point where, walking through the Union I almost got into a fight because I refused to sign a petition. I can't understand this. It doesn't fit my conception of a student. Student participation, as I see it, is an organized and objective movement where you try to improve things, make things better for yourself; not easier, but better. There's a difference, a considerable difference. (MC #26)

"Some students who were successfully working toward radical change in quieter, non-violent ways became disillusioned with those who would do no more than scream for change:

I know I worked over there (at College A) every day and by the end of the week I was very discouraged, because the radicals go over there and fill the room and yell and scream like they're doing right now, but they don't really want to get anything done. I think they just like what they're doing. This is their thing. . . . It's kind of discouraging after a while. (MR #28)

I could go into a meeting and agree with what was being said and come out objecting, not to what was being said but the way it was being said, and I did this many times. Not many times, but often enough to get sick of it, and quit. (MC #26)

"Others vacillated between doubt and confidence:

At times I'm very gung-ho. 'This concerns the students, this is our university . . .'—let's say a course, one of my teachers talked about this at one of our teach-ins. He was teaching a linguistics analysis course that the students hated. I mean, he said you have never seen such hate for a course in your life. He said that 5 years later you begin to realize that if you hadn't taken this course you would know so much less . . . people taking it would say, 'Gee, it's got to go.' But 5 years later people would say, 'Gee, I'm glad I took it.' So when you think about things like that you wonder. (FR #29)

You try to sort out everything that's happened and no matter what you do, you still come up with the 'I just don't know' type of situation. (FC #32)

"Students themselves were changing. When asked, 'What in your university experience has been of most value to you?' one replied:

The most value to me, I think—well, I have a feeling it's just been in the last few weeks with the teach-ins, really getting involved in the university, in the faculty members, seeing how they work and listening to some of the students' demands or complaints about the university.
These few radical groups who would spout off and everything, I'd always think they were wrong. They're just being radical. And, I guess that's the biggest change. I've just learned to listen. (MR #34)

"Some professors seem to be satisfying student cries for relevance in the classroom:

There's a few teachers who will—sometimes they'll even forget about what they're supposed to be teaching and discuss what's happening right now. It's almost like, 'What I'm teaching here is important but what's going on outside is even more important and we've got to discuss both; we've got to do both. You've got to learn about Descartes but you've also got to learn about what's happening here.' (MC #41)

Another student summarized the effects of protest:

Later, they realized that nothing had been done, that ROTC was still on campus, that Themis was still going up, that the construction still wasn't integrated, that there still weren't any more black students going to be on campus next year. Nothing was done. (MC #6)

While noting that most students remained primarily concerned about their grades and education, Ebert (1988) suggests that the temptation must have been strong for students to occasionally abandon academics and join the movement. "No one wanted to be branded out of the group, but it is not true that many days went by when no classes were attended because of student strikes," he recalls. When one of his geography classes was interrupted by demonstrators, "students started yelling that they [the protesters] should get the hell out. Ninety percent wanted the lecture to continue."

During the late sixties most UB faculty tried to behave as though nothing out of the ordinary was happening; some met their scheduled classes and left the campus or remained, unseen, in their laboratories. Many felt it was the job of the administration to deal with such situations, and that if officials did their jobs right in the first place, "none of this would ever have happened." A few tried to work constructively with students, but the faculty generally focused on the administration for allowing such events in the first place. All too often the majority of faculty members, even if sometimes interested and concerned, constituted an audience to the proceedings. "Faculty members can maintain their invulnerable positions by simply sidestepping issues as they arise, and refusing to become involved," suggests Political Science Professor Claude Welch (1989). "Many plead that they are 'individualists' or 'apolitical,' or that they are too busy with 'important work' to 'waste their time' on these matters. However, it is this very separateness that infuriates students and spurs them to greater group action. The alienation, separation, and detachment so often referred to in the existential literature that students are so fond of, is basically separation and alienation from the faculty."

"For its part, the faculty is distressed by the excesses of its academic offspring and frequently frightened by the flickerfusion of the frequently cryptofascist nature of the student activist," Rossberg (1968) believes. "The guilt that plagues the average faculty member's existence is partially assuaged by vicarious participation in the student demonstrations, by providing a vehicle for projection of the faculty member's own discomfort with his environment and an outlet for a partial release of guilt. The activist student hates/needs the liberal faculty member. The liberal faculty member fears/needs the activist student" (p. 63).

Today's unionized faculty will likely avoid involvement if universities are confronted with problems similar to those of the sixties. Most faculty—and administrators—were uncertain about what to do when confronted in the sixties by something they had never seen before. Accustomed to an orderly academic world, they suddenly discovered that there were no enforceable rules to influence decorum and classroom behavior, although they might have done some homework to understand better what was happening and the nature of the students who most wanted to change the university.

Biological Sciences Professor Morton Rothstein (1991), fearing the potential destruction of research projects by mindless militants, organized faculty into patrols to watch over laboratory equipment. He believes that his colleagues, faced with unfamiliar experiences and unpredictable student behaviors, were more bewildered than frightened by the activists. Other faculty who lived near the campus offered their homes as alternative sites for classes and seminars.

Professor Richard Cox (1991) was convinced that the principle of protecting the integrity of the university was at stake. He was among those who steadfastly refused to move his classes off campus and continued meeting with his students on schedule. Cox recalls one occasion when he was reading aloud a description of the French Revolution as demonstrators were marching and shouting outside his classroom windows.

Historian Robert Pope (1991) remembers when he held the crash doors in a large Diefendorf lecture hall and prevented demonstrators from entering to disrupt his class. "The overwhelming majority of students and faculty were angry over activist tactics," he said. "My American history class cheered me on as I stood at the door, with my head turned over my shoulder, and continued the lecture."

"A few stopped teaching their subject matter entirely and turned instead to student issues," Psychology Professor Joseph Masling recalls (1989). "Others saw students as adversaries, and more than a few faculty members began to carry concealed weapons to class. Some faculty began to dress as students did and a large number stopped giving differential grades based on student performance, awarding everyone A and B grades."

As Bettelheim wrote twenty years ago:

> In our universities today we have faculty members who are trying to remain aloof from it all, and others who are trying to anticipate even the most radical student demands so as to avoid confrontations. Worst of all, many professors are so intimidated that they cave in before the students exercise pressure. It is the continuous worry about what the militant students may do next, the anxious efforts to give them no offense, which saps the universities of their strength to the point of paralysis. And this anxious avoidance of taking a firm stand gives not only the militants, but also many noncommitted students, the feeling that they have the faculty on the run. (Bettelheim 1969)

As a concerned onlooker, Education Professor Gerald Rising (1991) found the period exciting, but disturbing.

> It was especially disturbing because of the lack of caring for the effect on individuals—professors whose academic and personal life was made miserable, administrators and teachers who tried to do their jobs in the face of student (and some faculty) anarchists, cleaners faced with graffiti-covered buildings, and students who needed required courses to graduate. None of the rioters cared for these or any other individual: they all had to be sacrificed to . . . And what was the object of that preposition? They seemed to feel that they knew, but did they? Their entire confrontation was negative and—granting that there were many bad things going on that deserved attention —they used all of their energy in this negative direction. If only some of that energy could have been harnessed to positive ends.

Rising learned firsthand the price exacted for espousing academic freedom.

Someone on campus scheduled a talk by a controversial psychologist who claimed that blacks were intellectually inferior through heredity. He had published several major studies that purported to show this, studies that were, of course, widely criticized and dissected. The upshot of this invitation was a strong reaction from students and even some faculty with the final outcome that the invitation was withdrawn. I took exception to this and wrote *The Spectrum* to complain about excluding any point-of-view from the campus. I made it clear in my letter that I was not a supporter of the proposed speaker, but that I thought he deserved a hearing and response. A few days later my wife and I began to get middle of the night phone calls and one morning I looked out the window to see formed in the snow in my front yard in fox-and-geese manner the pattern of a swastika. I went out and tramped around to obliterate the symbol. . . .

Kurtz (1989) maintains that the faculty "did not fully understand or believe the revolutionary goals of the militants. Although faculties are often high on intellectual talent, courage is a rare virtue on campuses. Dedicated teachers frequently find it difficult to use the rod of criticism on their students, particularly when so many of these teachers feel the need to be popular or well liked." He maintains further that under Meyerson's regime a working alliance was forged between revolutionaries and radical educationalists, "a new popular front, that was supposed to apply dramatic therapy to the university. In the ensuing struggle for power, the chief 'enemy' of the united front of radical educators and revolutionaries were those who defended academic freedom, tenure, and standards of excellence. Anyone—liberals or conservatives—who opposed new programs was said to be 'against progress' and expressing positions of 'entrenched self-interest.' "

Some faculty sincerely hoped to bring about reform and appropriate educational change but saw their efforts fail as they became trapped between opposing groups. English Professor Mac S. Hammond (1990) expresses the dilemma well for that segment of the faculty: "I was caught up in the middle between the student activists and the following administrative reaction. I was wiped out politically by both. My aim was educational innovation that all came to naught."

The faculty split was sharpest in the faltering arena of university governance. Initially influenced by Meyerson's leadership, the formerly elected, representative Senate was expanded into a full Senate of over 1,200 members. Concurrently, the Undergraduate Student Senate changed into a policy town-meeting structure, in which any student could attend to discuss and vote on issues, thereby replacing the previously better organized moderate leadership. Apparently better in theory than practice (but who knows how these bodies might have fared in different times) university governance alterations favored student/faculty activists. In addition to becoming extremely influential in undergraduate governance, militant students assumed control of the Graduate Student Association. Activists dominated the editorial policy of *The Spectrum,*

Radicals' artistic rendering of Dr. Siggelkow. Inset shows how the author believes
he looked at the time.

A demonstration opposing Mosley's appearance at UB, September 26, 1962. Used with permission of the UB Archives.

Sir Oswald Mosley speaking at UB, September 26, 1962. *Courier-Express* photo, used with permission of the Buffalo and Erie County Historical Society and E. H. Butler Library, State University College, Buffalo.

After a legal delay of two years, Herbert Aptheker speaks at UB on November 13, 1964. *Courier-Express* photo, used with permission of the Buffalo and Erie County Historical Society and E. H. Butler Library, State University College, Buffalo.

Demonstrators protesting the Selective Service Qualification Test. Used with permission of the UB Archives.

UB's first sit-in. Hayes Hall, May 2, 1966. Used with permission of the UB Archives.

Protestors against the Selective Service Qualification Test. Leon Phipps is in the foreground. Used with permission of the UB Archives.

Dow Chemical demonstrators marching to the Alumni office, December 18, 1967. Used with permission of the UB Archives.

Author with bullhorn at Norton Hall during the Dow Chemical demonstrations. Used with permission of the UB Archives.

Dow Chemical demonstrators, December 18, 1967. Used with permission of the UB Archives.

The remains of two construction shacks at UB that had been used for Project Themis. Used with permission of *The Buffalo News* library.

Bruce Beyer in 1969. Used with permission of the UB Archives.

Meyerson speaking at the March 3, 1969, convocation. Used with permission of the UB Archives.

Meyerson speaking at the convocation on March 3, 1969. Dr. Regan is to his right; Professor Connolly is to his left. Used with permission of the UB Archives.

The takeover of Hayes Hall, March 19, 1969. Used with permission of the UB Archives.

State University of Buffalo students inside Hayes Hall kept an eye on activity through the windows. *Buffalo Evening News* photo, used with permission of *The Buffalo News* library.

A *Buffalo Evening News* photo, March 20, 1969, of a barricaded side entrance to Hayes Hall. Used with permission of *The Buffalo News* library.

Demonstrators leaving Hayes Hall the morning after the take-over. (Anthony Lorenzetti is on the right and Fred Snell is holding the door.) Photo by George J. Butler, used with permission of *The Buffalo News* library.

Dr. Siggelkow conferring with William Payne of the Erie County Sheriff's Department, February 26, 1970. Photo courtesy of *The Buffalonian Yearbook,* 1970.

Campus police car damaged by students, February 25, 1970.

Buffalo TPU officer in damaged vehicle. Photo courtesy of Lt. Alfred McDonald.

Undercover deputy Russell Pecoraro "arrested" during evening of February 25, 1970. Photo courtesy of Russell Pecoraro.

Admissions and Records office files, destroyed by arson. *Buffalo Evening News* photo, used with permission of *The Buffalo News* library.

Dr. Raymond Ewell surveys the damage caused by vandals in his office in Hayes Hall. *Courier-Express* photo, used with permission of the Buffalo and Erie County Historical Society and E. H. Butler Library, State University College, Buffalo.

Part of the Buffalo police contingent occupying the campus. Photo by Ed Nowak, used with permission of the UB Archives.

Courier-Express photograph of Buffalo police arriving on Sunday morning, March 8, 1970, to occupy the UB Main Street campus. Used with permission of the Buffalo and Erie County Historical Society and E. H. Butler Library, State University College, Buffalo.

Buffalo police stationed at one of the entrances to Hayes Hall. Used with permission of the UB Archives.

Lt. McDonald discusses occupation with students near his police vehicle. Photo by Ed Zagorski, used courtesy of Lt. Alfred McDonald.

Peaceful march by demonstrators on March 8, 1970, to protest the arrival of Buffalo police that day. Used with permission of the UB Archives.

Professor Robert K. Dentan, pockets turned out, was searched as he and Dr. Snell, left, were booked together with other faculty members for Hayes Hall sit-in. Used with permission of *The Buffalo News* library.

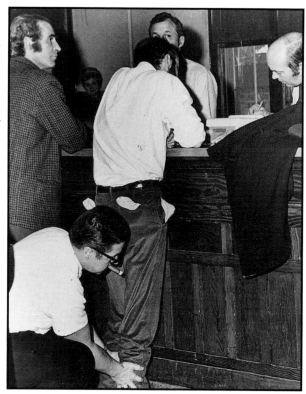

UB faculty members behind bars at the Kensington station. Federman is second from left in this *Courier-Express* photo, which later appeared in *Newsweek*. Used with permission of the Buffalo and Erie County Historical Society and E. H. Butler Library, State University College, Buffalo.

A *Courier-Express* photo from March 12, 1970, of Dr. Regan telling UB faculty of police withdrawal. Used with permission of the Buffalo and Erie County Historical Society and E. H. Butler Library, State University College, Buffalo.

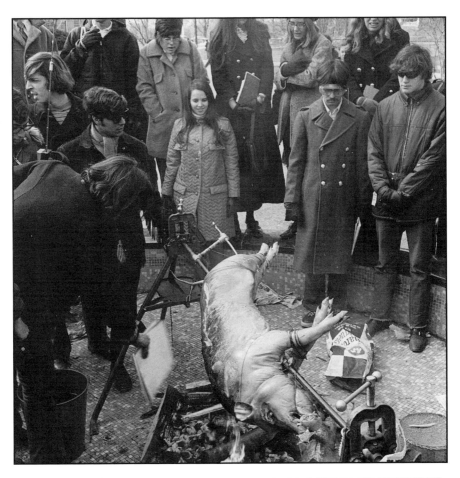

Students held a pig roast to protest the police occupation of the Main Street campus. Photo by Ed Nowak, used with permission of the UB Archives.

Bobby Faust pops out of coffin to address mourners. *Courier-Express* photo, used with permission of the Buffalo and Erie County Historical Society and E. H. Butler Library, State University College, Buffalo.

One of the casualties. Photographs like this influenced previously uncommitted faculty and students. *Courier-Express* photo, used with permission of the Buffalo and Erie County Historical Society and E. H. Butler Library, State University College, Buffalo.

Buffalo police prepare to fire another volley of tear gas onto the UB campus. *Courier-Express* photo, used with permission of the Buffalo and Erie County Historical Society and E. H. Butler Library, State University College, Buffalo.

Tear gas eclipsed buildings facing the UB campus from Main Street. Residents objected strongly to the attacks because tear gas fumes shifted away from campus. *Courier-Express* photo, used with permission of the Buffalo and Erie County Historical Society and E. H. Butler Library, State University College, Buffalo.

Students and onlookers
retreat from Main Street
to the campus after tear
gas attack. *Buffalo Eve-
ning News* photo, used
with permission of *The
Buffalo News* library.

manipulated and controlled mass meetings, and dictated what gatherings they would countenance in the halls of Norton Union.

Changes in student/faculty governmental structures accelerated the polarization process among and between campus constituencies. Lengthy and increasingly unproductive Faculty Senate meetings dragged on as activists invariably outlasted initial majorities of liberal-moderates. Effective opposition to militants gradually eroded, if only because dedicated activists never seemed to have to get home for dinner. Constructive legislation became impossible. Senate meetings were disrupted by shouts and obscenities from student observers at open sessions and from extremist faculty during closed ones. "It was difficult to vote without a sense of intimidation; many faculty began to boycott Senate meetings rather than suffer indignities and insults," recalls Kurtz (1989).

Vice Chairman Thomas Connolly provided direction as chairman of the faltering Faculty Senate, but for those hoping for organized faculty leadership that body functioned poorly. Frantz was secretary to the Faculty Senate during this period. "Its very size—1,200 members—caused instability, and the body was too cumbersome," explains Frantz (1989). "Since 12.5 percent constituted a legal quorum, a relatively small but determined minority consistently influenced debate and action on broad policy questions. The Senate became incapable of maintaining decorum at some of its most controversial meetings." Frantz recalls an early December meeting "when student dissidents packed the gallery and forced postponement of the final adoption of the Bennis prospectus for the development of the controversial college system." An aura of instability consistently permeated Senate deliberations.

English Professor George Hochfield (1989), elected to preside over the Faculty Senate several years later, is critical of his colleagues during this period.

> Some had a second chance at adolescence; they put on jeans and started calling everyone by first names. Then they got divorced. . . . They collaborated enthusiastically like radical prophets with whom history had finally caught up. The cheers of the crowd in Faculty Senate or departmental meetings made them feel heroic. . . . I wish I remembered in greater detail some of those meetings of the Senate when the gallery invaded the floor and turned the proceedings into a sort of menacing carnival. A kind of megalomania set in, making people feel that a revolution of the Senate was a way of ordering the world, and triumph there was a blow against evil society. I myself was guilty of such feelings. I had such a horror of the war, such a raging conviction of its evil, that there were times when I thought a Senate resolution was virtually equivalent to sending Lyndon Johnson to the guillotine . . . on the other hand, when these rampant emotions were transferred to academic matters, I tended to be on the side of caution and skepticism, and then I became aware of the violence and irrationality in the atmosphere. . . . To say in public that a course in "Automobile Repair for Women" didn't belong in a university curriculum, or that Socialism might profitably be studied in the library was to invite a barrage of dirty mail

and vicious phone calls. All in all, the lessons of that period for me were a profound attachment to the practice of democratic debate and a conviction that certain principles matter and must be defended, however strongly the wind might be blowing in the other direction.

Philosophy Professor W. V. Quine (1985) was at Harvard during the "disorders" at Cambridge. "Students occupied University Hall, ejected the authorities, and rifled the confidential files. President Pusey was compelled to call in the police, after many hours of waiting and warning. . . . He was unduly apologetic afterward about having acted thus responsibly, and the culprits were set loose on further mischief in the service of their headlong ideals. . . . Violence peaked with the fire-bombing of a center for international politics in old Divinity Hall." What Quine relates about the 1969 disruptions at Harvard foreshadowed similar developments at institutions like UB:

> There were demonstrations of solidarity with the Viet Cong; demands for severing the Reserve Officer Training Corps; demands for student participation in staffing the faculty, planning the curriculum, and planning the courses; demands for abolishing grades and for abolishing general examinations; demands for amnesty of apprehended activists. The demands for amnesty were crowned with success to the detriment of any self-image of heroism on the activists' part. So was the demand for severance of the ROTC, and so were other demands in varying degrees. Feeling ran high in the faculty between a radical caucus at one edge, which backed the vocal students, and a conservative caucus at the other edge, in which Oscar Handlin played a leading role and I an ineffectual one. Attendance at faculty meetings exceeded all bounds; we had to move them from the faculty room in University Hall to the Loeb Theater. In previous years I had seldom attended, but now duty called. . . .
> Standards sank in various departments. The preliminary examinations for the Ph.D. had been the major hurdle in our department and they were dropped by direction of the Students for a Democratic Society, who had found that the exams induced anxiety. Personal relations deteriorated. Professors who had shared their students' intellectual concerns in a friendly or paternal way were put off by student talk of students' rights and put to calculating their own rights and the limits of their obligations. The loss in rapport and fellow-feeling, as well as in academic standards, was not soon to be made up.

Some liberal, moderate, and conservative faculty may be faulted for lacking perseverance (and courage), but they could hardly be blamed for objecting to being called on frequently to consider antiwar resolutions and other items completely unrelated to university business. Presumptuous discussions neither altered world events nor pacified radical elements. "In effect, the center collapses," Kurtz (1989) believes, "pushed either to the right—with a resulting alliance of liberals and conservatives demanding law and order—or to the left —with resulting support for the radical assault on the university. The upshot was an extreme polarization of the faculty and a destruction of whatever liberal consensus once existed."

Open and subtle divisions among and between typically image-conscious administrators, myself included, were not conducive to unity. Both Regan and Bennis—along with another former key administrator who had just returned to full-time faculty status—vied openly for the presidency. Staff members experienced growing concerns about surviving to serve the next president, whoever that might be. Although not politically influential within the campus hierarchy, nonacademic and lower-level support staff—including the large and uniformly loyal civil-service secretarial component—remained united. With few exceptions this constituency consistently supported the administration, generally deplored student and faculty excesses, and related more closely to elements of the outside community that favored stronger enforcement measures, including the use of outside police. These personnel courageously and consistently reported for work, no matter what was happening around them at any given moment. Rallies, threats of building takeovers, and bomb scares were commonplace and finally accepted as daily routine.

Local and national media contributed to general confusion, campus discord, and polarization. Although participants in protest activities at any given campus were initially unaware of similar actions elsewhere, media coverage conveyed the impression that a nationwide conspiracy was behind localized campus disruptions. Administrators and activists—both eager to advance their version of events to reporters—were equally bitter about news coverage. Press accounts that generally seemed distorted and overly dramatic to university officials were never sensational enough for militant protesters.

UB student activists consistently charged media bias, claiming that Buffalo TV and local news coverage concentrated exclusively on transmitting outrage at the violent tactics of the movement, rather than analyzing the causes behind a demonstration. News stories became a simple damage and casualty report, emphasizing the students' "violent" character. "When students read something in the papers that they thought was unfair, it would often incite them to further violence," says Michael Jackson, an editor of *Ethos*, in an interview with *Spectrum* writer Adrienne McCann (1979). "The *Courier-Express* sensationalized the unrest to the extent of printing most of the articles on the front page, using enormous headline type and large photogrpahs," according to Jackson, who was often contactd by the *News* to express the students' point of view.

"Student perspectives on events made reportage difficult," explains Harlan Abbey (1991), a *Courier-Express* reporter. "It became an all-white–all-black issue. You were, in the estimation of student demonstrators, either *for* or *against* them." Michael B. McKeating, a then graduating senior and former member of *The Spectrum* staff, attended rallies and meetings unchallenged by the radicals. Because of his interest in journalism and knowledge about the campus, he was hired as a full-time reporter to cover the riots for *The Buffalo Evening News.* McKeating (1990) recalls being physically threatened by activists after he joined the *News.* "The strikers never understood or accepted the role of the outside press," he says. "We were always confronted with 'Where do you stand?' It was 'either you are for us or against us.' "

TV stations were not particularly interested in enhancing UB's image, reports McCann. "Most demonstrations started just for camera coverage," John Krieger (1979), then executive producer of WBEN News, explains to McCann. "If we didn't show up they wouldn't hold the demonstration." Krieger explained that WBEN "would film anything that moved," adding that "sometimes if we didn't appear at a demonstration, student leaders would call us, demanding to know why we weren't there." Because WBEN was "airing a lot of antiwar demonstrations, the station received a lot of phone calls from the Buffalo community questioning why we had so much coverage. Yet locally it took a great period of time for the establishment to be willing to go on air."

"An idea in itself may amount to nothing," Bettelheim (1969) reminds us, "but it becomes news by interfering with something else which is considered of public importance. In themselves, a couple of hundred demonstrators somewhere in New York or Chicago would amount to very little; but when fifty students march into a lecture hall, seize control of the podium, and broadcast their claims and philosophy to people who came to hear something quite different—then they have made news." (p. 26)

Miles (1969) referring to "the beginning of organized defiance," describes how activists capitalize on media involvement.

> The intensely alienated minority decides that the administration has no intention of taking action to deal with their complaints and that nothing the minority possibly do under the rules laid down by the administration will have any significant effect. The only way they can get action is to make a big stink, the biggest one possible. The theory is that institutional power structures do not like big stinks and will make concessions to avoid prolonged bad publicity and general disruption to the operation of the institution. The more news coverage the better, from the point of view of the minority strategists. (p. 361)

A "big stink" may involve the occupation of a building, or it may involve a strike. "In any event," Miles continues, "it has an overtly aggressive character, deliberately defiant of authority. Its purpose is to provide a confrontation before as large an audience as possible. It is believed by the provocateurs that what happens after the confrontation is almost certainly to be detrimental to the authority structure, and it is assumed that what is bad for the authority structure is likely to be beneficial to the aims of the alienated group." (p. 361)

While alienated people—particularly youth—may not fully understand or well express their reasons for their alienation or propose viable alternatives for what they do not like, Miles emphasizes that the administration is not relieved of trying to understand those causes more fully than they are understood by the alienated group and to find ways of reducing that alienation. "The standard behavior—it might even be labeled a cardinal principle —of most members of the authority structure of institutions is to seek to understand people's grievances solely by what they say, and to expect the aggrieved to propose feasible alternative courses of action which will alleviate their grievances," Miles explains. "If they have no such alternative courses of action and can propose none, the administration tends to think itself 'off the hook' and views the alienated members as demonstrably unreasonable. If there is any one lesson which deserves to be burned into the consciousness of university officials . . . it is that this cardinal principle is a false premise. The causes of alienation are deep and complex. Young people moving through the most difficult period of their lives may know *that* they are alienated without being expected to articulate well *why* they are alienated, and they most certainly cannot be held to account for devising mature and desirable solutions to the problems they identify (although they should be strongly encouraged to try)." (p. 357)

Despite general confusion and ever-increasing internal divisions, UB was still functioning as an educational entity on January 1, 1970. Unforeseen events would touch the university early in the spring term.

References

Abbey, Harlan. (1991). Interview.

Altbach, Philip G. (1990). Interview and Questionnaire.

Axelrod, Seymour. (1989). Interview and Questionnaire.

Banning, James H., and McKinley, Donna L. (1988). "Activism and the Campus Ecology," *Student Affairs and Campus Dissent: Reflections of the Past and Challenge for the Future*, Monograph Series Volume 8, National Association of Student Personnel Administrators, Inc., Keith M. Miser, ed., March. Reprinted by permission of the National Association of Student Personnel Administrators.

Bentivogli, Daniel. (1989). Interview and Questionnaire.

Bermudez, Brad. (1979). "From the Opposite Side of the Desk: Three Former Student Leaders Discuss Their Changing Perspectives," from "Through and Through the Looking Glass: The Shattering of a University, 1968–1972," a special edition of *The Spectrum*, May 11.

Bettelheim, Bruno. (1969). "The Anatomy of Academic Discontent," *Change*, May–June.

Bishop, Katherine. (1989). "From the Inside Out: The 60s Legacy," *The New York Times*, January 8.

Burke, Edward C. (1968). "Columbia Poll Shows Majority Oppose the Seizure," *The New York Times*, June 6.

Cox, Richard H. (1991). Interview and Questionnaire.

Ebert, Charles H. V. (1988). Interview and Questionnaire.

Frantz, Thomas T. (1968). "Research Review: Protest Prone Students and Institutions," *NASPA Journal*, October.

Dissent and Disruption

Frantz, Thomas T. (1989). Interview and Questionnaire.

Hammond, Mac S. (1990). Questionnaire.

Hochfield, George. (1989). Questionnaire.

Keniston, Kenneth. (1967). "Deans and Dissenters," *NASPA Journal,* October.

Kurtz, Paul. (1971). "Inside the Buffalo Commune: Or, How to Destroy a University," *In Defense of Academic Freedom,* Sidney Hook, ed. (New York: Pegasus).

––––––. (1989). Interview and Questionnaire.

Marquis, Don. (1950). *The Lives and Times of Archie and Mehitabel.* (New York: Doubleday).

Masling, Joseph. (1989). Questionnaire.

McCann, Adrienne. (1979). "Sheer Coverage: Buffalo Media Failed to Look Behind the Volatile Surface," from "Through and Through the Looking Glass: The Shattering of a University, 1968–1972," a special edition of *The Spectrum,* May 11.

McKeating, Michael. (1990). Interview and Questionnaire.

Miles, Rufus E., Jr. (1969). "The Pathology of Institutional Breakdown," *Journal of Higher Education,* May.

Pope, Robert G. (1991). Interview and Questionnaire.

Quine, W. V. (1970). *The Time of My Life: An Autobiography* (Cambridge, MA: MIT Press).

Rising, Gerald R. (1991). Interview and Questionnaire.

Rossberg, Robert H. (1968). "The Professor and the Activist," *NASPA Journal,* October.

––––––. (1989). Interview and Questionnaire.

Rothstein, Morton. (1991). Interview and Questionnaire.

Rubin, Barry. (1989). "Learning From Experience," *Second Thoughts: Former Radicals Look Back at the Sixties,* Peter Collier and David Horowitz, eds. (New York: Madison Books).

Ryba, Glen. (1970). "The University Experience," Office of Instructional Studies and Research. SUNY/Buffalo.

CHAPTER IX

Administrative Indecision—
Or, Who Called the Cops?

A social organization of any sort whatever, large or small, is what it is because each member proceeds to his own duty with a trust that the other members will simultaneously do theirs. A government, an army, a communal system, a college, an athletic team, all exist in this condition, without which not only is nothing achieved, but nothing is ever attempted.

—William James

On January 20, 1970, Meyerson announced he would become president of the University of Pennsylvania, effective in June 1970. During the spring term, he said, he would continue to satisfy his one-third-time administrative responsibilities at UB. Meyerson's parting contribution was a plea to the Faculty Senate to work out a parallel student-faculty governance system. He would virtually neither be seen on campus nor heard from publicly for the next five months. Regan, heir apparent as the search began for a new leader, was named acting president. Even as the University Council plunged into the presidential search process, a rising faculty dispute on new by-laws for the Senate opened, and student activists put together a plan constituting them as half a legislature, with no executive or judicial branches proposed.

Bennis (1972) identifies Meyerson's departure as a serious blow to UB's academic development. "The changes proposed by Meyerson depended on continued presidential support for their success," the former provost wrote. "The campus had, in effect, undergone major surgery and did not have sufficient time to heal before a series of altogether different demands, including a semester of unrest, a new president, and a major recession, were made on it. When Meyerson did resign in late January 1970, it was as though someone had prematurely pulled out the stitches" (p. 112).

Meyerson's new confirmed "abdication" was viewed within the university family as "untimely," "unfortunate," "inopportune," and "a disaster." Recently hired younger faculty, many attracted by Meyerson's glowing vision of UB's future, were the least understanding and most disappointed. Biologist Peter S. Gold (1989), who arrived in fall 1969, "wondered if Meyerson was a man of principle, or only just another opportunist who intended only to use the institution to further his own career." Bruce Jackson (1989), a newly appointed assistant professor in English, felt betrayed by Meyerson's evasion of his academic responsibilities and still harbors feelings of "anger and anomie." "It was like a father figure who doesn't live up to expectations," Jackson suggests. "Despite Regan's desire to give an impression of strong leadership, we were now never certain who was in charge—it was unclear who really was president."

Paul Lohnes (1989), Professor of Educational Studies, remembers he was "disturbed by the weakness and even cowardice of administrative responses. Our president actually left the campus." A disappointed Leslie Fiedler (1989), Professor of English, feels that the president, "ready to break and run, crumbled under pressure." Although noting that unrest was not well handled anywhere, Ronald Hauser (1991), Professor of Modern Language and Literature, observes that "Meyerson ran away when he took a hurried leave from which he never returned—and after all, Regan was Meyerson's appointee." Physiologist Robert B. Reeves (1989) describes the administration as "self-serving. Meyerson went on a hastily prepared 'sabbatic leave' and left behind an inexperienced, naive administrator. No one in the administration could summon the courage to speak out for and reaffirm the principle of a university committed to free and open exchange of ideas, free of doctrinal and physical intimidation, or the sanctity of the classroom from political disruption. One spark of inspired leadership could have saved the day. Only common sense had to be invoked but the Meyerson administration was utterly without conviction. No administrator would risk his personal advancement to save his institution from destructive forces whose effects would last for a decade."

Some faculty believe the university might have better weathered the storm had Meyerson remained or reassumed leadership at some point, but others are convinced that no chief administrator could have survived. Law Professor James Magavern (1989), a Buffalo attorney and legal advisor to the acting president in 1969–70, believes UB was in a no-win situation: "No matter who was there—including Meyerson—or what he did, the radicals would eventually have achieved their primary goal of provoking a massive response by outside police." Philosophy Professor Newton Garver (1989) feels that Meyerson's position was impossible and untenable. "He was a president designed for good times, who was caught up with the rest of us in the intense difficulties that grew out of the terrible Vietnam conflict," explains Garver, who remains one of a small number of Meyerson proponents.

"It is hard to say if it would have helped, but Meyerson's return would have removed Regan as a target and scapegoat for faculty who were disaffected by the president's departure," says Henrik N. Dullea (1989), then one of Regan's closest aides, who is now Vice President for University Relations at Cornell University.

The need to select a new president agitated demands from every faction, and student dissenters were the most vocal. "Dr. Regan's civilized suggestion that the university act like a center of learning and discuss its problems in a series of campus-wide forums was trampled before it sprouted," reported Ketter (1971). Regan—described by one faculty member as coming in a pope, but going out a cardinal—had little time for broader administrative leadership and few opportunities to become even moderately popular. From the beginning the acting president was considered a prime candidate for the recently vacated presidency, but the dual relationship was constantly in the background. It was immediately apparent that Meyerson would not interfere with Regan, who was determined to be a strong, independent leader. Bennis, whom Regan appointed acting Executive Vice President (the acting president's former role) was already preoccupied with full-time responsibilities as Vice President for Academic Affairs.

Experienced staff soon sense shifts in administrative winds; when Regan entered the presidential race in earnest, previously involved faculty and some administrators found themselves outside the innermost administrative loop. Staff members became alarmed and paranoid when their advice was not invited or desired, and they hesitated to make suggestions because they were not recognized as part of the decision-making process. Lacking presidential direction, mutually remedial trust levels gradually eroded. Only a few of the former hierarchy and faculty whom Meyerson had formerly consulted were informed about the acting president's feeling, attitudes about issues, and plans for dealing with potential unrest. New problems developed before old ones could be resolved, and periods of indecision increasingly paralleled the acting president's insolationist tendency. Perhaps he misunderstood, or took too literally Chancellor Capen's adage, "the skipper travels alone." Nor could the acting president rely on significant involvement by a disengaged—and uninformed— faculty, who generally tried to continue their teaching and research as though in a pre-Vietnam environment. Then, as now, there was not enough faculty interest in improving that most important of all balancing factors— the teaching process.

Early in February 1970 Governor Rockefeller ended the construction moratorium without complete reconciliation of the protesting minorities. A controversy over who had asked for the Amherst work stoppage in the first place cropped up and became disagreeably contentious. (Meyerson had publicly supported the moratorium, which did not sit well with a governor anxious for trade union support.) "Curiously enough, the university failed to advance its strongest point of defense, which was the belief that fair employment and labor practices were essential to a public enterprise in a democracy," Ketter (1971) points out.

Concurrently, the usually placid Engineering students began a peaceful protest and boycott of classes to pressure Regan into awarding tenure to several professors who had not been supported by their provost and the tenure committee. Perceiving UB as a "tinderbox" after his first week on campus, Gold (1989) began to think "there really was something wrong, if Engineering students could get excited enough to even consider anything like that."

A relatively minor issue is often the catalyst for major trouble: a dispute over modest differences in stipend levels for black athletes, coupled with an impercipient decision to call in outside police assistance, charted the course of the last three months of the spring term. The myth persists that white activists in the late sixties contributed significantly to increased efforts to recruit minority students and support their causes, but photographs of demonstrating students at UB reveal virtually no intermingling of white and black faces. "It is significant that although the issue of racism was repeatedly raised during the 1970 troubles, blacks generally did not join in the whites' definition of the issues of protest, or join in activities orchestrated by white activists, affirms Ketter (1971). "They conducted their protest and established their point quite apart—disturbingly apart—from the whites."

"Black students distrusted white radicals because they were unsure about what the activists stood for or were trying to accomplish," says Black Studies/Anthropology Professor David J. Banks (1991). "Whites tend to try to dominate black organizations when they join them. White leaders in the sixties too often believed that they understood black student concerns and automatically assumed that they were qualified to give leadership to minority groups," Banks observes.

Daniel Bentivogli (1989), an acknowledged leader of YAWF, reports that while the blacks occasionally consulted with his organization, "they had different goals which precluded relationships with the militant white leadership that wanted to destory the very society that blacks were trying to enter." Blacks religiously avoided such alliances for good reason. They feared being used and realized that they could accomplish more without help from non-black groups, whose leaders too often had hidden agenda unrelated to affirmative action. H. Warren Button (1991) recalls the late Edgar Z. Friedenburg's analysis at the time that it was as though entrance to the university was controlled by a huge revolving door through which whites were struggling to get out while blacks were striving to push their way in.

Nationally, as at UB in 1969, the two major groups in the vanguard of the unrest were the predominantly white Students for a Democratic Society and various associations of black students. "While SDS champions the black causes, the blacks rarely join forces with SDS except for brief tactical gains," explained *New York Times* educational writer Fred Hechinger (1969).

> But while the left-radicals seem to pick their issues with a view to maximum damage to the "establishment"—often with the bluntly stated goal of destroying the university at the brain of the power structure and as the prelude to bringing down the power structure itself—the black students generally fight for limited objectives which they consider of importance to their own cause and education: open admission of the minorities to college, protecting of black tenants against "university expansion" into their neighborhoods, student-run black studies programs. Far from wanting to destroy the university, the blacks aim at making it more responsive to their needs as they see them.

What began in January as a personality conflict between a black basketball player and the coach mushroomed by February into a dispute over a stipend that was slightly lower for athletes than for other minorities regularly enrolled in a special program for educationally disadvantaged minority students. The program inadvertently provided a larger subvention per student, but one which a bureaucratic NCAA enforcement committee would surely repudiate as a wage-scale violation for athletes. When the administration did not challenge the athletic department's unyielding insistence on conformance with NCAA regulations, white activists charged "blatant institutional racism." The blacks unilaterally confronted the administration with their own sports-subsidy demand that the athletic subvention be the same whether it came through some other source or the Department of Physical Education. "After a sit-in of white non-athletes on the gymnasium floor captured the issue in garbled form and brought about the cancellation of the (Feb. 24) game and the [uneventful] dispersal of the crowd of Campus Police, an all day meeting (Feb. 25) achieved an agreement with the blacks," reports Ketter (1971).

Another account, the Greiner Report (1970), covered later in this chapter, notes that city police had been alerted and appeared on campus to help campus security clear the gymnasium on February 24. "The person who placed the call is sure he did not ask them to come on the campus," states the Greiner document. "Nevertheless, the TPU [Tactical Patrol Unit] arrived and remained in the area for some time. The crowd dispersed, and the police left without incident." Outside police were clearly not required on February 24 (especially without warning); the contest had been canceled and activists were not about to "occupy" the gym.

Buffalo police at that time could not be requested directly by campus security without prior administrative authorization, but the acting president may not have been consulted in this instance. An advisory Security Task Force consisting of student-faculty-administrative representation, originally appointed by Meyerson, was designed to function if any situation developed that might conceivably require alerting and authorizing involvement of outside police. This vehicle was forgotten or deemed untrustworthy but no change in policy had been announced. There was ample time to convene this body since the administration knew trouble was brewing that might justify outside assistance. The untimely appearance of Buffalo police—if someone invited them on— underlines the need for effective lines of communication and clearly under- stood channels of delegated authority. The mysterious arrival and "on call" availability of the TPU, coupled with subsequent impetuous and questionable orders to an untrained campus security force did much to determine the fate of Regan and the university.

Everyone knew the black athlete negotiations were progressing well, but SDS sponsored a rally in Haas Lounge at Norton Union for the evening of February 25 to keep the embers glowing. Much to the disappointment of the radicals, black spokesmen announced that the athletes were entirely satisfied with how the situation was being resolved. The sparsely attended meeting wound down so quietly when radical leaders advised a rational "wait and see" policy that I decided for this one evening to participate in a down- town duplicate bridge session, an interest I had reluctantly denied myself for some time. Activities triggered by some forty demonstrators brought me back to the campus, after what *The Spectrum* (1970a) would call "the most terrifying night in the university's history."

"That evening I drove to my office in Hayes Hall," recalls Education Professor Robert Fisk (1988). "I was surprised to find a line-up of Buffalo police cars parked near the Campus Police headquarters, a puzzling phe- nomenon. Hayes was ablaze with lights and every window in view broken. When students began breaking windows someone called the Buffalo police, who were now on campus. I asked if you had been called. Finding you had not, I telephoned your home and gave a synopsis of events as I knew them to Lois." An account of the confusing events that resulted in two student- police confrontations is important, since many observers believe UB might have survived subsequent major disruptions had this single episode been avoided.

A confidential "Summary of Campus Security Activities" (1970)—cir- culated on March 4 by Regan to nine other administrators, including three of seven vice-presidents (but not to me)—constitutes one view of the eve- ning's events.

> In anticipation of a student demonstration at [another] basketball game to be held in Clark Gym at 8:30 P.M. this date, 20 members of the cam- pus security police were assembled and assigned crowd control. There were negotiations on demands between the black students and the coaching staff which were unresolved at game time and the game was postponed. At approximately 8:40 P.M. Lt. Dmowski received a radioed message to re- port to Hayes Hall and clear out the students there . . . arriving at Hayes Hall, students were in the process of smashing windows. Dmowski asked

President Regan what his orders were and was told to arrest them. The Lt. and his men pursued the crowd of approximately 40 persons toward Norton Hall.

"An angry white-faced Regan, standing on the Hayes Hall steps, shouted, 'I want those men arrested,' " report campus security officers John Boland (1989) and Jack Eggert (1989). (The report fails to note that the normally almost invisible safety officers were helmeted and in full riot gear.)

"This was completely counter to anything the campus security police had previously attempted," I observed in unpublished notes (Siggelkow 1970). "The action was carried out by untrained individuals who possessed little understanding about tactics involved, or the implications of their actions. . . . The campus security force, although unarmed, looked like city police because of their equipment. . . . Pursuit of these individuals was ill conceived, thoughtless, and a serious tactical mistake."

The officers, slowed by equipment and riot helmets, did not run after the students, but *marched,* in formation, after them. As one officer explained, they couldn't run because if they did the face shield would fog up. The rock throwers could easily outdistance the police, escaping either by running the short distance across Main Street or disappearing into the large residence hall complex adjacent to Norton. Two "identified" leaders chose, instead, to wait for the patrol to catch up with them. When previously uninvolved students moved furniture from the lounge to barricade the Norton entrance, the culprits had yet another opportunity to leave by one of several other doors. Director of Security Robert Hunt (1989) believes it was deliberate entrapment and that "some of the weapons that suddenly appeared among the attackers—such as lead pipes—had been smuggled earlier onto the campus."

According to officers Boland and Eggert, the confidential report—which neither saw until 1989—inaccurately describes what happened before they reached the union. It stated,

> When the campus security officers approached the fountain area between Lockwood Library and Norton Union, they were met by approximately 150 persons armed with bricks, bottles, stones, ice, clubs, and miscellaneous missiles. Some were in helmets and other protective gear in preparation for a confrontation. The campus security officers formed into a protective group and advanced through this crowd toward Norton Union. At this time they were being pelted with all the things that this crowd could throw at them, including waste containers.

Contradicting this account, Boland and Eggert recall that *no* opposition was encountered until their return trip *back* to Hayes and Winspear. Michael Valente (1990) of the Campus Security force concurs, but remembers his feelings of anxiety when the men arrived at Norton Union. "They don't expect us to go in there, do they?" he asked a fellow officer.

"When they reached Norton Union they could see people breaking up furniture and barricading the door," the original security report continues, "the persons barricading the door began to throw pieces of furniture at the officers, and using the legs as clubs to strike them. The leader of this group appeared to be Terry Keegan." (He now reportedly makes his living as a street musician in West Germany.) "He was apprehended along with two other persons, one believed to be Tom Kearns. Keegan and Kearns were subdued and handcuffed. The third person was handcuffed but broke away and disppeared into the crowd." (This was an undercover deputy, Russell Pecoraro, from the Sheriff's Department, who asked to be arrested to protect his cover, Boland reveals.)

> Just as Dmowski began to speak in a tone indicating the seriousness of their situation his radio went dead and we were unable to communicate with him. Other walkie-talkies in the area gave us conflicting information as to where they were. This information included Norton, then Lockwood Circle, then in Lockwood Library, but finally we were able to understand that they had retreated to Hayes Hall and at this point we called the tactical squad. Approximately 5 minutes elapsed from their first call for help until the tactical unit was actually summoned. . . .

Eggert, Boland, and Valente agree with the balance of the security account, which included reports of their fight to get back to Hayes with their two prisoners. Eggert recalls the incident "as if it were yesterday" and "wondered if [he] would get out alive." Eggert and Boland claim that urgent calls for outside help were ignored by the president's office and believe their outnumbered force was saved only because Officer (Willie) Nichols was on vehicle patrol duty. Nichols, listening to the chaotic interchange on his radio, decided to drive to the point of action. "When he turned on his bubble gum lights," Eggert says, "the attacking students temporarily thought the Buffalo police were arriving. They backed off just long enough for us to make it to Hayes."

"In the melee between Norton Union and Hayes Hall," according to the security report,

> 9 of our officers were injured . . . from being hit with clubs, bricks, garbage cans, large and small pieces of ice. The officer most wounded . . . was struck in the face; his face shield gave him major protection; however, he did receive lacerations about the mouth requiring several stitches. One tooth was extensively damaged. The other officers received injuries varying from very bad bruises from being hit with solid objects (rendering them barely able to walk) to shoulder separations, back strains, and so forth.
>
> Officers were picked up in our patrol cars along with the prisoners and returned to 196 Winspear. As they came in the back door the tactical unit from Buffalo came in the front door. Dr. Regan, Dr.Bennis, Hank Dullea, and others entered the building at this time.

The campus security detachment was now safely back from Norton and the T.P.U. had not as yet been ordered into action. Faced with this second decision concerning police involvement, it was apparently determined that two Pyrrhic victories were somehow better than one.

> Conferences with the above and Lt. MacDonald [sic] of the T.P.U. decided action should be taken to protect Norton Union. . . . The Buffalo tactical unit left 196 and proceeded to Norton Union. On their approach the students inside the Union began to leave. . . . After the Union was cleared campus security received a call to support the tactical unit by coming over to secure Norton Union. The tactical squad then began to be attacked by students who were also causing extensive damage to their cars. At this time the tactical unit selected those who seemed to be the obvious leaders, went into the crowds and arrested them. Our information at this point is that they arrested approximately 12 to 15 persons, very few of whom are students on this campus. Most of them are persons over thirty.

[This was later changed to note that "4 of 18 arrested were non-students."]

> Because of the arrests and conditions of the equipment, the tactical unit withdrew and turned the prisoners over to Precinct 16; had their equipment refurnished with tires, etc., and then returned to 196. . . . After a cooling off period, Lt. MacDonald instructed four cars, with four men, to make a pass through the Norton Union area to observe activities. . . . The caravan came back with a report that the Union seemed to be clearing out and that there was not too much activity there at that time. . . .
>
> Mr. Hunt sat in with the meeting of President Regan and the deans and provosts. This meeting dissolved at approximately 2:00 A.M. All campus security officers met at 196 at 2:00 and reviewed the day's proceedings step by step with each man contributing his information and corrections. All were advised not to be baited into any discussions and not to be surprised at the "paper attack" which would be heaped upon them by the rioting students. The campus was considered secure at 2:20 A.M. . . . The temperature was 11 degrees F. . . .

When authorities angrily overreact, communication breakdowns tend to occur, ill-conceived police tactics may be authorized, and bad decisions are petulantly reached under stress. The involvement of the tough Buffalo Tactical Patrol Unit breathed new life into an amorphous radical movement that was running out of issues. No one immediately assumed responsibility for authorizing TPU action, but Edward Doty (1970), then Vice President for Operations and Systems, did his best to protect the acting president, as his unpublished "For the Record" account reveals:

> On the 25th negotiations went on during most of the day under the auspices of the Select Committee between the black basketball players and the Athletic Department concerning the grievances. Shortly before 9:00 P.M. the game with SUNY/Albany was canceled to permit negotiations to continue.

> At approximately 9:00 P.M. an SDS group, led by (Terry) Keegan and (Arnold) Stanton, entered Hayes Hall. Keegan asked me if Regan was in. I said, Yes. He then called to his group to follow and they headed for Dr. Regan's office. Magavern and I stood in the doorway of his office and when they said, Can we pass?, we said, No. . . . After considerable verbal abuse . . . this group left the building and headed toward Norton. They immediately started throwing stones at Dr. Regan's windows, breaking a number of them. Dr. Regan and Dr. Bennis were behind those windows. In effect an attempt was made to assault them with rocks and flying glass. They also broke several windows in Dr. Bennis' office. I went down to my office. . . . I saw them break windows in Crosby Hall. . . . Dr. Regan called the Campus Police to try to restore order. The Campus Police pursued this group right into Norton Union. They made several arrests in Norton Union and then withdrew, pursued by students. There were fights between students and Campus Police. The Campus Police called for help. I was called from Security Headquarters and it was evident to me from what I could hear over the police radio that they were indeed in trouble, so I went out to check with Dr. Regan and came back and called the City Police to come to the assistance of our Campus Police, which the City Police did do.

(This is incorrect since the UB contingent had already successfully completed the mission without help; ironically, the Campus Police, who had fought back to Hayes so valiantly without outside support, were later ordered to assist the Buffalo police at Norton. Doty's account illustrates how perspectives of the same incident differ among various participants, even when located in adjacent offices.)

"About 11 o'clock, I felt that a reasonable amount of order had been restored and went home," Doty continues. "I learned subsequently that a number of arrests had been made by the City Police, after rather severe provocations by students later in the evening." Doty was criticized for requesting outside police involvement, but it was not the original *alerting*—with Regan's apparent authorization—of Buffalo police that caused problems, but a subsequent order (which Doty clearly did not give, and no one ever officially volunteered responsibility for it) that resulted in the move into Norton Union by a Buffalo Tactical Patrol unit. "It was an administrative decision," Doty explains to no one in particular in his "For the Record" notes, "concurred in by Dr. Regan, Dr. Bennis, Dr.Siggelkow, and others." (I was not there, and had no contact with Doty, but was probably taking a 1200-point set at the bridge table about then.)

The radicals needed help and they got it. The February 26 *Spectrum* (1970a) "EXTRA!! INVASION!" issue reported "what was called a police riot by some observers and excessive force by nearly all others as dozens of students were clubbed and kicked to the point of bleeding. . . ." The graphic *Spectrum* account provides yet another perspective:

> Campus and city police battled students here for at least three hours last night, resulting in at least 17 arrests and several injuries. Campus police

entered Norton Hall shortly before 9 P.M., scattering occupants of the main floor, and making two arrests. City police surrounded and eventually envaded [sic] the student union an hour later. . . .

The night began with a peaceful rally in the Haas Lounge supporting the demands of the black athletes for extensive reforms in recruiting and in the financial aid programs of the University's Athletic Department.

The Norton Hall rally broke up with the leaders of the original boycott calling on the assembled crowd to wait and see how the university administration reacted to the demands of the boycotting black athletes. However . . . a group of approximately 100 students began a march toward Clark Gym, where the Tactical Patrol Unit was reportedly waiting.

When they found that the freshman and junior varsity games had already been concluded [the games were, in fact, canceled], the group proceeded to Hayes Hall to confront Acting President Peter F. Regan over the issue of police on campus. The doors to Regan's office were locked. The group then talked to a presidential assistant and questioned him on the power and function of the Security Task Force in deciding and calling Buffalo City Police on campus.

As the students left the building about 20 Campus Police, garbed in full riot gear, were marching in formation toward Hayes Hall. An unidentified person threw an object, believed to be a rock, through one of the windows of Regan's office and the demonstrators began running toward Norton Hall with the cops following in pursuit.

Chairs and tables from Haas Lounge were stacked in front of the fountain entrance of Norton Hall in an attempt to erect a barricade and prevent further police sweeps into the building. Several individuals began to dismantle the furniture and heave the fragments at the University Bookstore picture windows. Three windows were smashed with glass and other debris scattered all over the floor.

Students entered Norton Hall shouting "the cops are coming." Some people in the Student Union looked out the windows and saw the helmeted Campus Police approaching Norton Hall. Numerous students grabbed furniture from Haas Lounge and attempted to barricade the doors. Campus police forced their way through the barricades and began chasing people through the lobby.

One of the Campus Police threw Kearns against the wall. A group of police began to club him to the ground. He was kicked, stepped upon, and clubbed by the police until his head began to bleed. He was then handcuffed and dragged out as students returning through the front door pelted the police with anything within their reach.

When the police got Kearns out of the building, the cop holding his right arm began to beat Kearns on the back of the head with his riot stick causing Kearns' glasses to fly off and blood to gush from his head. . . .

Numerous people . . . crowded the SA office to write down what they had seen. Many expressed shock and everyone appeared to be in agreement that the police had gotten totally out of hand and had clubbed people indiscriminately. . . .

City police began arriving on campus almost immediately after the first Norton Hall confrontation between students and the campus security forces. Approximately one hour after the campus police swept through Norton making arrests, the city police entered the building. . . .

Some people fell down and one was clubbed by a policeman. Rolled up into a ball, the downed student was hit several times by the policeman, who then let his dog loose.

Like a cat playing with a mouse the police continually advanced into the crowd, then retreated with the students at their heels. . . .

One girl was dragged down the steps of Tower and when a boy jumped onto the policeman, several others came over and beat him up as well. . . .

Police meanwhile regrouped in front of Norton Hall and periodically charged the crowd as it grew in numbers. Some dogs from the K-9 Corps were set free from their leashes by the police.

A meeting of high level administrators was called for 12:30 A.M. A *Spectrum* reporter was denied entrance to the Acheson Hall meeting which he reported was guarded by a "sea of blue."

During the two-hour meeting we all sought a scapegoat and took turns believing outrageous charges about police brutality. Some accounts from my own staff members, I am embarrassed to admit, were inaccurate, but some campus security men may have lost control. Baumer (1989) recalls that everyone present seemed "confused" and "overwhelmed" by reports of physical attacks on bystanders attributed to campus security personnel. (Such opposites as undercover deputy Pecoraro and radical leader Bentivogli concur that the only persons they saw clubbing anyone were the Campus Police. They suggest that security personnel were retaliating for the physical assault to which they had been subjected during the earlier student-police fracas.)

Hunt maintains that there was "no police riot" and that it is easy to believe almost anything when there is great confusion. He is still concerned that no one ever acknowledged how his men were subjected to unwarranted attacks by persons whose behavior was at least equally inappropriate. "I was not allowed by Regan to say anything then or later in defense of campus security, or their need to fight back," says Hunt (1989). Associate Professor Howard E. Strauss, then Assistant Dean in the Faculty of Engineering and Applied Sciences, was in Norton the entire evening; he concurs with Hunt that the UB officers acted appropriately and he observed no Campus Security actions that justified charges of a "police riot."

"We did the best we knew how, and received nothing but negative criticism for trying to save the university," complains Eggert (1989). "There was a total lack of concern for the safety and welfare of the Campus Police, who were in such low esteem that they were not even allowed to talk to students." Eggert adds that "no exercise similar to what we tried at Norton would even be considered today." Better equipped and with wiser leadership, "we wouldn't be asked to charge blindly over the top. There would be no attempt to arrest anyone under such conditions; suspects were not going to run away, and we should have waited until the next day to arrest them."

A week passed before the taciturn acting president on March 5 appointed three young faculty "to determine the facts and the temporal sequence of events on the night of Wednesday, February 25, when Tactical Police Units of the Buffalo City Police entered Norton Hall" (Greiner 1970). No moderate, older faculty member was included among the appointees, who were Lawrence W. Chisholm (American Studies), Konrad van Moltke (History), and Chairman William R. Greiner (Law and Jurisprudence), who was appointed president of the university in fall 1991. The trio was to ascertain how and when "the nightmarish events" happened; a broader and more appropriate charge could have centered on putting the affair behind us. Emphasis should have been placed on recommendations to safeguard against repetition of such events, how to ascertain better when such drastic moves are justified, ways to resolve inevitable communication problems when an organization is under stress, and the development of a workable mechanism for making sound decisions. The committee concentrated on administrative shortcoming instead of suggesting corrective measures, producing yet another incomplete version of the event.

"The acting president received from the committee a strong recommendation, not of the rioting, but of himself," says Ketter (1971). Hastily prepared within a week, "The Report to the University, A Reconstruction with Commentary of Critical Events on Wednesday, February 25, 1970," (Greiner 1970), was not presented first to the acting president who commissioned it. The release could not have appeared at a more inappropriate time, and was published in a March 10 *Spectrum* "Extra" editon, flanked by a shadowy photograph of sinister figures—recognizable as police because of their nightsticks—standing in front of Norton Hall at night.

Although presumably intended to reassure the university community, the Greiner report begins feverishly: "On Wednesday, February 25, 1970, 27 persons were injured seriously enough on this campus to report for treatment to the campus infirmary or one of the area hospitals. Five of these were police officers. This represents by far the most serious instance of bodily injury in the history of this university." The ending paragraph three pages later offers little solace: "The events of last Wednesday touch virtually every issue confronting this campus. Our students are full of distrust, our faculty in disarray, and our administrative leaders inaccessible. These conditions are making it extremely difficult to start talking with each other again."

Not unexpectedly, the committee found that "our administrative leaders" (all carefully identified by name, although other principals were not) "must share the responsibility, along with vandals and physical assaulters of every kind for the course of events. Administrative errors, whether errors of commission or omission, contributed to escalations of force and resulting physical injuries." The "presidential group" was found "negligent" for "prolonged ignorance of the events . . . given the ample communication opportunities and the considerable time available for inquiries." Neither the administration nor campus security were afforded an opportunity to respond concurrently to the published content.

As disclaimers, the committee "did not talk personally with any people who were arrested or who may be involved in litigation" (their anonymity could have been protected); furthermore, "we have avoided any investigations which might place any individual in legal jeopardy—even though our report is informal and our work is finished when this report is released." No attempt was made to find out directly from anyone allegedly assaulted exactly what happened, or what provoked police reactions. Considerable reliance is placed on tapes and information supplied by *The Spectrum* editorial staff. "Statements regarding attacks on bystanders were for the most part unavailable to us. We anticipate that litigation and further hearings [neither of which materialized] may shed further light on the incidents surrounding the arrests." Only one injury—that resulted not from direct police action but crowd density—was verified. "A university staff member [Robert Walker, a member of my staff who was not identified by name in the report] "sustained a severe injury to his right hand as he was pressed against a glass showcase."

The account correctly establishes that "confrontations between the Buffalo police and students and other persons on the campus that evening occurred outside Norton Union between 10:30 and midnight," *after* "things were settling down in Norton Union" and where "by 10 P.M. people were leaving, believing the trouble was over." Bentivogli (1989) agrees with others who report that the union had quieted down after the Campus Police left. "There would have been no further problems had the TPU not appeared," Bentivogli maintains. He disagreed with Arnold Stanton, who urged the march to Hayes after blacks assured students at the rally about the progress of negotiations. Bentivogli also confirms that no dogs were unleashed and supports reports from Student Health that no one was seriously injured or hospitalized.

Documentation in the Greiner report leaves much to be desired:

"Hurried instructions regarding the pursuit and arrest of the vandals were shouted by Dr. Regan, Mr. Doty, and others present in the (Hayes) hallway. On the basis of information available to us we were unable to reach a firm conclusion regarding the precise orders directed to the campus policemen." The committee did not talk to officers Dmowski, Eggert, or Boland, who were as anxious then, as now, to give their version. The committee also notes that "one crucial document, the campus security log for that Wednesday, has been mislaid," by campus security, and the investigators never saw the confidential campus security summary prepared the night of the event. The Greiner committee was "unable to clearly establish how the decision to call the Buffalo police was made," but the flawed report's most serious shortcoming is revealed by an admission that "We have not talked to Buffalo policemen." Even so, the authors could not refrain from adding, "At one point a policeman is reported to have drawn his gun." No effort was made to confirm this inflammatory allegation, although one person who could have responded was the easily available Lt. Alfred McDonald.

"It was a comedy of errors," McDonald (1989) says today about that "bitterly cold" night. His unit had been standing by near 196 Winspear since 6 P.M., when it was ordered to the campus facility around 10:00 P.M. where he met with Dr. Regan. He remembers "a beehive of activity" and observed "beat-up" Campus Police, threatening mass resignation. "There were all kinds of confusing reports coming in, including one that students were systematically wrecking the union and another that alcoholic beverages were still being sold in the rathskeller. Finally, a vacillating Regan—after asking about providing students escape routes from the union—told me to clear and secure Norton Hall." He believes now that Regan may have confused him with another Pct. 16 platoon lieutenant, who was standing nearby. "We were about the same size, dressed alike, and held similar rank, but people never really see the face of a police officer," explains McDonald. "I was off with my men, and if Regan changed his mind he informed the wrong person."

McDonald encountered no serious problems in clearing Norton and persons in the building were cooperative in leaving. He remembers feeling pleased when he called the Deputy Commissioner to inform him that everything was stable and that he would be leaving the campus.

"Clearing the building was one thing, but getting out was another," McDonald continues. After hanging up the telephone he discovered that all of his men—including those he had ordered to guard the parked police cars outside—had, "like the Pied Piper," followed him into the building. While his contingent was busy inside, "students were crawling over the cars like ants, smashing windshields, breaking bubble lights, letting air out of tires and trying to set vehicles on fire. The thought crossed my mind that I was probably the only policeman in America trying to get out of a university building instead of trying to break into it.

"We had to fight our way out to save our equipment as best we could," McDonald recalls. "Our skirmish line was met by a hail of rocks and an eerie chant ('Off the Pigs . . . Off the Pigs') came from the crowd. Someone was waving a large Viet Cong flag and another demonstrator sounded cavalry charges on a bugle. We finally got off campus, in some cases driving cars with flat tires and no windshields. One person even stabbed a K-9 dog, and we took some prisoners."

Supported in the Greiner report were *Ethos* (1970) and *Spectrum* (1970a) claims that dogs were "unleashed" to attack the crowd. This, McDonald asserts, would never happen, "since K-9 dogs are ineffective unless under control at all times." He knows of no gun being drawn, although "one of his men put his hand on a gun, but it was not removed from its holster." He claims "complete control" over his unit, and is disdainful about "rent-a-cop" campus police. "They were untrained, but tried to look and act like Buffalo police. Think about it—you don't wear riot equipment, sheep lined leather coats, and a helmet unless there is a riot. When you dress like that you set the tone for a potential riot." His review of photographs revealed helmeted police using batons, but no evidence depicting similar actions by his men, who were wearing garrison caps. McDonald is not naive. He was informed that "one of his men, when asked by someone if he had a search warrant, responded by hitting the questioner with his nightstick, and said, 'Here's your search warrant.' I really tried to find out if it happened and who did that, but it wasn't until months later that I accidentally overheard one of my men bragging about how he 'clubbed a UB student.' " McDonald insists that it was not a "police riot." He did not see anyone getting seriously injured, "although campus security men did tend to use their nightsticks freely."

McDonald experienced difficulty afterwards in keeping Sheriff Michael Amico and his deputies off the campus. "Amico appeared at my command post and told me that he had twenty deputies who were ready to enter the campus," McDonald says. "I stated that everything was under control and we had no need for his assistance. He said he would enter over my objections and I told him a further display of police power could turn the situation into a major crisis. He said he feared for the safety of his undercover men and he was going to clear out the union. I informed him that my unit had already done this and the campus was back in the hands of Campus Police. I stated that we had made 18 arrests, which were now being processed and stood my ground. The sheriff did make a driving tour of the campus, but he left."

Deputy Commissioner Anthony Custodi provided additional details to the *Buffalo Evening News* (1970) the next day. He had received the initial call for help from Mr. Doty, "one of those whose authority was needed for the Buffalo police to take action." Eight TPU, three K-9, and three Kensington Precinct cars had been employed. A campus patrolman's vehicle "had been overturned, a van was set on fire, and one K-9 dog (King) was being treated for a deep puncture wound." Custodi volunteered that no black students had been involved.

The Greiner committee's research was flawed, since neither hospitalized individuals nor Buffalo police representatives were contacted.

> Resort to police force was taken too soon in response to fears and anxieties which were exaggerated by serious failures in liaison. Scant effort was made to obtain continuous, accurate information before dispatching police to the general area of Norton Union or afterward. . . .
>   Official silence about . . . physical injuries to university members . . . makes that silence even more offensive to common standards of humane concern about fellow members of our university community. . . . (Greiner 1970)

Unaccountably, the Greiner committee did not check with the University Health Service to confirm claims of injuries reported by *The Spectrum* or radical leaders. A February 27 memorandum by Assistant Director Dr. M. Luther Musselman (1970), as reconfirmed today by Musselman and Dr. Marie Kunz, revealed no in-patient admissions. Musselman's roundup of admissions at six nearby hospitals turned up "three casualties," none of which was serious. Walker's hand laceration was referred out for treatment (Musselman 1989, Kunz 1989).

The Greiner report continues:

> In light of nationwide experience of police-student confrontations we find that anticipation of a peaceful outcome to police intervention, inside or around the symbolic center of student life, Norton Union, to have been at best naive.
>
> Risks involved in police participation constitute so grave a danger to our continuing life as a university community that only clearly established danger to human life can justify our own leaders supporting large scale police intervention, and then only with far more extensive safeguards than those then in effect. . . .
>
> An academic community is vulnerable because of the values it espouses. Free inquiry and human discourse, the bases of our enterprise, cannot proceed under coercion, whether aggressive or preventive. We must recognize that we are powerless to protect ourselves against certain abuses. It is better to be seen to be vulnerable than to jeopardize the freedom we live by. Only under the most extraordinary circumstances will the upbringing of a police force on campus contribute more to the protection of free academic life than it detracts from that life; this must instruct our decisions. We are defenseless against the breaking of windows; we had better learn to accept this truth, bitter to some, before we destroy the substance of this community trying to preserve its outward trappings. We realize that there must be limits to abuse, but we urge that the hurt must be commensurate to the risks which the reactions entail.

Those who believe that outside police involvement is invariably the most viable option overlook concerns related to timing, the need for clearly written policies, clarity of instructions, what constitutes provocation, and even such mundane considerations as understanding how some city policemen generally perceive college youth—whose opinions, lifestyles, and appearance conflict with accepted community mores. Rather than expressing appreciation for having been given an opportunity to help, the committee maintained, instead, that a presidential appraisal and review, "if it had been made immediately after the events, would have reduced campus tensions and would have made unnecessary this delayed inquiry." My own belated view in my unpublished memorandum 1970 was similarly limited and equally unfair: "Immediate administrative reactions would have helped. Investigation was indicated and a straightforward preliminary report by the acting president might have done much to cool off the situation before it escalated further" (Siggelkow 1970). My presence would not likely have changed the course of the rapidly moving events, but I felt guilty about returning after the worst was over. Had I been on campus earlier—and this is self-serving—I would have immediately proceeded to Norton, which is exactly where the acting president should have gone as soon as trouble was reported there. He was wasting time listening to rumors and second hand reports in what was far from a neutral setting. A president has no choice other than to be visible, arriving as soon as possible at trouble sites, and visiting injured or hospitalized personnel at the first opportunity. How easy it is to criticize administrative inaction; even now facts remain elusive. Prolonged executive indecision during crisis periods heightens confusion and disagreement, generating concern and bitterness among uninformed faculty and administrators. Communication with various constituencies becomes almost impossible, especially if the administration is locked into dysfunction and rumors go unanswered.

To overcome initial charges of inadequate administrative response, the acting president desperately tried to create a positive climate by issuing a series of lengthy single spaced bulletins; the first of which, dated February 26, was issued at the dramatic hour of 5:00 A.M. Unfortunately, these statements —signed by both the acting president and acting executive vice president— failed to result in desired reactions, but reflected instead, a less than reassuring administrative perspective, that had little impact on an aroused university community.

The stage was now set for events that would further undermine the stability of the university.

References

Banks, David J. (1991). Interview and Questionnaire.

Baumer, William H. (1989). Interview and Questionnaire.

Bennis, Warren. (1972). "The Sociology of Institutions, or Who Sank the Yellow Submarine?", *Psychology Today,* November.

Bentivogli, Daniel. (1989). Interview and Questionnaire.

Boland, John W. (1989). Interview and Questionnaire.

Buffalo Evening News. (1970). "UB Police, Student Melee Results in Arrest of 16; 11 Hurt, Halls Damaged," February 25.

Button, H. Warren. (1991). Interview and Questionnaire.

Doty, Edward W. (1970). "For the Record," Office Memorandum, March 8.

Dullea, Henrik M. (1989). Telephone interview.

Eggert, Jack T. (1989). Interview and Questionnaire.

Ethos. (1970). March 3.

Fiedler, Leslie. (1989). Interview.

Fisk, Robert S. (1988). Interview and Questionnaire.

Garver, Newton. (1989). Interview and Questionnaire.

Gold, Peter S. (1989). Interview and Questionnaire.

Greiner, William R., Chisholm, Lawrence W., and von Moltke, Konrad. (1970). "A Report to the University: A Reconstruction with Commentary of Critical Events on Wednesday, February 25, 1970." *The Spectrum,* March 10.

Hauser, Ronald. (1991). Interview and Questionnaire.

Hechinger, Fred M. (1969). "A Campus Crisis: Tough Questions Over the Rebels," *The New York Times,* "The Week in Review," May 4.

Hunt, Robert E. (1989). Interview and Questionnaire.

Jackson, Bruce H. (1989). Interview and Questionnaire.

Ketter, Robert L. (1971). "Report of the President, SUNY/Buffalo," *The Reporter,* February 11.

Kunz, Marie. (1989). Interview.

Lohnes, Paul R. (1989). Questionnaire.

Magavern, James L. (1989). Interview.

McDonald, Alfred F. (1989). Interview.

Musselman, M. Luther. (1989). Interview and Questionnaire.

———. (1970). "Campus Incident on Night of Feb. 25, 1970," Memorandum from University Health Service, February 27.

Reeves, Robert Blake. (1989). Questionnaire.

Siggelkow, Richard A. (1970). "Anatomy of a Disruption," unpublished office memorandum, SUNY/Buffalo, July 7.

The Spectrum. (1970). "EXTRA!! INVASION," February 26.

Strauss, Howard E. (1990). Interview and Questionnaire.

"Summary of Campus Security Activities." (1970). Confidential Summary oɪ Events, SUNY/Buffalo, February 25.

Valente, Michael A. (1990). Interview.

CHAPTER X

Pigs Off Campus!

When does one know if he has ever made the right decision?

—Millard Fillmore, thirteenth President of the United States and
first Chancellor of the University of Buffalo (1846–1874)

An uneasy calm that settled over the campus the morning after Wednesday's Norton Hall episode would be shattered by activist attacks on UB security officers and Buffalo police early Thursday afternoon, February 26. This would be followed by another confrontation between demonstrators and a large contingent of lawmen under the command of Erie County Sheriff Michael A. Amico.

Around mid-morning on Thursday, February 26, administrators in Hayes were instructed "for reasons of personal safety" to dismiss secretarial personnel, move temporarily to a rented office building across from the campus, and await orders from the acting president. Neither he nor anyone bearing instructions ever appeared. Bored, uninformed, and not knowing what was occurring on campus, I decided to return to Hayes after lunch, where I hoped to be of some help, or at least find out what was happening.

The Spectrum (1970a) describes the events of February 26:

The student-police confrontation, which erupted when campus police charged through the student union Wednesday night, continued Thursday as thousands of demonstrators attacked various "pig" buildings: Hayes Hall, Campus Security, Project Themis, and ROTC offices in Clark Gym.

The afternoon's actions began shortly after 1 P.M., when nearly a thousand individuals packed into Norton Hall's Haas Lounge and its adjacent corridors to hear speakers' reactions to the battles and arrests which occurred the night before. . . . Many reviewed the beatings which they had witnessed as the arrests, numbering about 18, were made. Terming the encounter "a police riot," one student claimed: "We were attacked and had no alternative but to defend ourselves." . . .

Shouts of "Off the pigs" were heard as the rally concluded and demonstrators decided to march on Hayes Hall. Regrouping outside, the numbers began to swell and marchers, led by two red banners, proceeded across campus into Hayes Hall.

"We want Regan," the group chanted. However, Dr. Regan's office was locked. . . . As the group began to head back toward Norton they spotted 25–30 officers of the campus police in full riot gear at the Winspear entrance to the university.

(The demonstrators were unaware that campus security had been augmented by twelve Buffalo police.) "The group," estimated by *The Spectrum* at more than double the 300 figure cited in *The Courier-Express* (1970a) and *The Buffalo Evening News* (1970a), "slowly began to approach the police across the ROTC drill field yelling to 'Stay together, stay together.'

"When they reached the baseball fence at the far end of the field they suddenly began to charge the police with makeshift weapons chanting 'Off the Pigs.' The police slowly retreated off the campus as the crowd approached throwing asphalt, ice, and sticks. Two policemen were hurt in the confrontation."

Witnessing this was Professor William H. Baumer (1989), who, backed by a conservative-moderate faction, had by eight votes become Chairman-elect for the coming fall term of the embattled and divided Faculty Senate. Concerned about the escalation in violent tactics and a deterioration in rational and more controlled behavior, Baumer firmly believes today that outside police in sufficient force to control such situations should be immediately employed. "The mob literally drove the police off campus with stones and anything they could find for weapons," he recalls." At one point within two minutes they totally dismantled a wooden dugout at the baseball field to get weapons to attack the retreating police. I fully expected to see shooting, and had a Buffalo police officer gone down we would have had serious student casualties then and there."

"The radicals speak loudly of achieving their primary goal—'Pigs Off Campus'—when they ran 30 policemen into Winspear Avenue with a hail of rocks and chunks of ice," reported Dan Hertzberg (1970) in the *Buffalo Evening News*.

A detachment of campus and city police under Lt. James Goss of the Buffalo police moved onto the campus to protect Clark Gymnasium. The protesters sighted the police force and 300 began a wild charge across an athletic field in front of the gym.

"Come on, Come on!," they screamed. "Power to the people!"

The students met the police contingent with a barrage of chunks of ice and rocks, forcing them to retreat to Winspear. "We were greatly outnumbered, so we gracefully and very rapidly got out," Lt. Goss explained later.

Campus Security officer Jack Eggert (1989) was with the retreating force. "After we moved off campus and stopped at the other side of Winspear one angry Buffalo policeman unholstered his revolver, but he was immediately ordered by the officer-in-charge to 'Put that back,' " Eggert recalls.

"An hour later," continues Hertzberg (1970), "70 sheriff's deputies . . . assembled in the traffic circle at the Main Street entrance to the university. Several of the deputies carried tear gas rifles. Six hundred students stood within 20 feet of the police, repeatedly shouting 'Pigs off campus.'"

The Spectrum (1970a) reported, "Amid chants of 'Power to the people' and shouts of 'Pigs Go Home,' Dr. Richard Siggelkow entered the street and began talking with the police. Several minutes passed and the crowd had grown to about 1500."

Seventy men and ten vehicles were immobile, surrounded by what I fervently hoped were primarily curiosity seekers instead of hostile radicals bent on demolishing police cars. Possibly irked by the firm rejection of Buffalo police to his offer of help the previous night, Amico (1989) acknowledges he had not been requested to enter the campus; he decided on an "independent mission" after hearing reports that the campus was "out of control." The helmeted lawmen, in full riot gear and armed with guns, nightsticks, and tear-gas equipment, were unlikely to remain passive. Continued interaction between nervous deputies and irate, name-calling demonstrators was potentially explosive. I was concerned that both the radical leadership and the sheriff might welcome provocation by design or accident, leading to physical retaliation.

Deputy William G. Payne encountered me in front of the lead vehicle, where we studied each other like two boxers receiving final instructions before the opening bell. He was in contact with the sheriff, he said, and could relay messages directly to him. I suggested that continued police presence at this time and place appeared unnecessary and could become inflammatory. Payne disappeared to confer by radio with Amico. He returned shortly; the troops would leave if the roadway ahead could be cleared.

I was pleasantly surprised—and temporarily relieved—when a path miraculously formed and the crowd cooperated, stepping back on my request. Several minutes (seemingly an hour) elapsed, but the convoy did not move. Restless observers returned to occupy the roadway, and we were back to our starting point. When I asked him about the delay, the deputy explained that Sheriff Amico was hesitant about moving forward, concerned that his men and vehicles would be vulnerable to attack. I observed with false confidence that the overall mood of the onlookers did not, in my view, suggest such an extreme possibility, and offered an alternative—could the convoy, even more easily, back into Main Street, only a block away? It took another five minutes (another eternity) to reject this point: "It would look as if we were retreating, and we would never do that," Payne informed me.

Sandwiched uncomfortably between heavily armed deputies and potentially volatile demonstrators—surrounded in turn by too many curious by-standers—I became increasingly apprehensive. As the deputy and I were talking, Robert Dombrowski (1989), a member of my staff, joined us and was immediately hit in the middle of his back by a piece of asphalt which he describes as "larger than a baseball, but smaller than a football." The missile, hurled by some fool hiding in the crowd, was more likely intended for me or the deputy. Dombrowski grunted but did not panic. "It was very painful," he remembers, "but I didn't want to react openly and start something if we didn't have to. The police were just waiting for something to erupt, and I hoped they would leave before anything serious happened." (I hope he received a merit raise that year.) Had an officer been struck we might have experienced our own Kent State—the second such possibility that afternoon. As Payne and I continued to seek agreement two local radio news reporters, armed with live microphones, arrived and asked me for a statement. I put an arm around each one, inquired about their health, asked them what they were doing, and promised to get back to them.

I warned the deputy that we could be down to our last chance to relieve the growing tension. Payne explains that Amico sent his men onto the campus because he felt the Buffalo police were ineffective and not firm enough in handling the situation. "I was not clear about our mission and never knew exactly what we were supposed to do after we got there," says Payne (1990). "It was like a Chinese fire drill, and I felt like one of a cast of characters pushed onto a stage without knowing my lines. Lacking a specific mission, it did seem foolish to remain standing there to agitate the crowd, so we finally accepted the suggestion to leave."

Now the crowd had to be moved back again. Enlisting a red-bearded demonstrator (I believe his name was Fisher) who was carrying a red baton, I symbolically suggested that he open the left side while I cleared the right. Accompanied by cries of "Sieg Heil" and "Power to the People,"—and the national anthem—the vehicles slowly weaved through and off the campus. The standoff had lasted for around thirty minutes.

In the page-one lead story of *The Buffalo Evening News* (1970b) it was reported that "the students felt they had gained a victory" when the police, "who had concentrated in front of Hayes Hall—marched off campus at the request of UB authorities. Dr. Richard Siggelkow asked the police to leave and accompanied the column of marching and riding policemen from Hayes to Winspear Ave." During his 6 P.M. telecast Channel 7's Irv Weinstein (1991) observed that my intervention had "prevented serious problems," but to the press and most outsiders it was another example of weakness and the lack of cooperation between UB and outside police authorities.

Hoping for major violence, hard-core radicals concentrated on luring outside police onto the campus to inflame the issue and gain support from uncommitted students. The next day "Wanted" bulletins for me and other similarly honored officials were posted throughout the campus. Beneath the unsympathetic artistic rendering of me was this message:

> Pigglesow—Wanted for Police Collaboration: Pigglesow has a deep passion for the Buffalo Pigs who visited our campus all day Thursday and put many people in the hospital the night before. Good Old Pigglesow had a beautiful heart-to-heart rap with the "boys in blue" for three hours Thursday afternoon before they decided to leave the campus. Piggly has a naughty habit of speaking out of both sides of his snout. From one side he told us the pigs were leaving campus while from the other he slanders us by urging the pigs to stay and put down the "dissident, radical, hippie property-destroying students" (or in our terms people who value life over property).

"Wanted" posters, with equally unflattering caricatures, were posted simultaneously with mine, for:

"Peter F. Ray-Gun" for "institutional Violence . . . as the man who signed the current ROTC contract which allows the killing of women and children of Vietnam and other third world countries . . . and for his pig-blindness toward the destruction of lives."

"Bennis the Menace" for "Academic non-development, another of the many puppets being manipulated at most times and other times . . . doing an excellent job of portraying a pig."

"Puppet Howdy Doty" for "having the pig sense to call the pigs into the union . . . and for his complacency in the savage beatings of . . . many students."

"Dory Fiend" (Friend), for "Counterinsurgency, the worst type of pig . . . smiling, cunning and 'semper fidelis.' "

"Albany (Bill) Austin" for "Co-option of Justice who is studying HOW TO SUPPRESS THE STUDENTS IN ANY ATTEMPT TO UNDO AND REDO THIS PIG SYSTEM."

Others similarly honored were "Big Brother Mary Jane Amico" (Michael Amico), "World Lord Argentina Rocky" (Rockefeller), and "See More Knocks" (Seymour Knox), "Culture Vulture."

Amico, a graduate of the University of Buffalo Law School, was incontrovertibly the university family's single most despised law enforcement official. He claimed that "the Mafia and other organized crime elements have little do to with drug traffic on the Niagara Frontier; UB is the real center for drug sources" and labeled the university "a center for the supply of narcotics in the county" (*Courier-Express* 1970b). On February 28 in the *Courier* (1970c), the sheriff "emphasized that police have the right to go on campus where a crime is being committed," claiming further that he "was often challenged by UB officials on his right to go on that campus to investigate a drug abuse and make arrests. . . . It is no secret that . . . most of my undercover men are on the UB campus." Our response in the next day's *Cou-*

rier (1970d) was, "we have said over and over again that the campus cannot be used as a sanctuary from the law." In the same item I quoted from our rules and regulations that "any student found to be in illegal possession of drugs must be reported to appropriate civil authorities," and cited instances of recent arrests, including one a week earlier when we turned an alleged dealer over to outside enforcement agencies.

Ironically, Buffalo police objected more than we did to the sheriff's intervention in university matters. Elected on his prior reputation with the Buffalo police as a "crime fighter" (especially on narcotics), the lawman departed from the time-honored tradition that Erie County sheriffs did not challenge the jurisdictional responsibility of city police over UB, which is located just inside city limits. The university was caught in a complex territorial dispute between two law-enforcement units with different policies and procedures. Buffalo police were concerned about Amico's self-appointed peace-keeping role. Former Division of Patrol Inspector Fred Platek (1990) and then Deputy Commissioner Thomas Blair (1990) point out that Amico's presence threatened unity of command. "When another law enforcement agency interposes itself into a jurisdiction that is clearly your responsibility," Blair explains, "the impression is that you are unable to handle the situation. The sheriff was an elected official who was not responsible to local city government. His men were not under our control or subject to our policies, and you can't have two separate, competing enforcement agencies operating independently in this type of situation."

"Buffalo police do not go on the UB campus unless they are called," Commissioner Frank N. Felicetta explained in the February 28 *Courier-Express* (1970c). " 'Only three top people have the right to request police assistance," said Felicetta, who declined to identify them lest they be harassed'. . . . Amico took a sterner approach, stating that he would not wait to send in his deputies if the situation became 'serious enough.' " The dispute continued as long as Amico was sheriff, even though journalist Millard Brown (then responsible for editorial comment in the *News*) called Amico into Felicetta's office to discuss the issue. "In front of Felicetta," asserts Amico (1989), "I was advised by Brown not to come on the campus."

The former sheriff believes that his adamant refusal to fold under pressure resulted in unfavorable news coverage and "a negative editorial campaign" that cost him an unanticipated defeat in the following election. Amico remains consistent today: "As a duly elected law enforcement official, pledged to protect property and individuals, I had no choice other than to pursue, and seek out flagrant wrong-doers, independently if necessary."

The sheriff's men were safely away when I returned to Hayes, but my day was not complete. I arrived as smoke was seeping into the first floor and Anthony Lorenzetti, Gilbert Moore (Education), and an omnipresent graduate student (Frank Kurtz) were running down the stairwell to put out a fire in a large basement room that was used as an informal staff lounge.

Also located in that area were vending and photocopying machines. It was futile to alert Buffalo firemen, who by now were understandably unenthusiastic about responding to a myriad of real/false fire alarms. They had tired of losing fire-fighting equipment and coping with harassment that resulted when they were on campus. I took one step into the room and couldn't see anything. As acrid smoke filled my lungs and my eyes began smarting, I instinctively followed my first impulse, which was to leave immediately and let the building burn. How my colleagues extinguished the flames I will never know but they were welcome to it. "Fire may have already interacted with [chemicals], because we were all coughing," recalls Lorenzetti (1988). "The room was so black with smoke that it was impossible to see anything but a glow in the far corner. I was so desperate that I threw the contents from a cold pot of coffee on the flames while we were stamping out the fire." The fire department never responded, and campus security arrived after the fire was out. They had wisely taken time to don protective clothing because of the known supply of dangerous fluid in the area.

The February 27 *News* (1970a) quoted optimistic statements by university officials that "most classes were being conducted as scheduled." The same item included a temporarily encouraging report about a mass meeting of "approximately 1,000 students (in contrast with 700 militants at a rally the previous day) who called for an end to violence on campus." William Austin, a black (who did not have support from the Black Student Union) was president of the Undergraduate Student Association. Sensing strong opposition to indiscriminate "trashing" he "received a rousing 'No' to his question to the crowd: 'Do you want this university burned down?' . . . Many students wore armbands saying, 'Fires won't rebuild America.' " The moderate student leadership, threatened by the radicals and not impressed with administrative support, disintegrated a few days later. One effective radical strategy was to schedule a counter rally each time the moderates decided to hold a meeting. Few students voted then or now (under 20 percent) to elect representatives to the Student Association, which always raises questions about who legitimately speaks for undergraduates. The Strike Committee pushed aside the divided, intimidated, and ineffective student leadership and soon had control of the budget. Organized opposition to militant elements by responsible students was virtually over.

"Gangs of militant students continued their assault on the University of Buffalo campus Thursday night, setting small fires in several buildings, ripping telephones from walls, and breaking windows" constituted the lead paragraph in the page-one story in the February 27 *Courier-Express* (1970e):

> About 200 policemen equipped with tear gas masks and shotguns stood by Winspear Avenue adjacent to the campus, available if needed. . . . Buffalo police and sheriff's deputies patrolled the campus on several occasions during that afternoon, but remained off the campus at night for fear that

their presence would incite the students to even greater destruction. . . .

Police said firebombs touched off a small fire in Hayes Hall . . . a librarian narrowly escaped injury when a firebomb exploded near him and destroyed about 1,000 books in the Spanish collection. . . . Sheriff Michael A. Amico, who was at the scene for most of the day and late into the night, said he was fearful for the safety of several undercover men he had on campus.

Now an Erie County Court judge, Michael L. D'Amico (1990), then a member of Amico's staff, "could not recall one single life-threatening or injurious incident involving any undercover agent." Not unlike deputies of Western frontier days, some were unpaid student volunteers, often recruited "on the spot" by the sheriff, D'Amico explains. "No official training was required, or even considerd necessary. These young men were able to lie convincingly while looking another person in the eye," which may have created occasional credibility problems for their superiors, to say nothing about counter-infiltration.

Full-time undercover agents were a different story and the potential for infiltration undoubtedly troubled radical leadership. Captain Kevin Caffery and Lt. Russell Pecoraro, two of the sheriff's most effective undercover deputies, blended easily into the activist structure because they had been stationed on campus as narcotics undercover personnel before the radicals predominated. "It was a distinct advantage to be perceived as a drug dealer by the militants," says Pecoraro (1989). Neither Caffery nor Pecoraro ever faced any life-threatening situations and neither expressed serious concern about being exposed. "We always ran with the mob. Everyone did his own thing and paid no attention to anyone else, but there were times when mob frenzy took over that I certainly hoped they didn't find out who I was," Pecoraro concedes. Gaining overnight respect for "escaping" from campus security during the Norton Hall incident, he became trusted to the extent that he stayed overnight at the homes of radicals and drove the car for one YAWF leader.

Caffery, then full-bearded, went under the name "Skip" Ried. He achieved instant student adulation after hitting Amico in the head with a well-aimed snowball when the sheriff once appeared on the campus. Caffery (1989) claims he attended YAWF meetings where instructions were given on how to assault —or even kill—police officers. "You were supposed to isolate an officer, incite the crowd into making the first contact, and then shout 'Kill the pig!' Mob psychology was expected to take over." (Some psychologists maintain that getting people to chant slogans may inhibit and reduce higher mental processes and judgment. When protesters are busy chanting slogans they can't think very well—the human brain has limits and speaking makes a difference in performance in another channel, such as reading.) He helped make grenades by filling baby bottles with glass, stones, cherry bombs, and other explosives—and then worried that they might be used against fellow officers. "We tested one in a wooded area, and the explosion ripped the bark off trees 100 feet away," he says. Significantly, neither he nor Pecoraro ever saw any full-time faculty members participating with or exhorting revolutionary radical groups to commit violent or illegal acts. Pecoraro also refutes claims that drugs were offered or sold by College A students to high-school youth in or around the Main Street store-front facility.

Some undercover deputies complained that Amico's frequent announcements about deploying his men at UB added to the general campus paranoia and complicated their jobs. "Students began to see agents behind every tree and bush," Pecoraro explains. "I was more concerned about being caught by a Buffalo patrolman in hot pursuit than being exposed by the radicals. You would get clubbed if a policeman caught up with you, because he couldn't take time to find out who you really were. A battlefield mentality often takes over under such conditions. Police sometimes get out of control, even to the point where they riot within their own ranks."

Philosophy Professor Peter Hare (1989) recalls his "major role in the admission of one of the most influential militants, Robert Cohen." Cohen, derisively referred to by students as "Bullet Bob," was a standardized conception of an irresponsible radical. His self-assumed leadership stance was never fully accepted by UB activists who mistrusted him despite the fact that he had been expelled from the University of Wisconsin for his radical activism. Snell (1989)—"Cohen always avoided me and there was never anything constructive in his suggestions"—notes that Cohen was overeager to advocate violent extremes and physical confrontation.

"I was director of Graduate Studies in Philosophy when Cohen applied," Hare explains.

> Since he had been dismissed from the University of Wisconsin for his political activities, it was apparent from the beginning that my decision would be controversial. His academic credentials were recognized by the Admissions and Finance Committee to be high enough to justify admission with aid. He also had a strong letter of support from a distinguished philosopher at Wisconsin. On the matter of his dismissal, we had a supportive letter from the Assistant Dean of the Wisconsin Law School. I felt strongly that the decision should be made solely on the basis of Cohen's intellectual credentials, which were solid. . . . We resolved to take whatever flak resulted from the decision. Not surprisingly, Bill Baumer became upset . . . and tried without success to prevent Cohen from coming to Buffalo.

(So did I. Former colleagues from Wisconsin warned me about Cohen before his arrival. I alerted Meyerson and argued that we were not obligated to consider the application of any graduate student "dismissed for cause" from another institution. The president did not, or could not, overrule the departmental decision and the Graduate School admitted Cohen as an advanced degree candidate.)

"Upon his arrival, when he was willing to take time from his political activities, Cohen did good work with me on the philosophy of William James," Hare says.

> I found him to be bright and easy to talk to when the subject was not politics. Perhaps because of my role in his admission he always treated me considerately. However, one needs no confidence in psychoanalysis to recognize that Bob had a traumatic effect on my psyche. For some ten years after his dismissal from UB I had (with gradually decreasing frequency) dreams in which Cohen was the central figure. In the dream I was seated in an airport waiting for a flight. Bob Cohen and a couple of his militant colleagues came up to me and calmly said, "Peter, it's your turn. . . ." I understood that statement to mean that it was time for my execution and that's when I always awoke from the dream.

English Professor George Hochfield (1989) has not forgotten his altercation with Cohen after an evening meeting on "Socialism" convened by College A.

> The speakers . . . were talking pure nonsense, and there were many expressions of contempt for mere book knowledge. . . . When the floor was opened for comment, I couldn't resist saying that most of what I had heard seemed to me to reveal considerable ignorance of the subject, and it might not be a bad idea to do a little reading about it. This was received very unfavorably, and after the meeting I was accosted by Bob Cohen in a most aggressive manner that almost led to fisticuffs. Two days later I was referred to in a *Spectrum* editorial as "the voice of the reactionary faculty."

A powerful, overdrawn, and occasionally inaccurate February 27 editorial appeared in *The Spectrum* (1970a), fueling rising tension and catching the attention of confused and bewildered students:

> When you see a cordon of campus cops charge into a crowded student union . . . grabbing and beating people as they go—you're radicalized.
>
> When you look out the window and for as far as you can see in both directions caravans of patrol cars, TPU cars, and K-9 trucks are cruising through the campus—you're radicalized.
>
> When you can't see the police, but you can hear the screams and you look out the window again, only this time some guy carrying his books is having his head beat against the guardrail because he couldn't decide which way to turn fast enough—you're radicalized. . . .
>
> A police riot is what it was, and if you don't believe that—look at the pictures or ask the dormitory girls who got dragged to the ground by their hair. . . .
>
> There is no reason why the Tactical Patrol Unit had to be called in Tuesday night to combat a peaceful sit-in at . . . Clark Gym. But they were there, and they didn't leave happy. "You might have won this tme, but wait till the next time," one cop was heard saying. Next time came the

next night and the cops didn't make the trip in vain Wednesday. They got to bust their heads.

Thursday morning Edward Doty . . . finally owned up to calling the police. He cited the rock-throwing at Hayes Hall and the request of campus police for outside assistance as his reasons. Who gave Doty that order and who first ordered the campus police into Norton Hall to vacate the building? Who outfitted them in riot gear? . . .

No more lies, no more bullshit! Pigs off campus now—and that includes the pigs in Hayes Hall who make the phone calls and then sit back and let their liberal hearts bleed over the casualties. Pleading no control over police conduct is no excuse—they shouldn't have been here in the first place.

Days blurred together as national news vanished from the front page and Buffalo area media concentrated on UB. On February 28 both local papers highlighted the acting president's decision to obtain a broadly worded temporary injunction, which would soon become permanent. "State Supreme Court Judge Frederick M. Marshall late Friday issued a temporary restraining order barring demonstrators from acting in any way to disrupt normal operations of the University of Buffalo," reported the *News* (1970c). "Most copies of the court order were torn down by militant students Friday night before they vacated administrative and classroom buildings they had occupied during the day." (No buildings had been "taken over" at this point because the demonstrators had neither the numbers nor organizational capability for doing so; the administration may have overdramatized the situation to reinforce arguments for granting the injunction. The acting president said he had been physically blocked and not allowed to enter Hayes at 9 A.M. Friday, but I and my staff (although some did not enter through the front door) put in an unimpeded "normal" day's work during regular office hours. The acting president may have tested the front entrance to make his point.

"The writ was obtained after three days of violence," the *Courier* (1970f) reported in its lead story February 28. The same article highlights the increasing outside pressure on the beleaguered acting president: "Also Friday afternoon a group of area state legislators . . . issued a statement that 'unless complete order' was restored to the campus . . . they would ask Governor Rockefeller and State University Chancellor Samuel Gould 'to make available all necessary force' immediately to stop the disorders." College presidents are paid to make difficult decisions, but few chief executives remain unmoved when barraged by influential outsiders who become angry when a public institution is perceived as being held hostage by a radical, undisciplined student body. University officials maintained (accurately) that "much of the window breaking Wednesday and Thursday night had been done by area high school students lured to the campus by reports of the disorders. . . ." More hurtful were additional details about "1,000 books in the Spanish collection that had been damaged when firebombs were thrown into Lockwood Library Thursday night. Many of these books, some dating to the eighteenth century, are priceless and irreplaceable. . . .

"Many demonstrating students criticized Dr. Regan's actions during the periods of violence," the *Courier* added. "They pointed out that President Meyerson had effectively 'called off' a similar tense situation by calling a mass meeting in Clark Gym. 'We came to see Dr. Regan, and he told us to get out of his office,' the students claimed."

A March 2 editorial in *The Spectrum* encapsulated the action: "Police arrests, beatings, fear, tear gas [untrue], burnings, rocks, helicopters [untrue], clubs, Molotov cocktails, marches, Hayes, Themis, ROTC, rallies, boycott, strike. Where is Dr. Regan besides swearing out affidavits for an injunction?" (Bachmann 1970a).

Although we are not informed about the demography of the sample, or how many interviewees participated, the *Courier* (1970g) dispatched an unidentified reporter "to ferret out some of the underlying causes of the recent unrest and interview students involved in the turmoil or who supported it":

Students who demonstrated or tacitly supported last week's protests wonder if the campus administration and the community want to know the reasons for their winter of discontent. Conversations concluded Saturday with students on the quieted Main Street campus indicate that the sharpest thorn in the student side was the Buffalo police presence and their behavior.

All of the students questioned, from freshmen to seniors, on their reasons for revolt, agreed that the arrival of Buffalo police triggered the turmoil which erupted Wednesday and subsided Friday . . . Another irritant, students say, is the university administration they regard as uncommunicative with students and unresponsive to their pleas for meaningful change. Instead of changes, they say "phoney" communications are established . . . as pacifiers but not satisfiers.

Students contend that their peer representatives were not consulted when Edward W. Doty . . . summoned police Wednesday in violation of a 1969 administrative-faculty-student agreement that all three parties would confer if police should be called. A group of students sitting on the floor in a circle in Norton Hall charged Buffalo police with "clubbing indiscriminately" and with "brutality" . . . frightening many youths who did not participate in the fray but got caught in the action.

One youth related that a policeman had ordered Norton Hall occupants Thursday night to leave by the front door, and when a group arrived at that door they were clouted on the head by club-wielding police. . . . Dissident students readily concede that they comprise a minority. . . . they regard the majority as comatose and uncommitted.

Dr. Regan, a psychiatrist . . . drew sharp criticism . . . and was accused of being "incommunicado" during the turmoil and with "hiding" from students who reportedly sought to talk to him.

None of the students in the opinion sampling said he or she would leave UB despite their grievances. Why? The consensus was that the campus is "alive."

"Moving picket lines, a 'strike solidarity' convocation, and the continuing leafleting of demands will highlight today's strike activities as students aim for a total shutdown of all regular university procedures," the March 2 *Spectrum* promised on page one.

> Demands for this strike began after students and police battled in and around Norton Hall last Wednesday night. Since then, vast numbers of students have been boycotting classes while unidentified "midnight ramblers" have been using guerrilla tactics on certain university buildings.
>
> Elaine Kolb, undergraduate from College A, spoke at Saturday night's strike meeting and warned students "not to be fooled by people like [Student Association President] Bill Austin, who will try to co-op [sic] this strike like they did last year and dissipate our energy into teach-ins."
>
> . . . the College A convocation, scheduled for 3 A.M. today in Clark Gym will definitely be a forum to gain solidarity for the strike and will not be controlled by administrators or "student representatives." (Bachman 1970b)

Psychology Professor Dean G. Pruitt (1970) was not an activist or a participant in demonstrations, but in 1970 the young faculty member was interested in people who became involved in such activities. When trouble first erupted in late February Pruitt sensed a unique opportunity to conduct first-hand research about student dissent and maintained a daily log about ongoing events. Pruitt's knowledge of details is also based on 1970–71 interviews he conducted with involved faculty and staff, including those who worked closely with Regan.

Interspersed in **bold face** are portions of Pruitt's comprehensive diary, which he wrote with the assistance of his graduate student James Gahagan, covering that period between March 2–8:

Monday, March 2

The Spectrum **reported that 1500–2000 students** [twice the number cited by local media] **marched around the campus and burned an effigy of the acting president in front of Hayes. This was extinguished by the Peace Patrol, which may have indicated to the strikers that the patrol was less than neutral, because the fire was not endangering anyone or any building. Around 3:20 A.M. some 4,000 students (*The Spectrum* figures) or 3,000 (*The News* and *The Courier*) attended a convocation in Clark Gym. Engineering students announced that faculty for whom they had been fighting had been awarded tenure and urged a "non-violent" approach. Black demands were reviewed but student association president Bill Austin was not permitted to speak at the meeting which was controlled by The Strike Committee. About half the audience was either uninterested or disgusted with the way the meeting was conducted, and left. Demands almost unanimously adopted by those remaining included the right of self-determination by the colleges; the BSU posi-**

tion on institutional racism; dropping all past or pending disciplinary charges stemming from any demonstrations; complete and immediate abolition of ROTC, Project Themis and all other militarily-related research; the immediate removal of the acting President with a new President to be named democratically by students and faculty; an open admissions policy for all people of the general community wishing to attend; and the immediate lifting of the injunction.

"No one called the continuing demands insolent or woolly-witted; it was believed that the situation was too tense and dangerous," explains Ketter (1971). "The effort at dignity, tolerance, and patience did credit to the university, showing what standards ought to be and why they are maturely admired. But what was overlooked, sometimes willfully ignored, was the evident fact that such values were little esteemed by some of those to whom they were extended. It was plain that these persons were Yahoos." (In Swift's *Gulliver's Travels,* Yahoos were a race of brutes who had the form of man and all his vices.)

On March 2 the *Courier* (1970h) lead story carried Regan's announcement of a "one day postponement of classes in all divisions except the professional schools to allow students and faculty to come up with a program for cleaning up our messes internally. When classes resume Tuesday," Regan hoped, "we can go on, change, and improve in an atmosphere free of intimidation." His statements included no instructions or staff direction concerning where and how the university community would come together for this purpose. (Meanwhile, the radicals seized the free time to announce a "University-wide Convocation" at Clark that afternoon.) Subheads announced that days off had been cancelled for Buffalo police, and the sheriff placed his men "on alert."

Other *Courier-Express* items on March 2 included a report about President Meyerson's reasons for non-involvement in the fast-moving events and the formation of a "Campus Peace Patrol." An enterprising *Courier* reporter caught up with Meyerson, with the following result:

> Martin Meyerson, president of the University of Buffalo, said Sunday night that he has not been involved in administration attempts to calm tension on the campus . . . the acting president "preferred" that the situation be handled in this way.
>
> Although Meyerson has been in the city . . . he has spent his time on faculty recruiting, the Amherst campus, and details involved with the lifting of the construction moratorium on the new campus.
>
> Currently on leave from the State University to serve as chairman of the Assembly on Goals and Governance of the American Academy of Arts and Sciences [he] declined to "second guess" administrative handling of the events of the last several days.
>
> He did identify deeper causes for the unrest—"a very elaborate pattern:

the war, the draft, the kinds of pressures young people are under today, the pressure to get into a good school and then pressure to get into a good graduate school."

He does not believe that there is a large group of radicals on campus . . . the figure of "30 to 40" true radicals is probably correct. However . . . "they can build up to a thousand sympathizers." (*Courier-Express* 1970i).

Regan also announced that Dr. David G. Hays, Chairman of the Linguistics Department, would be in charge of student-faculty volunteer patrols. "Keep it open, keep it safe, keep it human . . . We are a non-violent crowd of faculty and students who carry no weapons and make no arrests," explained Hays (1988). "The tradition of not calling police on campus stems from the tradition of trust between students and faculty in a university. That trust has been greatly eroded, and it is time to start building it again."

Tuesday, March 3

The weather was cold and many students were passing the pickets and attending classes. Pickets remained around doors until 2 P.M. when a rally was scheduled at Newton fountain, although it was evident by 11:30 A.M. that morale was flagging. A petition calling for a class boycott was signed by 47 professors and teaching assistants in the English Department.

Regan agreed to a rare public campus appearance in 147 Diefendorf Hall on March 3 to discuss the ROTC issue. While visibility may have been desirable, his advisers picked a room that was far too small for the occasion; worse yet, discussion was limited to the one issue. The fate of ROTC did not as immediately concern students as did the injunction—which Regan barred from any consideration. It was a disaster. Pruitt describes firsthand what happened:

Seats and aisles were already filled by a hostile hissing crowd when Regan entered. He tried to shout over the interruptions. One female said, "He is an asshole, but let the asshole speak." When asked when the injunction would be removed, he responded, "That depends on how this meeting goes." Heckling became overwhelming, the crowd could not be silenced, and Regan abruptly left. About 40 students followed him back to Hayes where he made a statement to the effect that he was a prisoner.

Pruitt believes that when hostile students prevented him from making his point Regan became defensive and closed off student contact. "He also missed the sense of this meeting and was hung up on procedural matters," says Pruitt (1989).

The March 5 *Spectrum* (1970c) reported on the ROTC fiasco:

The stupidity of his actions over the past week has more than boggled the mind. . . . Speaking amid the shouts of 500 striking students chanting "Off the Injunction" and "Pig, Pig, Pig," Acting President Peter F. Regan refused Tuesday to lift the court injunction against them, citing that such action would lead to "further disruptions" on campus.

Dr. Regan appeared at a packed meeting in Diefendorf Hall originally scheduled to discuss the issue of ROTC . . . but which became metamorphized into a verbal battle over the continuance of the injunction. . . .

A mass picket line was formed in front of Hayes Hall by some 200 of the demonstrators. A small one engine plane was seen circling repeatedly overhead as was a helicopter reportedly equipped with tear gas. [The reporter must have known that it was a "traffic-copter" reporting traffic patterns of a local radio station.]

Regan now appointed the Greiner commission, asking for a report "within 48 hours," and promising to release the findings as soon as he received them. (The committee later chose, instead, to send the report directly to *The Spectrum* and local media, gratuitously adding warnings about bringing police on the campus after learning that they had already arrived.)

Sarah Gallagher's letter in the March 3 *Spectrum* typifies the unrelenting attack on Regan:

We might consider exactly what it is that Dr. Regan has accomplished —he has mobilized the right wing, the community, the left wing, the radicals and the people in the mdidle against him with more success than could have been achieved in a month of protests. (Gallagher 1970)

The March 3 *Ethos* (1970) was editorially unsympathetic to the radicals and unappreciative about the efforts of the president:

If a small group of radicals had not urged on the rally . . . Wednesday night, the violence and destruction may never have occurred. The black students had already expressed their desire to wait, but it seems that some white radical leaders are more concerned with instigating violence than with protecting their fellow students' lives.

Little of Thursday's actions can be justified; they must be viewed as student reaction to their hate and fear of police on campus. However, again, not all of the action was reaction. Those who were leading the crowd on Thursday knew exactly what they were doing. If anyone is to be blamed for the damage that occurred, they should be.

Looking at the administration, we find that they have done little good and a lot of harm.

Acting President Peter Regan's official statements have been flowery and poetic but have hardly dealt with the issue at hand. It is unfortunate that the Acting President is unable to empathize with students. By acting without understanding the students' emotions and reactions and by remaining unavailable for discussion, Dr. Regan has not only alienated himself, but also made serious blunders all the way around with his policy statements in the context of the situation that existed.

In critical situations, dialogue and understanding can be the keys to peace. As Dr. Regan himself said, we should "walk together, talk together." He has not followed his own advice.

The Student Association made an inept and unproductive attempt at coping with the situation before it became worse last Thursday. The coordinating Council could not even agree on a policy statement, much less a positive course of action.

"On March 3 an estimated 200 to 250 pickets were dispersed in small groups in eleven locations on the Main Street campus," writes Ketter (1971). Class attendance was reported to be about 80 percent."

According to Geography Professor Charles Ebert (1988):

Many students still adamantly opposed the disruption of classes; serious students were determined not to get involved. Still, it was a daily battle to carry on the routine that had been taken for granted on the campus. Instead of waking up to a day of teaching, teachers would wake up wondering what would happen that day. The atmosphere was constantly tense and most of the faculty were between the one extreme of conservatives who protected the system and what it represented and the other extreme who wanted to destroy it.

Wednesday, March 4

At 9 A.M. the number of pickets around various buildings was considerably smaller than the day before and chanting had noticeably decreased . . . . The strike was dying out. . . . At most 20 percent of students were staying out of classes. . . . Around 9:45 A.M. a bomb scare emptied Acheson—the faculty-student peace keeping patrol began searching the building, because firemen would not come on campus. . . . A rally scheduled for 10:30 A.M. was moved back to 11:30 to capture a larger audience, but only 300–400 persons showed up. Because of the poor showing on the picket lines in the classrooms the theme was one of discouragement. It appeared that the strike was dying.

There were two feeble attempts to build up morale among strikers. At 2 P.M. in Haas Lounge the "People's High Triubunal" was called on "Behalf of Life vs. Peter Regan and co-conspirators in Defense of Death." This was attended by a small band of demonstrators who then moved to Hayes Hall and attempted to exorcise the evil spirits inside Hayes. The chanting group circled the building three times, but the building withstood all efforts to levitate it.

The March 6 *Spectrum* (1970d) gave its version of the bizarre activities of Wednesday, March 4:

At least 200 demonstrators marched in the pouring rain to Hayes Hall and then to Campus Security Headquarters at Winspear Avenue to personally serve injunctions on Acting President Peter F. Regan and his "co-conspirator," the police.

The order was issued at about 2:30 A.M. Wednesday, during a session of the "People's High Tribunal" in Haas Lounge. This "court"—comprised of all those who jammed into the lounge—unanimously agreed to enjoin Dr. Regan and all police from conspiring against the "People's University at Buffalo" and from "Fucking over people's lives."

Charging the defendants with "reckless endangerment of life itself," the injunction ordered them to "stop employing unlawful force and violence" . . . against the People of the World and to "stop institutional violence and genocide against our brothers and sisters everywhere."

To dramatize how strikers are now defying Dr. Regan's authority as President, a small group presented a brief political theater performance near the front of the lounge. In this skit, Dr. Regan was portrayed as a live robot-like puppet, joyously exploiting and manipulating university students. Eventually, the students joined together and put him "up against the wall" until he crumbled to the floor mumbling "This is not programmed."

The March 4 *Courier-Express* (1970j) reported that "most classes were continuing" (on March 3) and "pickets appeared to be dwindling, partly because of the rain which forced them to huddle closer to building entrances and may have discourged others." In the same issue Hays expanded on the role of the Peace Patrol: "In the event police are called to the campus, those who felt the call 'unnecessary' would position themselves between police and students 'not to do battle' but to give one last measure of protection.' "

The faculty-student patrol followed a model I had heard of from other places," explains Hays (1988):

I felt that I stood *in loco parentis* to the students and their safety was a great responsibility. Other faculty members stepped in quickly. . . . My information was that 600 persons were wearing white armbands that week. . . . We got word from time to time that an activity was planned, and called out our forces. On one occasion I found a doorway where a column of police were hidden, or at least tucked away. They were wearing protective gear and carrying clubs. The first in line looked to be the same age as the students, and he looked frightened. I reassured him, and we walked between the doorway and the students. . . . For a week we were the only security force on the campus. As far as I knew, there was no significant crime that week. In the end, of course, the patrol could not prevent a riot. Surely there must be cooperation from both adversaries if the peace is to be kept. Without the cooperation, the peace-keeping force needs superior weapons, and we had none. I called a press conference to tell Buffalo that the faculty as well as the students feared the police. The press did come, and printed some of my remarks, but not that one.

The March 4 *News* (1970d) reported Regan's determination not to lift the injunction until UB "cools down." An undercover deputy sheriff claimed in another item that "UB aides [graduate assistants] used Molotov cocktails during the campus trouble," and there was this headlined warning: "Leaders at UB Unrest Face Suspension Threat." The campus patrol was still "keeping the peace" but Regan became increasingly inaccessible. His absence did not go unnoticed by *Ethos,* which in each issue now ran several photographs of the acting president, captioned "Where is this man?"

Between 1:30 and 2:00 A.M. Bennis met with some of the strike committee at a conference arranged by graduate students. Regan would not meet with any of the group because he felt that this would legitimize the strike committee as a bargaining agent or representative in future discussion with students. . . . Arts and Letters were now attacking Regan from a pro-strike orientation while other faculties were attacking him from a law and order position. The acting president continued to discount faculty opinion as irresponsible or not relevant.

At 2:30 P.M. Dr. Rowland read aloud a list of 20 students suspended for alleged interference with academic and non-academic functions of the university on one or more occasions since October, 1969. All student privileges and financial aid were stopped for those named.

Gahagan, in his portion of the daily log, reports that a rally followed the suspension edict, against which some students retaliated that evening by smashing plate glass windows of the M&T Bank in University Plaza, as well as "a few more" on campus (Pruitt 1970).

Suspension of twenty activist students may have been welcomed by the outside community, but the action was ill conceived. Any of several Student Personnel staff (including myself or the directors of Admission and Financial Aid) could have helped whoever drew up the flawed list from committing serious errors that would soon result in the cancellation of the suspension action. Included were two students who had not been in the city at the time and some non-students over whom we had no jurisdiction. Two others named were not currently registered; they had left the previous term and were not physically present to defy the injunction. An innocent bystander was incorrectly identified because his name was too similar to that of another individual who qualified for punitive action; worse yet, another person was one of the "good guys," who was working against the radical cause. Lacking entirely was any semblance of due process. Counter to university policy governing such drastic administrative action, the "students" were suspended without a (required) preliminary hearing—a vital step that would have prevented needless embarrassment. I was concerned because our office, bypassed in the process, was credited with the fiasco even though none of our staff had anything to do with it. SUNY Chancellor Samuel B. Gould informed the *Buffalo Evening News* (1970e) that the suspensions were the first ever in SUNY on charges relating to campus disturbances involving student unrest.

Thursday, March 5

The strikers (125–150) wearing masks and scarves to avoid identification, locked arms and stood in front of entrances to Hayes to prevent people from entering the building. Some individuals persuaded the strikers to let them through. [Arriving at 7:30 A.M. I had no trouble going to my office, possibly because the blockade was not yet fully in place.] **Between 8:00 and 8:30 A.M. Dr. Gilbert Moore, Executive Assistant to the acting president, was drowned out by catcalls and chants as he went from door to door to read the temporary restraining order to the students. Bennis and other administrators then took turns (unsuccessful) trying to get into Hayes.** [As I watched from inside Hayes, I was relieved not to have been asked to participate in this strange, demeaning exercise and wondered if they had forgotten about the heating tunnels.]

Over two and a half miles of underground passageways interconnect most of the Main Street campus buildings. The radicals never fathomed how to invade this network which was used extensively by university security and Buffalo police and occasionally by administrative staff. A special key is required to unlock the metal doors at each entrance. We incorporated the heating tunnel system into our plans the preceding year when Meyerson spoke at Clark Hall. If the president experienced serious difficulty, Eugene Martell, one of my staff who was once a lead blocker for Paul Hornung on an undefeated Notre Dame football team, had special instructions to whisk Meyerson out of there through a tunnel located behind the platform.

The strikers were still refusing to meet with any administrative group until two demands were met: (1) the injunction had to be lifted and (2) police would not be called to the campus. The *Courier-Express* (1970k) reported that 150 students, their faces masked, had tried "without much success" to prevent entry into Hayes Hall during the day. Pruitt arrived at noon and estimates that the number of strikers at doorways had dwindled to 50–75, since many who left for lunch were not replaced. Three demonstrators in ski masks whom Pruitt interviewed told him that anyone who did not respect the blockade was "selfish" and "misguided" (Pruitt 1989).

Phone calls, letters and telegrams were pouring into Regan's office and area and state legislators were calling for police involvement.

Friday, March 6:

Regan attended (with Bennis and another of his advisers) a 9 A.M. meeting of the UB Council at the Statler Hilton Hotel in downtown Buffalo. Despite the lack of a quorum (only four members attended) the meeting began with a motion, immediately seconded, asking for Regan's resignation. [During the ensuing discussions a thoughtless call from an administrative assistant informed Regan that the Arts and Letters faculty by a 92–6 vote

had passed a resolution objecting to the way Regan was handling the crisis.] A noon meeting [which I attended] **of administrators, faculty and selected students not involved in the strike was scheduled for noon at the home of Warren Bennis. He arrived at 12:30 P.M.; the acting president had stopped off at Command Headquarters and did not appear until 1:30 P.M. In response to a direct question from a student** [Dennis Arnold] **the President stated that there were no plans to bring police on campus. This may have been disingenuous on his part since on his way to the meeting he had stopped at Command Headquarters where planning for a police call was already underway. It was implied that police would not be on campus and the acting president seemed to agree. It was agreed that interdepartmental faculty-student meetings would be held Monday morning, March 9, to open up communication between students and faculty.**

Class attendance was reported as practically normal and the strike as a widespread movement appeared to be dying out. The *Spectrum* (1970d) asked for Regan's resignation and editorially supported both the strike and a continuation of strike activities.

In another of many memoranda Regan (1970) deplored violence, concluding with a veiled warning that "Some members of the public understandably wonder whether to insist, allegedly for our protection, that martial law be imposed; to protect our right of free inquiry. . . .We reject this alternative. We can continue to reject it only if our way of discourse returns as the single style on this campus."

"There are still some of us who love the old university," Hays had informed *The Buffalo Evening News* (1970f) on Tuesday, March 3. By Friday, March 6, the *News* would report that Hays, wearing an "On Strike" button, had resigned. "Regan refused to talk with me for 38 hours straight," he explained. The patrol would continue to function until its members were later physically endangered by elements from student *and* police groups, but the loss of leadership did not auger well for continued calm. Why did Hays resign? "It was the difficulty of getting to the administration," he writes in 1988. "The administration was not above it all as I thought they should be . . . they were an adversary in the conflict. They lacked wisdom and perspective. However, I doubt that a wise, rock-solid administration could have moderated the conflict; certain students and certain police wanted a fight; yet the administration might have saved the university—at least in part—by different conduct. Or had the administration already lost the university before the conflict?" Hays (1988) believes "there were crazies and crooks on both sides, but among the activists there were certainly some who wanted honest and compassionate government."

Criticism also came from within the university. Paul Kurtz was quoted extensively in the March 6 *Courier-Express* (1970m). The campus had become "a jungle because of lack of courage by UB administrators," he charged. "There has been a failure of leadership resulting in the breakdown of civilization at the university," and "the administration even tried to suppress reporting the amount of 'vandalism' and 'violence.' " According to Kurtz, "30 to 40 students want to bring down the system and we are helping them. How do you save democracy when those who wish to destroy it are using it?"

On the next page a Buffalo assemblyman announced his intention "to demand immediate consideration of his bill to suspend students in state supported schools who are found guilty of violations leading to campus disorders." *The Courier* concluded its coverage by adding, "The campus was quiet today as the normal pace of activity entered the week-end lull" (*Courier-Express* 1970n).

The Faculty-Senate executive committee met this evening [Friday, March 6] at the home of its chairman. The acting president was not there but a member of the committee was in touch with him by telephone. . . . They discussed the pros and cons of bringing in the police either to contain individual wrongdoers or as a kind of peacekeeping occupying force. Committee members felt that they did not want to make a statement on the issue that would limit administrative options. They also did not want to say police should never come on campus nor did they wish to suggest that they would be welcome. The outcome was an ambiguous compromise statement. The resolution to some of the members was apparently intended as a statement with policy implications leaving the final decision up to the acting president in consultation with the committee. Regan did not in fact consult the committee but later referred to the resolution as supportive of his decision.

While this meeting was going on, another—attended by selected members of the inner administrative circle was concurrently taking place in the home of the acting president. The acting president went over his reasons for asking the police to come on Sunday and said he wanted to give the people present a chance to back out. At that time nobody opted not to back the decision although a little later the acting Executive Vice President (Bennis) argued that it would be worthwhile waiting until Tuesday to see whether the blockade would continue.

Everyone present at the meeting assumed that the police would have to be called unless an alternative could be agreed upon, since the strike would not die by itself, community pressure was mounting, and there was a developing danger of clashes between striking and non-striking students.

Doty (1989), who was at the meeting, remembers going to the kitchen where Walter F. "Bud" Stafford—a local M.D., and a trusted and close confidant in Regan's unofficial cabinet—was seated. Stafford did not participate in the discussions, but had been listening to the arguments. "Peter sounds as if he is going to call in the police," Stafford said to Doty. "Can't you talk him out of it?" Doty replied that he "wouldn't even try" because he consistently and strongly supported the prospect of outside police involvement. Doty had the impression that the final decision was reached that night, but Inspector Platek points out that logistics for such a major operation required detailed plans that had to be completed several weeks earlier. "In fact, we we ready a week earlier, but were held back. The rumor was that the governor felt it should be postponed for another week."

An unusual, clandestine meeting took place early on Saturday, March 7. Deputy Commissioner Thomas Blair of the Buffalo police met privately with Meyerson in the university's rented Main Street facility at the corner of Heath and Main Streets across from the campus. "Meyerson said there were reports that the radicals planned to take over the campus on Monday. 'We don't want them to do that,' " he told Blair (1990). "I was relieved to hear him talk like that because I had the impression he supported radical efforts to reform the university. It changed my perspective on him." Blair's account contradicts a generally held impression that Meyerson was not involved directly in the decision to invite outside police to occcpy the campus.

It was a quiet day. Strike activities were in abeyance for the weekend. The Council of Provosts (Academic Deans) met that afternoon and discussed the crisis. There seemed to be general agreement that police should be brought in only as a last resort, but that it looked as though they probably would be called in the near future. That afternoon at an important meeting of selected faculty and administrators Regan announced his decision. . . . The group discussed practical arrangements for quartering police, duties to be assigned to them and how they were to patrol the campus. . . . No general announcement was made to the university; the acting president believed that police should come at a time when the campus was quiet, but took no steps to warn the strikers for he believed that warning would deter their actions and that those strikers who wanted a confrontation would get it.

The Saturday, March 7 *Buffalo Evening News* (1970h) reported that "Dr. (Ira) Cohen stressed the hope that the meetings (to be held Monday) will bring together the 80 to 85 percent of the students who have been attending classes and the strikers for beneficial dialogue."

The March 7 *Courier* (1970p) ran a revealing page-one photograph of "a bewildered Dr. Raymond Ewell (Vice President for Research) surveying damage by vandals to his office in Hayes Hall," which accompanied the lead story, "Hayes Hall, Gym Area Targets of UB Vandals." Between midnight and 1:30 A.M. on March 6 unidentified persons broke into Ewell's office and the floor was covered with file papers and two inches of water. "They were apparently on a blind rampage, just like the Japanese when they evacuated Manila," Ewell explained, adding "We adopted a policy of not having any classified research in 1961. When I arrived in 1957 there were two classified projects, one in Physics, the other in Electrical Engineering. Both were terminated in 1960. Harvard was then about the only other school in the country with such a policy. The SUNY Board of Trustees adopted this policy in 1966 from the Buffalo campus." He volunteered his own firm conviction about the threat of the "military-industrial complex," but believed that ROTC was a necessary program. "It might not be as efficient as West Point, *et al.,* but we would be more secure from national domination by the armed forces." Significantly, ten athletes, flanked by Major Robert Garwood, Commandant of the Aerospace Program, and football coach Robert Deming, were reported as standing on the steps of Clark Gym on March 6 where they successfully prevented a group of radicals from entering the building.

The campus community went to bed Saturday night—with only a few individuals aware of the police occupation that would take place at UB the next morning.

References

Amico, Michael A. (1989). Interview.

Bachmann, Sue. (1970a). "One Year Later," *The Spectrum,* March 2.

———. (1970b). "Student Strikers Organize for Complete University Shutdown," *The Spectrum,* March 2.

Blair, Thomas R. (1990). Interview.

Buffalo Evening News. (1970a). February 27.

———. (1970b). "UB Militants Continue Destruction," February 27.

———. (1970c). February 28.

———. (1970d). March 4.

———. (1970e). "UB Suspensions 1st in State," March 8.

———. (1970f). "His Love of UB Motivates Head of Campus Patrol," March 3.

———. (1970g). "Hays Quits as Head of UB Patrol," March 6.

———. (1970h). "UB Sets Aside 2 Hours for Discussions," March 7.

Caffery, Kevin. (1989). Interview.

Courier-Express. (1970a). February 27.

———. (1970b). "1% of UB Faculty Are Drug Users, Amico Charges in Speech to Editors," February 10.

———. (1970c). "Police Have Right to Enter Campus," February 28.

———. (1970d). "UB Official Disputes Amico Talk," February 29.

———. (1970e). "Assault on UB Persists, Gangs Set Small Fires, Police Mass 200 Strong Near Campus," February 27.

———. (1970f). "Restraining Order Bans Further UB Disruption," February 28.

———. (1970g). "UB Students Say Police Arrival Triggered Strike," March 1.

———. (1970h). "Most UB Classes Called Off Today," March 2.

———. (1970i). "UB Head Stays Out of Action," March 2.

———. (1970j). March 4.

———. (1970k). March 6.

———. (1970m). "Professor Charges UB Leadership Is Failure," March 6.

———. (1970n). "Hausbeck to Push Bill on Suspension," March 6.

———. (1970p). "Hayes Hall, Gym Area Targets of UB Vandals," March 7.

D'Amico, Michael L. (1990). Interview and Questionnaire.

Dombrowski, Robert. (1989). Telephone Interview.

Doty, Edward W. (1989). Interview and Questionnaire.

Ebert, Charles H. V. (1988). Interview and Questionnaire.

Eggert, Jack T. (1989). Interview and Questionnaire.

Ethos. (1990). March 3.

Gallagher, Sarah. (1970). "Talk Fans Vandals' Flames," *The Spectrum,* March 3.

Hare, Peter H. (1989). Questionnaire.

Hays, David G. (1988). Questionnaire.

Hertzberg, Dan. (1970). "UB Radicals Claim Victory: Exit of Police from the Campus," *The Buffalo Evening News,* February 27.

Hochfield, George. (1989). Questionnaire.

Ketter, Robert L. (1971). "Report of the President," SUNY/Buffalo, *The Reporter,* February 11.

Lorenzetti, Anthony F. (1988). Interview and Questionnaire.

Payne, William G. (1990). Telephone interview.

Pecoraro, Russell. (1989). Interview.

Platek, Frederick J. (1990). Interview.

Pruitt, Dean G. (1989). Interview and Questionnaire.

Pruitt, Dean G., and Gahagan, James P. (1970). "Chronology and Personal Notes, February 25–April 1."

Regan, Peter. (1970). Memorandum, March 6.

The Reporter. (1988). "Ed Doty Retires from UB," January 26.

Snell, Fred. (1989). Interview and Questionnaire.

The Spectrum. (1970a). February 27.

———. (1970b). March 1.

———. (1970c). March 5.

———. (1970d). March 6.

Weinstein, Irv. (1991). Interview.

CHAPTER XI

The Police Occupation—March 8

No matter how bad things get on campus, police should not be called in. They cannot be trusted, and an invitation to them to enter in the name "law and order" is evidence that the university has given up trying to become a center for independent thought and criticism, for such a center can live only by discussion. The Reagan-Hayakawa syndrome produces a university that is worse than none at all.

> —Robert M. Hutchins (May 3, 1969), then President
> of the Center for the Study of Democratic
> Institution and formerly President of the University
> of Chicago for twenty-two years

Students at UB during the 1969–70 school year probably recall the prolonged police presence as the most memorable and controversial episode of the spring term. Triggering events are soon forgotten, but the police were called in by Regan "to protect the safety and rights of individuals on campus, guard university property, and arrest any violators of the injunction" (Hertzberg 1970). Veteran faculty still argue over the timing and merits of inviting several hundred armed, riot-equipped police to patrol the campus on twenty-four-hour shifts for over two weeks. The massive police occupation further polarized the campus.

Vice-Chairman of the Faculty Senate Professor Thomas Connolly (1989) was more surprised than pleased when a telephone call awakened him around 4:00 A.M. Sunday, March 8. Late night interruptions were not unusual, but this one—a message from the acting president—was. Connolly was informed that Buffalo police, invited to occupy the campus for an indefinite period, would be arriving in full force at UB early that morning.

"I had been relaxed, because it was our first peaceful weekend for some time," Connolly recalls. "No student rallies were imminent or scheduled, no group had taken over any buildings, and we were only two weeks away from spring vacation. There was no need to call the police." Because he and the Senate Executive Committee—which he chaired—had not been consulted when the decision was made, Connolly rejected Regan's early morning request to join a select group of UB staff and faculty to meet and accompany the police onto the campus from the Winspear entrance. (He became more incensed upon learning that Senate Vice-Chair elect Baumer had participated in preliminary discussions the preceding afternoon.) "Of course they knew I would oppose police on campus," Connolly asserts. "It was a *fait d'accompli* by the time I learned they were on their way and, remember, the greatest violence of the year would occur (March 12) after the occupation." Connolly maintains that Regan wanted the job too much, which was dangerous. "As acting president, he should have made himself ineligible, or temporarily moved aside for another interim president appointed out of Albany [not an unusual practice], thereby freeing himself to pursue the position unencumbered by his administrative role," Connolly believes.

At 5:00 A.M. I fumbled for the ringing telephone. Ed Doty's call was not an invitation to join the welcoming party, but he had insisted to Regan that I should be one of a select few to be alerted prior to the imminent police appearance. Among others not consulted—who learned about the action after the police arrived—were Vice President for University Relations A. Westley Rowland, the Provosts (including Professor Ira S. Cohen, Provost of Social Sciences and Administration and Chair of the Council of Provosts), the President of the Undergraduate Student Association, the Director of Campus Security and Environmental Health, and members of Regan's immediate staff, including Assistant Executive Vice President Charles M. Fogel, Assistant to the Vice President Lawrence A. Cappiello, and Executive Assistant to the President Theodore Friend. The acting president's legal adviser, James Magavern (1989), maintains that neither he nor I were consulted beforehand "because they knew we would be opposed to police involvement." He heard the news on the radio that Sunday and was also among those not involved in prior discussions or informed in advance about the March 8 occupation.

"The acting president appeared to be more heavily influenced by his administrative assistants," conclude Pruitt and Gahagan (1974). "His personal style was to take a great deal of responsibility himself, rather than looking for consensus or listening to contrary views. Some vice presidents and other key personnel found themselves losing influence as they advocated political and/or personal measures for dealing with the crisis other than those the acting president chose to follow. Opposing views were not welcomed. As time went on, the group around the acting president progressively narrowed and dissenting forces were dropped out, or discounted" (pp. 379–80). A chief executive officer who bypasses or does not share information with senior staff who are not afraid to challenge erroneous assumptions and sort out false information is deprived of valuable insights.

Friend (1970), concerned about his lack of involvement, resigned on March 16, and wrote an open letter to Regan: "Your awareness of my feelings has made you want to shield me from consultation on such decisions [the police occupation]. . . . I know you believe with me that the university is not a sanctuary from the law but a citadel of the spirit. I fear, however, that in proving the first we have not sufficiently shown the second."

"The police arrived shortly after 6 A.M. March 8," the *New York Times* (1970a) erroneously reported on March 9, since it was closer to 9 A.M. "They walked in groups of two to six, equipped with helmets, nightsticks and two-way radios." Each squad of twelve men was commanded by a lieutenant. Two or three squads—depending on the sensitivity of a patrol point—made up a platoon under the command of a captain. "Conceding that peaceful efforts to end the demonstrations had failed, the acting president called the police patrol a 'preventive' measure that would continue until peace is restored.' " The *Times* added that "the call for police was a reversal of earlier university policy which had kept police off the 180-acre campus for the past several days."

The March 9 *Courier-Express* (1970a) headline "Police March onto Campus at Request of UB's Regan" was supported by four photographs depicting the arrival of one police contingent, a student-faculty "solidarity" march Sunday afternoon protesting the intrusion, police guarding the Hayes Hall entrance, and Peace Patrol members standing uneasily between students and the police. Also featured was the ill-timed and hastily prepared Greiner report with its strong, if belated, warnings against involving outside police. Carried over from Sunday's issue was Provost Cohen's uncoordinated announcement canceling Monday's classes "so that the University community could examine the issues." Governor Rockefeller's consent for the action and SUNY Chancellor Samuel B. Gould's expression of complete confidence in the acting president rounded out major front-page items.

In similarly dramatic style, the March 9 *Buffalo Evening News* reported: "Three hundred Buffalo police today are patrolling the Main Street campus. They moved unannounced onto the campus Sunday morning answering a request by Acting President Peter F. Regan. . . . Joining the city police were nearly 150 Erie County Sheriff's deputies" (Hertzberg 1970).

Pruitt (1970a) reports:

> at least 78 police cars were counted surrounding the campus before the police moved in. . . . Over 100 deputies of the local county sheriff moved onto the campus at the same time, and entered several dormitories and other student areas. These men were uninvited, and there were later reports that many of them removed their badges. The sheriff was known to be trying to turn events on campus to his own advantage. Indeed, one factor in the decision to call the Buffalo police was the fear that the sheriff would at his own initiative bring his men on campus and engage in actions against students.

"Sheriff Amico ordered his deputies off the campus late Sunday afternoon," Hertzberg continued. "He said everything seemed orderly, and his men were apparently not needed. He added, however, that they would be ready to return. . . ." A divided Faculty Senate Executive Committee "issued a statement supporting Dr. Regan's calling of police 'as necessary and inevitable under the circumstances.' But Thomas F. Connolly, Chairman of the Committee, told a meeting of students and faculty that he was 'sick' over the presence of police at UB and had refused an administrative offer to accompany the police when they entered the campus.

"Dr. Regan made the decision Friday afternoon after consulting by telephone with Dr. Gould and aides to Governor Rockefeller," Hertzberg writes. "Regan met Friday night with eight or nine top UB administrators and with the Faculty Senate Executive Committee." In his request to Commissioner Felicetta, Regan wrote that the university "finds itself in a most disruptive condition in which our normal academic and administrative processes cannot be relied upon to restore conditions of safety to our campus." Felicetta responded that police would remain on the campus only until University authorities are convinced that police presence there is no longer necessary. The *News* explained that by bringing in police Sunday, the quietest time of the week, "Dr. Regan hoped to get them on campus with as little hostile opposition as possible, and then use the police force to prevent the outbreak of disruptive demonstrations this week."

Hertzberg also described on March 9 how some students and faculty spontaneously reacted: "Late Sunday afternoon nearly 2,000 students and faculty members [figures ranged up to 5,000, depending on the periodical] demonstrated in opposition to the police occupation on the campus, staging a peaceful 'solidarity' march.

"The protesters chanted 'Power to the People,' 'Pigs Off Campus' as they walked behind a cluster of red flags, [an unwelcome touch for many of the participating faculty, including Connolly] past Hayes Hall on a line that stretched a quarter mile across the campus."

Developments at the university edged state, national, and other local events off the front pages of the two Buffalo newspapers. From February 26 to March 21, two-thirds of front-page coverage in the *Courier* and the *News* concerned UB, and there were many related items on inside pages, according to David Chodrow's (1989) study. The *Courier,* which then published the city's only Sunday paper, carried 104 first-page articles about the university—with 14 banner headlines— in contrast to 108 other items of local, state, or national significance, Chodrow reveals. "Thirty-seven of 67 front-page photographs highlighted campus unrest. During the same period the *News* devoted 33 of 109 front-page stories, six with banner heads, to the university."

It was rumored that the *News* softened coverage on UB after an appeal to the owner of the newspaper by Seymour Knox, then Chairman of the SUNY/Buffalo Council.

Magavern (1970) expressed his concerns in a memorandum to Dr. Regan, with copies to me, Dr. Bennis, and three of the acting president's administrative assistants, Dr. Theodore Friend, Dr. Gilbert Moore, and Mr. Henrik Dullea: "Of all the ways to disaster, I believe the presence of the police on campus is most inevitable. They will offer perfect targets for the crazies in their attempts to provoke violence. . . . The presence of the police will greatly broaden and deepen the bitterness of many of the liberal left and moderates." He suggested "a reorganization of the present communication and decision-making process . . . to minimize breakdowns in communication" and deplored the "preoccupation with tactics to the exclusion of strategy, isolation from the attitudes of the liberal left" and "a war room mentality."

During the first week of the crisis Regan established his off-campus "Command Headquarters," effectively distancing himself from events about which he was making decisions. Individuals answering telephone calls identified their location with a crisp "Command Post" greeting. "Instead of retreating into bunkers, Regan should have made himself available at an open campus meeting similar to that held by Meyerson a year earlier," argues Connolly (1989). "No one could reach him. All incoming calls were screened in advance by his people and only those with special code numbers could contact him."

When I later asked Regan why he called in the police when he did, he answered "to seize the high ground." Abandoned in this otherwise military format was a chain of command concept, essential to military efficiency. Although Vice President for Finance and Management Edward W. Doty (1989) was involved with inner circle discussions, including the police intervention, he remembers complaining to Regan about the acting president's unwillingness to use established administrative channels and his reluctance to delegate appropriate authority to administrators within either the new or previously existing management structure.

Pruitt and Gahagan (1974) contribute their analysis: "The head man is often an important key to effectiveness and morale. If he becomes discredited or distracted with the details of conflict, the organization may lose its capacity to make meaningful decisions, as apparently happened in our crisis. . . . When the head man becomes a defendant within his organization he is likely to become cut off from the dissenting portions of the organization and therefore to lack critical information about what is going on. Also, because he is angry he may misconstrue certain critical issues. Such a state of mind may make him an unreliable decision-maker. Yet, it may be hard for him to reverse his decisions because he is the head man." At UB "the Acting President and a number of his associates withdrew from the campus, psychologically as well as physically, and apparently did not comprehend the true nature of their position," Pruitt and Gahagan conclude (p. 379–80).

I would have advised against calling the police in full force because the strike was dying and the university community was inadequately prepared for the shock. Someone forgot what happened when police were involved at Columbia and Harvard. There were major differences at UB: the radical movement was not in control, no buildings were being occupied in defiance of authority, and the radicals were groping for viable issues.

Hechinger (1970) was the first outside, qualified observer to suggest that UB may have moved to strong police action too quickly. "The uncertain administration," he maintained in a *New York Times* article, "faced too divided a constituency to be able to weather the police presence as a more solidly supported administration might have. Moreover, Buffalo is surrounded by a conservative town whose law-enforcement agencies, after much provocation, longed to be unleashed."

Director of Norton Union Dr. James Gruber and his staff, in daily contact with the radicals, were generally aware of activist plans, moods, and aspirations since hard-core leaders were headquartered in the Graduate Student Association offices at Norton. "YAWF/SDS strategy revolved around bringing in outside police and hoping for physical confrontations to involve uncommitted moderate students," maintains Gruber (1989). "Radical leaders deliberately spread false rumors and distorted information within the dormitories to stir up resident students. Reports about total numbers injured, hospitalized, or participating in demonstrations were highly exaggerated and 'incidents' were carefully planned. As one radical leader told me, 'Revolutions do not take place in nice velvet boxes.'" Gruber is still bemused about how major disruptive activities were successfully orchestrated by no more than eight to ten of the dedicated hard-core, but support for the strike was not evident that weekend. "Regan obviously intended to establish law and order, but he played directly into the hands of the radicals who needed the police on campus to regain momentum." Bentivogli (1989) concurs with Snell (1989) that the demonstrators were "slowing down" and "running out of steam."

Then Assistant Professor of Education J. Ronald Gentile (1989) believes the show of force made things worse. "Demonstrations started again with more vigor. I was reminded of this when Li Peng called in the troops as the students were beginning to disperse at Tiananmen Square."

A Strike Committee member informed Pruitt (1970b) that student support and sympathy had pretty much dwindled by Friday, "until Regan's decision gave us an essential boost." Testifying before the Henderson Commission in 1970 Pruitt's impression was that the student movement and the disruptions were disintegrating and the crisis had very nearly burned itself out. "Bringing in the police caused it to flare up again." He maintains that pressure from political leaders in Buffalo and Albany to bring in police was a disservice to education—and the acting president.

Justifying his decision in a two-page letter to the university community, Regan (1970a) cited "the intolerable violation of the rights of individuals, the destruction of property, and the disruptions of the vital functions of this university. During the last two days a small group of people, approximately

200 in number, repeatedly blocked buildings in defiance of a court order,"
he wrote, "terrorized secretaries and other personnel, forced the closure of
Admissions and Records, and disrupted peaceful meetings and other forms
of classroom activities.

"Over the past ten days fire bombings and other forms of vandalism
have destroyed thousands of dollars worth of our property, including some
irreplaceable books in the library," Regan's letter concludes. The police, he
explained, were invited in on a quiet Sunday morning to minimize dangers
of panic, confusion, or thoughtless crowd action, which might lead to bloodshed. Although down to the skeleton crew of a handful of close advisers,
the acting president claimed "the decision was taken after the most thorough
appraisal and wide consultation and in the belief that it is the proper course."

The occupation would be uniformly attacked both by those who argued
that outside force should have been called in earlier and others who were
as firmly convinced that conditions and timing did not then justify police
involvement. What actions are open to chief executives when individuals cannot be protected from illegal behavior, classes are disrupted, harassment and
threats of physical assault are reported, files are broken into, building entrances are blocked, and property is extensively and deliberately destroyed?
How long should such conditions be tolerated?

Militant tactics of using transitory issues created difficult situations that
caused administrative errors and resulted in mass support for dissidents by
previously uncommitted students and faculty. Regan was now coping with
militants, an aroused citizenry, competing law-enforcement agencies, and politicians—state and local—who are always eager to join the procession. Caught
too long between the need to take a stern, realistic stance to deal effectively
with violence and parallel dangers of repression and overreaction, erosion of
the acting president's influence became apparent. Unable to control the dem-
onstators, he became the target of blame, losing influence over large segments
of the campus community. Some administrators resigned and joined faculty
members who tried to go over Regan's head and establish communication
with the Chancellor of the State University and members of the state legislature.
"With his authority and capacity to exert informal leadership on campus largely
eroded, the acting president was forced to rely almost exclusively on coercive
power wielded by the Buffalo police . . . whose right to be on campus was
widely disputed," concluded Pruitt and Gahagan (1974, p. 381).

Another persistent belief—along with the general impression that an overwhelming majority of students was consistently and actively involved throughout the disruptions—is that radicals and their followers literally closed down
the university. The libraries—despite threats of firebombs—always remained
open. The Admissions and Records Office, in fact, had not become inoper-
ative on Friday, March 7—or at any other time—either upon my instructions

or because of any decision by Dr. Arthur Kaiser (1989), the Director of the unit. "Some radicals came into our office, but James Schwender [his Assistant Director] and I escorted them out without any problems. I assigned a male staff member to the reception area to reassure secretarial staff, but that was about it." The power of unconfirmed rumor was reinforced by the acting president's off-campus perception of a besieged campus, but none of his advisers contacted me or Kaiser to ascertain our true condition. Student Affairs policy throughout the crisis was to keep all services functioning; this included the obviously inviting target of the Placement Office, which was still serving "military-industrial complex" recruiters and was interconnected by a hallway with the Admissions Office. "We never shut the doors during the entire period," reports Placement Director Eugene Martell (1989).

The views of Kurtz—a consistent advocate for early intervention of outside civil authority to protect higher education from unjustified assault—remain unchanged after twenty years. He remembers his hate mail and threatening phone calls in 1970, and being shouted down and prevented from teaching by chanting demonstrators, who rattled bats and clubs around his classroom windows. "Academic freedom was threatened by those who prevented others from entering buildings and disrupted normal educational activities," maintains Kurtz (1989). "If a university is allowed to be politicized, the first casualty is bound to be academic freedom."

Kurtz (1971) had warned that:

> Militants either do not genuinely believe in academic freedom or they only believe in it for themselves. It does not apply to ROTC, liberal or conservative professors, or speakers with whom the militants disagree. Militants reject the ideal of an open campus, a free and pluralistic marketplace of ideas, or the interplay of opposing viewpoints.
>
> Radicals and revolutionaries are the first to complain bitterly, when their academic freedom was compromised by criticism from the "far right," yet they are indifferent to pleas for the academic freedom of those whom they hound. What they fail to see is that *if* ROTC or Themis can be banned from campus on "moral" or political grounds, then the same argument can be used to ban teaching of revolutionary socialism, or remove the SDS from campus. Radicals demand the untrammeled right to teach what they wish, but they think nothing of interrupting classes of liberal professors with whom they disagree. (p. 242)

"Those who believe in the integrity of the university," he warns today, "must be prepared to defend it against enemies from without and within. McCarthyism of the left, or right, which is the greater danger today—can only be neutralized by applying sanctions and enforcing suspensions and expulsions at the first outbreak of violence, intimidation, disruption, or harassment. If the university cannot protect those within it, it must be prepared to summon civil authorities and to use the injunctive power of the courts with police to enforce it. It must be willing to face the whimper of protest from faculty or students. Outsiders of both extremes embrace a similar objective; they seek to antagonize and inflame public opinion against the university and gain ultimate control over the educational process as we know it" (Kurtz 1989).

Doty (1989) believes the situation would have been much worse had the police not been employed. "The major problem wasn't property damage, although it measured in the hundreds of thousands of dollars. The problem was that the university simply wasn't conducting classes. . . . We were paying everybody's salaries, but we were not getting much teaching done. Or learning. The kids were being shortchanged in their educations. That was the real cost. With the police on campus at least UB was conducting classes."

After the police arrived group after group of faculty announced that they would do no more teaching until the officers were removed, later to break ranks at the realization that if they withheld their services Albany might withhold their pay. "Protest resignations attained one day's fame, then lapsed into oblivion," observes Ketter (1971).

On Monday, March 9, the History Department demanded Regan's resignation for calling police on the campus, suspending students "without a shred of due process," and for a consistent lack of candor and unavailability to the university community, Pruitt (1970a) reported. "The police presence," a majority of the historians concluded, "is utterly incompatible with an academic situation. So long as they are here, we are unable to meet our classes." English Department faculty members recommended that all regular English classes be suspended or used to discuss present conditions until police were removed. The School of Social Welfare defeated by one vote a motion calling for the immediate suspension or dismissal of the acting president, but repeated a call to boycott classes until the injunction and suspensions were lifted and the administration entered into negotiations with the striking committee. Mathematics by a 16 (in favor), 3 (opposed), and 3 (abstained) faculty vote and a 77-2-3 student action condemned "the unwarranted presence of police on the campus and will not conduct classes until the police are moved and the administration initiates discussion with the students on the substance of their demands." Normally conservative School of Management students voted to continue holding classes, but overwhelmingly favored removal of police from the campus. Neutrally political Dental School students were temporarily caught up in the action—thirty-five walked out after a lecturer refused to yield the podium to one of them. The local AAUP was calling for an observer from national headquarters (which later resulted in a condemnation of the use of police).

Ethos (1970) editorially noted that "Regan has handled the situation badly from the first. Many believe that the strike was dying, only to be brought to life by the presence of police on Sunday morning." A *Spectrum* (1970) lead article announced that "Support for the student strike, and resolutions concerning student demands and the action of Acting President Regan have been voted upon by the Faculty of Arts and Letters, Biology Department members, the School of Social Welfare, and the Anthropology Department," concluding with: "Others have noted that supsensions, court injunctions, and arrests are to be expected, because those in the administration are beginning to realize the demonstrators are a part of a world-wide movement to uproot American capitalism on all levels."

At 9:00 A.M. Monday morning Bennis (1970), in an open letter, disassociated himself from the decision to call the police and resigned as Acting Executive Vice President while carefully preserving his office and salary as Vice President for Academic Development. "Calling of the police . . . was premature," he chided,

> because the administration had not bent itself, did not take the necessary risks of self-exposure to communicate . . . To assign all blame to an amorphous group of "radicals" is to avoid admitting our own involvement in this awful escalation of force. . . . What started as a relatively small group of dissidents has become a massive group of angry students and faculty. A simple reading of recent history should have indicated that the responses this administration chose would lead to such escalation. We must recognize that whatever the causes of this anger, surely among the various components are the lack of perception, accessibility, and compassion evidenced by this administration.

Bennis explained that he was moved by a terrible sense of joint responsibility for these events after reading the Greiner report, and added: "We were vulnerable to mistakes of fatigue, pressure, unpreparedness and the self-doubt that prevents men from dissenting in crisis." Maintaining that he was always totally against police coming on the campus, he emphasized that his resignation was not politically motivated to enhance any personal bid for the UB presidency.

Regan (1970b), accepting the resignation, noted prior agreement with Bennis about the need to involve police. "If there is a fundamental difference between us, it is clearly on the issue of whether the timing was right," he wrote back. "On listening to your argument that police action should be delayed until Wednesday, I chose Sunday because of the ineffectiveness of the positive educational efforts we were able to mount during the past week under chaotic circumstances and confusion, demoralization, and fears which were gripping so many members of this academic community."

On the university's radio station (WBFO) that evening Pruitt recorded an interview between a student announcer and Bennis. "Regan had been under a big information overload," the vice president volunteered. "We are not used to managing crises in the university; what happens at a time like this is you get a sort of war room mentality, one's time must be carefully husbanded, and such divergent advice is given. Some people wanted Regan to become visible, others wanted him to avoid visibility for fear of inflaming things. It is true that Regan was afraid to go out and talk to groups but the reason for this was that he was afraid it would inflame them—that he would get nothing accomplished, that he might be misunderstood." Bennis concluded by saying that he had been advised that you need sleep in such a crisis and he wanted to go home to bed.

Throughout the spring turmoil WBFO—under the direction of William Siemering from 1962–70—remained on the air. The station courageously broadcast all of the action and a full spectrum of opinion. Coverage included live sessions of the Faculty Senate, student demonstrations, and interviews with faculty, staff, and students even as tear gas fumes drifted over the campus.

Siemering (1991), who developed National Public Radio's "All Things Considered," recalls that hectic period as "a test of WBFO's journalistic independence." Several top administrators wanted to close the station down but the *Courier-Express* would later commend the broad coverage as a "beacon of light" amid chaos. The station provided an important communication link both on and off the campus.

Pruitt and Gahagan (1974) report that many relatively neutral faculty, students, and staff diminished the role of members of the Strike Committee—whose blockade of the Administration Building had precipitated Regan's action—and blamed the acting president, instead, for calling in the police. "The 'punishment' of having 400 policemen occupying the campus did not seem to fit the 'crime' of blocking the doors," Pruitt and Gahagan point out. "The moral seems clear: to avoid blame that may erode his power, an administrator should employ a *measured response* to provocation from his adversaries" (p. 383).

Sociology Professor Lionel Lewis (1989) warns, "While law and order are essential, there are real dangers when there is no sense of the true mood of moderate faculty and uncommitted students. A president must establish a level of trust so that any dramatic move—such as calling in outside police—is understood by a majority of the several campus constituencies."

Hechinger (1969): "Confrontation politics escalate by their own means. Administrators and faculty are not oriented to such combat. Faculties are seriously divided, with strong factions often siding with the idealistic goals of students and, because of liberal convictions, loath to resort to any form of suppression or counter-violence. When police are used, these sentiments tend to be reinforced." This does *not* mean, if circumstances clearly require such involvement, that outside police in force should never be called.

Print and electronic media featured Monday's only demonstration, a mock funeral at which the university was laid to rest before 350 mourners and watching police. At 1:24 P.M. a hearse, containing a flag-draped coffin, arrived on campus. When the cortege reached Hayes, Robert Faust, a diminutive sophomore, popped out of the coffin to proclaim, from the shoulders of another student, the death of the State University of Buffalo. In his eulogy he promised the rebirth of the student body at the new institution, henceforth to be called "PUNY/Buffalo," the "P" standing for people's. Those attending the service were awarded "Nth degrees," which they dropped into the open casket. The solemn marchers carried only one sign: "Regan Repent: The World Is Coming To An End."

Tuesday, March 10, was highlighted by a pig roast. Four students carried the 135-pound pig, donated by the farmer father of a striking student, to the waterless fountain oval facing Norton. The *New York Times* (1970b) reported that the event was billed as a "Totemic Feast of Welcome" for Jerry Rubin and Rennie Davis, two Chicago conspiracy trial defendants scheduled to speak on campus that evening. The pig had a traditional apple in its mouth and a non-traditional sheriff's badge on its snout. A hi-fi with two speakers at full volume played music from a window in nearby Foster Hall. When police patrols ventured near the fountain area the Beatles' song "Piggies" was played for their benefit. Several officers became agitated, but most of them studiously ignored the festivities. Rubin, the featured speaker that evening, addressed a crowd that ranged from 5,000 to an impossible 10,000—again depending on which local publication you believed. Careful not to expose himself to charges of inciting to riot, he made few specific references to UB during his fifteen-minute speech. There were no incidents before, during, or after the presentation, which was followed by a dance, sponsored by the Strike Committee.

Regan now rescinded his March 4 suspensions of the twenty "students," an announcement that received extensive media coverage. A new task force was established to deal with the issues and Ira Cohen and Warren Bennis, in his capacity as Vice President for Academic Development, scheduled the first meeting of the group in Lockwood Library. Generally viewed as a liberal ploy to co-opt the movement, the effort received little notice and no support from the student body. It came too late, even for moderate and conservative students, to impact on the current situation.

On Wednesday, March 11, the *Buffalo Evening News* (1970a) reported that Tuesday's meeting of the Buffalo Common Council was marked by sharp criticisms of the university. "Alfreda W. Slominski . . . blasted the UB administration. 'If they had stuck to their guns and permitted our men to arrest those breaking the law, we wouldn't be in the fix we are today. The campus disorder is separating the men from the boys.' "

Professor Connolly (1989) contended that there was no adequate place on campus to accommodate the full Faculty Senate, and the March 11 session was moved downtown to Memorial Auditorium. Regan's announcement that he was planning a withdrawal of the police did not deter the Senate from voting overwhelmingly to remove the occupying force immediately. Biology Professor Harold Segal, in a long speech, called for the acting president's resignation and charged the administration with miserably handling situations that could have been resolved long ago. "Police action was the final outrage," Segal said (1991). Invoking the Greiner report, he accused Regan of being more concerned with the breaking of windows than students' heads and praised the student blockade of Hayes as an honorable and courageous act of civil disobedience. Other speakers faulted the administration for failed leadership and charged that Regan's recent appearance on television escalated community pressure and further distanced the university from the community.

A motion by Edgar Z. Friendenberg to remove both campus and city police and use the Winspear security offices for educational purposes—"if they could pass inspection by the City of Buffalo Health Department"—was hastily referred to committee. Pruitt describes what happened after the no confidence vote on Regan was defeated by a standing vote, 417–263: "Students [seated in the balcony and not allowed on floor level] began chanting, 'Strike! Shut it down!' interspersed with shouts of 'Bullshit' and 'You wonder why we shut this fucking place down?'" As he left the building, Pruitt "saw many uniformed police—most of them big fellows—a rather frightening sight. It looked as if they had prepared for a riot. At a mass rally that evening, in response to the failure of the faculty to vote no confidence (on Regan) the (divided) Strike Committee issued an ultimatum calling for the administration to meet all strike demands by 9 A.M. Thrusday March 12, or face the outcome of a 'War Council' " (Pruitt 1970a).

On Thursday, March 12, both local newspapers concentrated on the acting president's cancellation "pending appropriate notice and correction of names" of the suspension of twenty students. Area legislators could not comprehend such administrative confusion and indecision, the "disastrous reversal of policy."

Flanking the *Courier's* lead story, "Faculty Senate Defeats Bid to Oust Regan," were reactions by livid legislators. "I know what will happen when I get back to Buffalo," Assemblyman Albert J. Hausbeck said. "Everyone will ask me what we are going to do about UB." His pending bill in the state legislature would "take the blackjack out of the hands of the campus revolutionaries and put an end to this grotesque Jacobin blackmail . . . by gangs of street ruffians masquerading as students." Assemblyman James Mc-Farland expressed "great disappointment about the action, which has plunged us deeper into permissiveness. If this is education, taxpayers should ask whether they want to continue spending that kind of money for this kind of result." He had driven around the campus the previous Sunday afternoon, he said, and observed thousands of broken windows and the most vicious obscenities spray-painted on those beautiful buildings. He had taken his eight-year-old son with him and "was sorry he learned to read so soon." McFarland concluded by inviting taxpayers to tour the campus and look at the destruction by the students, where "damage estimates have gone as high as $300,000" (*Courier-Express* 1970b). State Senator Thomas McGowan informed both newspapers, that "we are witnessing a conflagration of something we have held extremely dear to us. Motherhood, the American flag, and education have assumed a statuesque and monumental status in our city. . . . We are witnessing the death of education, and the ironic part is that we are paying for it." He added, "an anarchist student in Buffalo recently told me, 'I would not hesitate to kill you.' " Assemblyman Chester Hardt warned, "At UB we are on the verge of a full scale all-out riot" (*Buffalo Evening News* 1970b; *Courier-Express* 1970b).

An unidentified Buffalo-area Republican informed the *Courier-Express* (1970b) that the governor wanted to move directly and personally into the situation. "Continued UB unrest represents political dynamite in a city area which has never treated him [Rockefeller] kindly in the previous elections and in a suburban area which is generally conservative Republican," he said. "There is concern among Republicans that the area would swing to a Democratic opponent in November if the situation is not remedied fast."

A page-three item in the *News* (1970c) reported Meyerson's "full confidence" in the acting president's judgment and decisions. All of the day-to-day decisions, including the one to bring Buffalo police on campus to end the lawlessness, were made by Regan, he explained. " 'When February 25 came Peter Regan felt the difficulties were such that there couldn't be any divided responsibility and he ought to take full command. I agreed.' Meyerson said that he was devoting his one-third assignment largely to recruiting and the university's national contacts," adding that he had never taken the position that it would be wrong to bring police on the campus under any circumstances.

Political Science Professor Lester Milbrath (1989) joined one of several faculty delegations that visited Meyerson to ask him, in light of Regan's continuing problems, if he would reassume university leadership. "Meyerson listened attentively and showed us every consideration," Milbrath recalls, "but when we asked him if he would come back the visibly perturbed president said, 'No, I can't . . . I just can't.' "

M. Robert Koren (1989), the current president of the UB Council, and then President of the General Alumni Board, believes that Meyerson—"who has been erroneously blamed for many things he did not do"—was willing to return and had not wanted to leave UB in the first place. "The Governor took away his scepter," Koren explains. "Martin lost Rockefeller's support because of his position that the new campus should be built by an integrated work force. The Governor had been wooing the strongly organized construction unions, who were impatient with the delay so Meyerson was informed by Albany that he had better seek employment elsewhere. This made it impossible for Martin to continue, let alone rescue Regan." It was the second time Meyerson had crossed the governor about constructing the new Amherst SUNY/Buffalo campus complex; immediately after arriving in 1962, Meyerson—envisioning an entirely different campus architecturally—suspended all plans and designs previously proposed by President Furnas.

Pruitt's (1970a) account reveals that the activists repeated the ultimatum of the previous evening, Thursday morning, sparking a series of hourly contacts between the Strike Committee and various faculty groups who hoped to forestall the "War Council" rally scheduled for that evening. Faculty members tried to persuade the acting president to negotiate or reflect some flexibility, but repeated efforts to contact Regan were rebuffed. Early reports were optimistic, but pessimism grew as the day progressed. The last announcement, which was that the administration had nothing to say, did not come from the faculty members involved, but was apparently transmitted through the peace patrol.

While a response was being awaited from the administration, 150–200 strikers—after a sparsely attended noon rally—carried on sporadic demonstrations at the usual places, Themis, Clark Gym, Winspear, and Hayes Hall. Pruitt recalls that police were present at all points, and while no significant police-student violence occurred, tension remained high. Obscenities were exchanged and some police had to be restrained by their colleagues.

Pruitt and Gahagan (1974) discovered that the concentric-circle structure influenced the strategy of the Strike Committee. "Inner room" members of the first circle, perceiving themselves as experienced and more politically astute, focused on policy and educational aspects. An "outer room" cohort worked more or less full time on details, and was expected to recruit sympathetic outsiders (a third group) to demonstrate and attend rallies. Outer room activists tired of their routine and felt entitled to make major determinations. They viewed the inner ring as too elitist and resented the decision makers, who were conspicuously absent at mass meetings and appeared only periodically at the office. The successful "Solidarity March" had been conceived by the outer room group, who were alone in the office when the Buffalo police surprised everyone March 8; after that, some of them began attending inner group sessions. Heated arguments marked the meetings as the student leadership—emulating several faculty/administrative structures—became factionalized and uncoordinated. Two slogans, appearing side-by-side (graffiti on Foster Hall), reflects the confusion: "MAKE LOVE, NOT WAR" vs. "KILL THE PIGS!"

Dissension between these two male-oriented groups was acerbated by growing dissent among female activists, whose leadership potential was ignored. Consistently relegated to secondary tasks, the women established a separate entity which contributed to the Women's Studies Program at UB. "Just like the outside world, we were just too macho in those days," explains Bentivogli (1989). "There was no consciousness among men about the rights of women. We drove them out."

When the Strike Committee met on Wednesday night, March 11, Pruitt and Gahagan report (1974), "the inner room split became overt as the outer room presented a proposal for a War Council." The plan was to issue a twenty-four-hour ultimatum to the acting president demanding removal of the police, unconditional amnesty to involved students, and agreement in principle to such demands as dropping ROTC. If he failed to do this, the strikers threatened a war dance and a mass march which held the possibility of violent confrontation with the police. "The idea was that the danger of student-police violence would move Regan to act on some of the demands, so the confrontation would not actually take place; meanwhile, strike activities would have led to concrete political gains. . . . Those opposed to the War Council argued that they did not believe that the Acting President would give in on any of the demands; he would probably let the confrontation run its course to teach students a lesson and lots of strikers would get hurt. . . . At the meeting the people in favor of the War Council won out." The proposal was approved at a mass meeting, which was not attended by the inner room people. The ultimatum was issued after the inner room people, who opposed it, had not come up with satisfactory alternative proposals.

A noon rally at Norton attracted only 150–200 strikers, who sporadically demonstrated at the usual places during the afternoon. Regan announced that a "phased withdrawal" of police would begin the following Tuesday. Concerned over the potential student-police violence if the administration offered no conciliatory gestures, considerable faculty pressure from various sources was exerted to encourage the acting president to negotiate, but repeated efforts to breach Regan's administrative structure were rebuffed. By late afternoon the stage was set for the high watermark of UB's campus violence.

The police presence had not stemmed the rising tide of criticism from the community, legislators, and alumni. J. William Dock (1989) had assumed his new job with the Alumni Association during the week of the police occupation and now wondered about the wisdom of his career decision. As it so often happens, the Loyalty Fund Drive had been launched just before the Norton Hall episode. With few exceptions, alumni were not in a giving mood. Dock feels that comments scribbled on the face of the first return that came to his attention summarized the general reaction: "I'm with those who feel there are a thousand other schools I'd send money to before giving one cent to UB. Take a walk around the old campus (if you dare) and take a look at old UB. Most of the students major in 'Rock Throwing' and 'Sloppiness.' While you are at it, check out the professors, if you can tell them from the students."

Examples of other letters, returned with checkless Loyalty Fund mailers, were courageously reproduced in the March 12 *Reporter:*

"While some returned were of the vicious 'Get rid of the Yids' variety, many were content to hit the 'law and order' theme":

"As an alumnus, I am ashamed I graduated from there."

"I shall withhold all financial support from the school which has done so much for me."

"We wish we could recall our tax dollars."

"Only when every kook has been thrown out of the University, and jail doors are closed on every person instrumental in causing damage . . . will I consider giving of my hard earned money."

"No contribution—would this destruction have been tolerated in the 40's or 50's? Of course not."

"Get rid of the cancer that is ruining the school and the campus."

Editorial comment in the March 12 *Buffalo Evening News* (1970d) was not reassuring:

The administration, in vacillating between firmness and concession, has found its efforts to restore stability admittedly frustrated. . . . Events pushed [Regan] to the point where he would be damned by the faculty and students if he brought in police and doubly damned by the community and political power structure, which supports and has ultimate authority over the university, if he did not. . . .

The question remains unsettled whether Dr. Regan's position has been so undercut as to be untenable. Indeed, the serious question arises whether any course firm enough to suit the community would be tenable on the campus. What would make it least tenable either place is the blow-hot-blow-cold ambivalence evidenced by the suspensions of 20 students followed by the abrupt revoking of the suspensions. . . .

Until this crisis occurred, there is no doubt that Dr. Regan was a leading contender, if not front runner, for the presidency. . . . But as we read the Faculty Senate votes, he can now maintain that candidacy only at the cost of keeping the faculty deeply divided. . . .

There is also now a very serious question whether the things Dr. Regan must do to make his position tenable on the campus will not render it untenable in the community, or vice versa. . . . Any solution smacking of appeasement or submission to those Dr. Regan has branded "vicious" disruptionists will bring proper cries of outrage from here to Albany and widen the cleavage both on campus and with the community. . . .

As demonstrators arrived that evening, March 12, for the rally, Lorenzetti (1989) recalls that the Student Affairs staff—who knew UB students better than most university officials—were concerned about outsiders, which included high-school youths, visitors from other area colleges, and some derelicts from downtown Buffalo who mysteriously appeared. Pruitt (1970a) covers the action:

Around 9:00 P.M. an estimated 1,000–1,500 people attended the Norton rally. Several men in war paint spoke briefly, and the crowd followed them to Clark Gymnasium. Those dressed in war paint danced around the flames of a small bonfire. A kerosene soaked sheet painted to resemble the Ameri-

can flag was burned as the crowd chanted, "Ho, Ho, Ho, Chi Minh, the NLF is going to win." Some watching police wanted to break up the ceremony at this point.

Student activists saw the police as "pot-bellied storm troopers"; the police could not repress their hatred for "long haired, flag-burning draft dodgers." Municipal police, not accustomed to having authority figures questioned, did not know how to react to rebellious and disrespectful college youth. What is clear is that putting protest down with force invariably increased student support for radical causes.

The demonstrators moved to another side of the gym and began pelting the police with ice, snow, rocks, and firecrackers. At no time did the police move against the crowd. The students continued to chant and snake-dance around the building, breaking windows, and taunting the police. Crowds of students were followed so closely by police that at times it almost appeared to be a mixed contingent. The mob marched across campus to Hayes where demonstrators gathered on the grass in front of the building, facing the police who lined up close to the building. Both sides shouted epithets at each other, but there was no significiant interaction between the two factions. The police were pretty well in control of themselves. The students then went back to the Themis project area, where they were met by some 75 police. Students threw rocks at windows as demonstrators and police surged back and forth. Peace patrol members interposed themselves between the two groups as much as possible and the police leadership was advising their men to remain calm. Anger was rising on both sides; the crowd stormed a police car, grabbing helmets and temporarily disarming one officer.

After an inconclusive foray, the students and police moved back to the administration building. It was around 11:00 P.M. Students and police continued to exchange verbal insults. About 1,000 demonstrators faced Hayes Hall. When the evening began, there were about 150 police on campus; reinforcements raised the total to 200.

Then Associate Professor of Education Stanley H. Cramer (1988) was a faculty observer on duty in Hayes.

> The police showed great restraint, but their lines began to bend. Some officers in the rear broke ranks, walking back and forth and talking to each other in an increasingly agitated manner, their obscenities matching those of the demonstrators. Another officer used a bullhorn to retain control, but maintaining authority became increasingly difficult. A rock broke a large plate glass window above the already shattered front door, showering glass on a contingent of police standing directly behind the entranceway. Shouting, they spontaneously broke ranks. Other officers exhorted them to return to Hayes, but they were temporarily out of control, and charged into the

crowd, clubbing as many of the retreating crowd as they could reach. Whatever the cause, all hell broke loose.

"The police, who had won Commissioner Felicetta's commendation for keeping their cool throughout 2½ hours of torment, formed up inside Hayes, then burst out with scattered shouts of 'Let's go!' " (*Courier-Express* 1970c).

Lorenzetti (1989) remembers that some police were yelling, "Kill! Kill!" as their lieutenants tried to turn them around.

The media reported that ambulances raced to the campus throughout the night to take those injured—either by police actions or the crowd's rock and bottle throwing—to several area hospitals.

According to the *New York Times* (1970c):

> the principal outbreaks of violence took place outside the Administration Building when about 15 policemen swinging clubs charged into a group of students marching on campus buildings to protest the administration's failure to meet a deadline for responding to student demands. . . .
>
> Members of a student-faculty peace patrol, who had tried to place themselves between the police and the students during the confrontations, announced today that they would send out no more patrols until the members could meet to discuss their position. Professor McAllister Hull, Jr., a leader of the patrol group, said it had been accused unjustly of aiding the police in the clashes.

By March 19 *The Reporter* (1970b) summarized the confrontation from a broader perspective:

> It happened again on Thurdsay, March 12—a violent police-student confrontation on campus—this time leaving an estimated 58 injured and leading to several arrests. . . . Acting President Peter F. Regan characterized Buffalo police actions during this latest confrontation as displaying "remarkable restraint under very provocative circumstances." . . .
>
> The Strike Committee, earlier on Thursday, had informed the administration that they could not be responsible for what might happen if *all* the demands of the strikers were not met by 8 P.M. Thursday. . . .
>
> Some observers indicated that until a major encounter at Hayes Hall, police used "great restraint" in handling the crowds. . . .
>
> In one of two reported charges, the police chased students across the front lawn as far as Main Street. A K-9 Corps van was seen careening wildly across the lawn in hot pursuit.
>
> The *Buffalo Evening News* reports that the police were out of control at least at one point, not heeding the shouts of the lieutenants to keep ranks. . . . WBFO (the University radio station) said that one even uglier incident was avoided after a Hayes Hall encounter as milling students began gathering in the North Fountain area around midnight. According to the station, police were advancing on the area when Dr. Claude Welch, Dean of Undergraduate Studies, struck a bargain with the officers. . . .

"It was a case of two opposites inevitably conflicting—conservative policemen and liberal students," Inspector Fred Platek (1991) of the Buffalo Police Department says today. "We had tear gas available but decided not to use it." According to Platek, Buffalo police never expended as much manpower before or since the UB occupation. "It was an excellent operation overall when you consider what was happening throughout the country," Platek believes.

Early in the morning of March 13, Dean of University College Claude E. Welch (1970) described his impression of the March 12 episode—"a most difficult set of hours" in a letter to his parents in Belmont, Massachusetts: While he and his wife were returning from the play, *Uncle Vanya,*

> we heard on the radio that troubles had erupted on campus. . . . I returned to the university finding about 150 policemen in front of Hayes Hall drawn up in a tight cordon, and perhaps 400–500 students taunting, jeering, hurling epithets, and generally abusing the Buffalo Police. As a member of the university administration strongly sympathetic to the Peace Patrol I attempted to interpose myself in as many ways as possible, such as removing rocks from the hands of students, arguing and or discussing the various issues, and trying to keep them from further inciting the police with the obscene language into which they readily lapsed. My efforts, and those of many, many others ultimately proved fruitless.

My own experience was typical of frustrated faculty and staff, who engaged in the hopeless task of trying to keep peace. At one point I tried to reason with a well-dressed young man, who seemed in a hypnotic trance, his eyes transfixed on the police cordon in front of Hayes. I was literally unable to pry a fist-sized stone from his hand, which he held in a deathlike grip. I might as well not have been there. I don't think he was aware of my presence or verbal pleas—and I am sure that rock hit somebody.

"At approximately midnight, the police, filled with rage and frustration, charged," Welch continues.

> Unlike almost all others, I did not run, but walked. Perhaps my trench coat, my relatively short hair, and my tie kept me from being clubbed, which happened to other observers, as well as striking students. On the second police charge I was able to have handcuffs removed from a Professor of Anthropology, who was a member of the Peace Patrol with a white armband, but who was not recognized as such by the police and was about to be arrested.
>
> The third charge was to me the most horrendous. I overheard at least seven policemen, as they ran past me in hot pursuit of students saying that they would "get those *** bastards this time," that they would chase them into Norton and give them what they deserved, that they would no longer tolerate the abuse heaped upon them but would deal out their revenge forcefully. I saw some lieutenants struggling to keep their men under control, and sensed that a police riot was very close to the surface. Fortu-

nately, the inspector in charge managed to line his men up in formation beside the library, facing the Student Union, the rallying point for radicals and obviously the prime target of police. . . .

I asked the police to withdraw completely from the area and return to their headquarters, in return for which I pledged to remove students voluntarily from the area outside the main classroom buildings. The bargain was struck—and adhered to. It may well have saved 100 skulls from being cracked and it is hard for me to write this without crackling a bit with the emotion of 12:30 A.M. I finally left the university shortly before 3 A.M., and hope never again to experience such a series of events. . . .

To me . . . it was more than a passing episode. It was a sickening condensation of the abusiveness and abrasiveness that have characterized this campus for the past two weeks. . . . The cycle of escalation and counter-escalation has severely jeopardized our educational foundations, and there seems to be little basis on which the administration might re-establish a working basis of trust with at least a portion of the student body . . . but do not let me sound unduly pessimistic, for I may be reflecting fatigue. (Welch 1970)

The media reported that a series of ambulances raced to the campus throughout the night to take those injured—either by police actions or the crowd's rock and bottle throwing—to several area hospitals. *The New York Times* (1970c) reported "at least 42 persons injured," and *The Courier-Express* (1970c) casualties totaled "28 Buffalo policemen, one campus guard, and 17 youths, most of them UB students." "The President of the Police Benevolent Association claimed publicly that over 50 policemen had been injured," reports Pruitt (1970a). "He called for more support and said that if the situation was not cleaned up quickly, the university should be closed and National Guard or state police should be brought in."

Many injuries reported by the police were not from thrown objects, or sufficiently serious to require hospitalization, Pruitt (1989) believes. "When middle-aged men try to keep up with college-age youths who, abetted by darkness, are running ahead of them on rough, uneven and unfamiliar campus terrain," Pruitt observes, "lameness, skinned knees, sprained backs and miscellaneous bruises are inevitable."

Dr. Musselman and Dr. Marie Kunz, then staff physicians with the University Health Services, are most qualified to evaluate the extent and severity of injuries sustained either in the Norton Union incident or the confrontation of March 12. Disquieting rumors, reinforced by radical charges, were not true. "Despite claims to the contrary, no one was ever seriously injured or hospitalized overnight in any area hospital," says Musselman (1989). "We would have received reports if our students had been treated, especially if the case was serious and required extensive medical involvement or an overnight stay." While not dismissing the potential for serious injury, he points out that large amounts of blood tend to result from relatively minor scalp wounds. "People think someone is being killed when they see a victim, because bleeding from head wounds is typically intense." Dr. Marie Kunz (1989) agrees that no one was seriously hurt in either encounter. "Typically, our treatment consisted of cleaning up the wound, applying salve or antibiotic cream, and sending the patient home." The Student Health Clinic—which established three sub-installations during this period, including one in Norton—functioned effectively throughout the period, in large part because of the dedication of Dr. Musselman, a reassuring sight at every rally and serious confrontation.

The campus quieted down around 1:00 A.M. On Friday, March 13, a meeting was held by faculty and Strike Committee members, reports Pruitt (1970a), where participants concluded that the confrontation could have been avoided had the administration made some concessions. From this group of faculty came "The University Survival Group," formed by two dozen deans, department chairpersons, and senior professors. "This Administration is leaving too much undone," they announced the next day. "Students and faculty are losing all confidence in the system." On Friday morning the Senate Executive Committee reminded the acting president about the earlier Senate resolution requesting removal of the police.

How some city police feel about student activism is captured by interviews between New York City police officer William Phillips and Leonard Shecter (1973). Phillips believes that he and other New York City police, by disobeying orders of their "namby-pamby" superiors, ended the 1969 riots at Columbia University in one grand stick-swinging charge. "What bothered Phillips most were crimes committed against property: 'I couldn't see them desecrating property, setting the buildings on fire. I couldn't see how they could get away with it. If they had any beefs, I'm sure there's a process they could have gone through, but to burn records, shit all over the office, shit in the drawers, that's god-damn wrong. . . . they shouldn't be allowed to do what they did' " (p. 198).

"Late Friday afternoon some faculty members and striking students met and criticized the Acting President for 'not having responded in some fashion to have avoided the War Council,' " says Pruitt (1970a). "Some proposed that new faculty leadership should be established and that faculty should sign a declaration of independence from the administration. Part of the group at this meeting held a rump session at which the notion of a faculty sit-in at the President's Office was probably discussed for the first time. The University Survival Group met with the Acting President and asked him to resign. He refused, stating that his strategy was to stay on for the present as 'the bad guy' until things calmed down, then fade into the background so that a 'good guy' task force could take the front of the stage. The Acting President was asked repeatedly by the Survival Group to resign, but always refused."

Delegations from other groups asked Regan to step down. Connolly (1989) believes "such overtures only made him angry and indignant. He asked us who on campus was better equipped to handle the situation?" On April 1

Chancellor Gould designated a ten-member faculty-student committee, chaired by Ira Cohen, to work with Regan, but Connolly believes "that only angered Peter further, driving him deeper into isolation."

Fall (1990) blames the administration for its inability and unwillingness to establish lines of communication to students and faculty. "The administration," he says, "was in place as a structured entity, while the students were disorganized and unable to communicate even within their own ranks." Bentivogli claims that the strikers were now so disorganized and unstructured that it would have been impossible for the faculty or the administration to establish effective channels of communication with the diverse elements of radical leadership.

Pruitt (1970a) reports no significant student activity on Friday, March 13. "At an evening rally there was much discussion about the events of Thursday night and general agreement that another such confrontation would be counter-productive. More students would be hurt, students would be blamed, and police tactics justified. This would strengthen the administration's 'vicious vandal' theory." On Saturday morning the Survival Group decided to get through to the SUNY administration in Albany, with a complete picture of events as they perceived them," Pruitt says, but continuing efforts to get Regan to resign failed.

The acting president met Saturday with area legislators to explain the situation and his policies. At a press conference he announced that classes would be held and withdrawal of the police would continue as campus problems decreased. There was little campus activity and the second week of the crisis ended quietly. The Faculty Senate executive Committee and a student-faculty group scheduled sessions for Sunday morning, March 15. Both meetings would be interrupted by the unanticipated arrest of 45 faculty members who naively expected to restore normalcy to UB.

References

Bennis, Warren. (1970). Letter of resignation to Dr. Regan, March 9.
Bentivogli, Daniel. (1989). Interview and Questionnaire.
Buffalo Evening News. (1970a). March 11.
———. (1970b). March 12.
———. (1970c). "Martin Meyerson Says Regan in Full Command at UB," March 12.
———. (1970d). "Now Pull UB Together," March 12.
Chodrow, David A. (1989). "Report on the Riots at the University of Buffalo, Feb.–March, 1970," May 1.
Connolly, Thomas E. (1989). Interview and Questionnaire.
Courier-Express. (1970a). "Police March onto Campus at Request of UB's Regan," March 9.
———. (1970b). March 12.
———. (1970c). "Police Battle as Violence Grips UB," March 13.
Cramer, Stanley. (1988). Interview and Questionnaire.
Dock, J. William. (1989). Interview and Questionnaire.
Doty, Edward W. (1989). Interview and Questionnaire.

Ethos. (1970). Editorial, March 12.

Fall, Charles R. (1990). Interview and Questionnaire.

Friend, Theodore. (1970). Open letter of resignation to Acting President, March 16.

Gentile, J. Ronald. (1989). Interview and Questionnaire.

Gruber, James J. (1989). Interview and Questionnaire.

Hechinger, Fred M. (1969). "A Campus Crisis, Tough Questions Over the Rebels," The Week in Review, *The New York Times,* May 4.

———. (1970). "Why One Campus Blows Up and Not Another," *The New York Times,* March 22.

Hertzberg, Dan. (1970). "Police Patrol UB Campus at Invitation of Dr. Regan," *Buffalo Evening News,* March 9.

Kaiser, Arthur L. (1989). Questionnaire and Interview.

Ketter, Robert L. (1971). Annual Report of the President, *The Reporter.*

Koren, M. Robert. (1989). Interview and Questionnaire.

Kunz, Marie L. (1989). Interview.

Kurtz, Paul. (1989). Interview and Questionnaire.

———. (1971). "Inside the Buffalo Commune: Or, How to Destroy a University," *In Defense of Academic Freedom,* Sidney Hook, ed. (New York: Pegasus Press).

Lewis, Lionel S. (1989). Interview and Questionnaire.

Lorenzetti, Anthony F. (1989). Interview and Questionnaire.

Magavern, James L. (1970). Memorandum to Dr. Regan, March 8.

———. (1989). Interview and Questionnaire.

Martell, Eugene J. (1989). Interview.

Milbrath, Lester W. (1989). Interview and Questionnaire.

Musselman, M. Luther. (1989). Interview and Questionnaire.

New York Times. (1970a). March 9.

———. (1970b). March 10.

———. (1970c). "Buffalo Campus Has More Clashes," March 14.

Platek, Fred. (1991). Interview and Questionnaire.

Pruitt, Dean G. (1970a). Unpublished Chronology and Personal Notes, February 25–April 1.

———. (1970b). Testimony before the Henderson Commission, New York, October.

———. (1989). Interview and Questionnaire.

Pruitt, Dean G., and Gahagan, James P. (1974). "Campus Crisis: The Search for Power," *Perspectives On Social Power,* James F. Tedeschi, ed. (Chicago: Aldine Publishing Company.

Regan, Peter F. (1970a). Letter to University Community, March 8.

———. (1970b). Letter to Warren Bennis, March 10.

The Reporter. (1970a). "Alumni Respond Negatively to Disruptions on Campus," March 12.

———. (1970b). "Strikers Reject Violence After Fracas Injures 58," March 19.

Segal, Harold. (1991). Interview and Questionnaire.

Shecter, Leonard. (1973). *On the Pad: The Underworld and Its Corrupt Police, Confessions of a Cop on the Take* (New York: G. P. Putnam's Sons).

Siemering, William H. (1991). Interview.

Snell, Fred M. (1989). Interview and Questionnaire.

The Spectrum. (1970). March 11.

Welch, Claude E., Jr. (1970). Letter to parents, March 13.

CHAPTER XII

The Faculty 45

I got the Peter Regan Hayes Hall 45 Blues,
I got the Peter Regan Hayes Hall office Blues,
I was there 10 minutes, got 30 days to lose.

—Chorus from "The Hayes Hall Blues," by The Vicious Vandals*

During the spring semester of the 1969–70 academic year "no other issue in the welter of 'violent' and 'dissenting' and 'radical' and 'polarizing' and 'fascist' and 'kid' controversies of these bitter months produced such an irreconcilable division of opinion as that of the forty-five," wrote Ketter (1971). The episode, generally ignored in official UB history, began on a cold, bright Sunday, March 15, 1970, when fifty concerned persons assembled shortly after noon on the Main Street campus at the steps of Lockwood Library. They were preparing to participate in an inadequately planned "peaceful protest" against the continuing occupation of UB by Buffalo police.

Sixteen of the original contingent who filed into Hayes Hall later that day are still full-time members of the faculty. Unidentified with previous physically disruptive actions during the 1960s, only a few of them had a prior activist reputation. They hoped that a nonviolent, nondestructive, nonhostile sit-in by a predominantly apolitical group could re-establish communication with the inaccessible administration that had been operating from secret off-campus "command posts" since February 26.

Getting arrested was furthest from the minds of most of the demonstra-

---

*All stanzas that appear in this chapter are from "The Hayes Hall Blues: 45 Revolutions per Minute," a record cut and privately produced by members of the UB Faculty 45 (who recorded under the name The Vicious Vandals) to help defray their legal expenses.

tors, who expected to return home in time for dinner and other social engagements. Although they could hardly have failed to notice injunction warnings posted conspicuously around the campus, a distinct majority would not have become involved had they foreseen their legal and personal problems. State Supreme Court Justice Frederick M. Marshall, at the request of the acting president, had issued a temporary injunction February 27, which State Supreme Court Justice Gilbert H. King continued on March 5 for another month. Justice King's order enjoined "all persons from acting in an unlawful manner so as to disrupt or interfere with lawful and normal operations" of the university (*Courier-Express* 1970a).

Within two hours after entering the administration building—and without meeting with the acting president—forty-five names were recorded on the police blotter. Michael H. Frisch, then an Assistant Professor of History, "did not think we would be arrested."* He maintains with many others that the strike had been "sputtering out until 400 police in full battle gear arrived at UB Sunday morning, March 8. It was more than the radicals could have hoped for to restore a spark to the dying movement," Frisch says. "Most faculty have a strong sense that a university cannot function under martial law; what Regan had done, whether he realized it or not, provided great impetus to the politicization of the university."

Although prior to Kent State, where deaths resulted from National Guard gunfire, it was feared that someone might get killed, Frisch explains. "The 45, a relatively small group, had become concerned and felt they had to do something. We wanted to break the cycle of violence and counter-violence and draw attention to the continued police presence on campus. The idea was to go to the administration building to talk about designing a university. We decided a sit-in would be more effective than a strike—you really can't strike against yourself. The university was unraveling, the administration had evaporated, and we were under a form of military government. Worse yet, occupying police are among the least capable in understanding with any real sensitivity the dynamics of what goes on in a university."

Stefan Fleischer, an Assistant Professor of English in 1970, believes the students were still basically harmless and not really interested in dismantling the entire educational enterprise. "Our motives were varied, and often unclear, but we wanted the police off campus," he says. "It was an 'experiment' to see what would happen when previously uninvolved faculty took such an action. We thought it would be perceived as so absurd that the administration would be forced to re-evaluate its rigid stance."

The group apparently formed spontaneously at an impromptu faculty

---

*Unless otherwise indicated by a parenthetical source citation, all direct quotations and paraphrases in this chapter are taken from personal interviews between the sources and the author. All such sources are listed in the References section at the end of this chapter.

meeting held shortly before the climactic confrontation between police and demonstrators on March 12. Some of the 45, including Assistant Professor of Mathematics Nicolas D. Goodman, were motivated by the recent disbanding of the Peace Patrol. Confrontations between the police—whom Goodman perceived as "provocateurs" to students—and demonstrators had exposed the ineffectiveness of the patrol, and some former members of that group were searching for other means to reduce campus tensions and restore normalcy. "More or less by default," Goodman led preliminary discussions about possible ways to reach the "invisible" administration. "I also wanted to divert the community's attention from the university and take the initiative away from the administrative and student 'crazies.' " He acknowledges that the group had no carefully designed plan, "but the great majority of the faculty were generally pretending that nothing was happening to the university." Given the chance, Goodman would not do it again: "In fact, at my age and because of my present university status, I'm the kind of person who would be targeted by demonstrators today."

Christine R. Duggleby, then a lecturer in Anthropology and one of three women arrested, expected to be home in time for dinner that evening.

Raymond Federman, then a full professor in the French Department, had served briefly with the Peace Patrol. "There were no leaders and the 45 were working for no ideology," he says. "We really didn't know what we were doing," recalls Fred M. Snell, the other full professor in the group and Master of the controversial College A. He describes the group as "disorganized and playing it by ear."

Charles A. Haynie, then with Tolstoy College, believes that "neutrality had been ineffective, and it was time to make a definitive stand. A 'sitdown' was considered to be the most appropriate action." He remembers one earlier proposal that the faculty should don academic gowns and parade solemnly around Dr. Regan's home in downtown Buffalo. That suggestion was discarded because "it would have too sharply distinguished faculty from students; besides, it was cold outside." An experienced civil rights worker in the South, Haynie welcomed the possibility of arrest to publicize the cause. "Most of the faculty were naive and disregarded warnings that they would be arrested," Haynie says. "I had a genuine fear of ending up in jail, but my major motivation was to dramatize the issue of having police on campus."

The faculty version of the failed effort to meet with the acting president was uniquely captured in a single titled "The Hayes Hall Blues: 45 Revolutions per Minute," that was cut and produced by members of the group in 1970 to help meet legal expenses. Chorus and back-up were credited to "The Vicious Vandals," a pointed reference to the acting president's ill-advised description of student radicals during a television appearance a week earlier. In the first stanza,

> On March 15, ya all know why
> A group of faculty decided to try
> To have a talk with one another in a friendly place
> And maybe get a view of the acting president's faceless face.

"We hoped for 100 participants," Philosophy Professor James M. Lawler recalls, "but when we reached 50 [five would quickly drop out] we decided to go ahead." Eighteen of the heterogenous "45" were in their late twenties, 23 in their thirties, and four were over 40 years of age, the oldest being 48. Nine came from the English Department, four each from Mathematics and Philosophy, and three each from French, History, and American Studies. Other disciplines represented were Anthropology, German, Biohysics, Social Work, Library Information Services, Social Philosophy/Historical Foundations, Physics/Astronomy, Music, and Medicine. Two full, 11 associate, and 23 assistant professors participated. Four were lecturers, one was a graduate student. Names of four others were not listed in the 1969–70 university directory. "Nobody knew us and, with few exceptions, we didn't know one another," Fleischer says.

"Suits and ties" was the suggested uniform of the day, Goodman recollects. Older faculty were encouraged to lead the procession ("Greybeards to the front!"), neatly complemented by Lawler's conservative dark suit and matching tie. The amorphous faculty contingent more closely resembled churchgoers than wild-eyed activists as they stood in front of the locked entrance to Hayes Hall. An original total of 46 entered the foyer after one of them produced a key to his office in Hayes.

> It was a quiet Sunday, nothing going on,
> Four hundred cops were policing the calm,
> As we walked into that office, like reasonable men,
> And you wouldn't believe the things that happened to us then.

When the late Thomas J. Schillo, on administrative watch, asked how he could help, someone informed him that they were going to a faculty meeting to see either the acting president or President Meyerson. A perplexed Schillo ("I recognized several of the people there and kept asking them what was going on," he later testified. "I was as mystified as everybody else in the room.") He accompanied them to the open presidential suite, which was not being used as an executive office by the acting president. At the president's office, Schillo was handed what was later described by attorneys representing the 45 as a statement indicating dissatisfaction with the administration:

Peter Regan and this administration have defied the will of the Faculty Senate expressed Wednesday, March 11, for the immediate removal of police from the campus, thereby making themselves responsible for Thursday's events [The student-police confrontations of March 12.]. Hence, we members of the faculty will occupy these premises until (1) the police are removed from the campus and (2) the injunction is lifted.

We are in sympathy with the general principles of the strike and will be formulating new structures of university governance—to follow Regan's resignation—for the consideration of the university community.

We call on all faculty members to join us here.

(*Buffalo Evening News* 1970a; *Courier-Express* 1970b)

Schillo took the position paper to his superior, Vice President for Operations and Systems Edward W. Doty, in a nearby office. In his sworn deposition, Doty (1970) stated he felt that the intent was to violate the preliminary injunction. He heard that other faculty members were arriving and was fearful that large numbers of students would also assemble "with the threat of further disruption." After calling the acting president at home for instructions, Doty informed the waiting group that they had no appointment with the president, or reservation for the use of the office. Then he added: "If you do not leave in five minutes, you will be subject to arrest for trespass."

Doty called up Regan, he was in a daze.
He said, Fred Snell is here with his 40 T.A.'s,
And they're standing on your carpets, sitting at your table too,
It's just an awful situation, only one thing to do.

Call the cops, stop playing games,
Throw them all in jail and give the papers their names,
We got to show the city we ain't afraid or effete,
I mean this whole place would crumble once you start letting teachers meet.

A rumor persists that Doty thought he was dealing with teaching assistants, but the vice president realized he was not confronting graduate students; he remembers asking the acting president twice if he really wanted the group arrested.

The sixteen current UB members of the 45 variously described Doty as "furious," "red-faced," and "very angry" . . . "the epitome of an angry administrator." Goodman asserts that the encounter was "traumatic—his reaction was what one might expect from a policeman who had been pushed to the edge and has no training for coping with difficult situations when his authority has been challenged." Seymour Axelrod, then an associate professor and psychologist in the Psychiatry Department, and Lawler concur that Doty put them in a challenging mood. (Lawler invokes the quotation, "a liberal is a conservative who has been arrested," and adds, "a radical is a liberal who has been arrested by another liberal.")

"He approached us in such a way that we couldn't leave," maintains English Professor Martin L. Pops. James H. Bunn, also in the English Department, argues that "Doty's approach only confirmed the general feeling that the administration seemed almost as reactionary as the townspeople. The minute he began his red-faced harangue there was no way for us to back out; we felt impelled to stay."

Following the ultimatum, Doty left to give the faculty a chance to reconsider. Within five minutes, another vice president, Albert Bush-Brown, appeared. Doty reports that Bush-Brown tried to intervene and reverse the arrest order.

> Regan said to Doty here's the way to put them down,
> I think the time has come to send in Albert Bush-Brown,
> Why don't you climb down Albert from your family tree,
> Cause with your kind of sweet talk we can pacify these faculty.

> Bush-Brown came in with an elegant glide
> Says I want you boys to know that I'm really on your side,
> I want to help you save our university too,
> So when I throw you all in jail you know it's hurting me more than you.

Described by some of the 45 as "pompous" and "ineffective," Bush-Brown (who came "to hyphenate," according to another member of the 45), stretched the deadline to thirty minutes, but was unable to convince anyone to leave. He promised to meet them over a glass of sherry almost anywhere else on or off campus. To the 45 he was just another unknown administrator, as equally unacquainted as Doty with the faculty group. Lawler recalls, "He tried to smile us out of the building. He used a carrot on a stick approach, and wanted to be reasonable, but he lost his chance when he also said we would be arrested."

Recorded in the Buffalo police log at the basement command post in Clark Gymnasium were these notations:

12:45 P.M. Three K-9 wagons and a booking team dispatched to Hayes Hall. Campus police ordered to Hayes by Mr. Doty to make the arrests before turning those arrested over to Buffalo police. Doty's order gives them five minutes to clear—if they don't, there will be arrests made.

1:11 P.M. Campus police ordered to Hayes by Mr. Doty.

1:17 P.M. Occupants of Hayes given five minutes to clear. If they don't arrests will be made.

1:50 P.M. Capt. Mahoney reports about 50 persons have been arrested and are being taken to Pct. 16. [Although not noted by the police, Max A. Wickert (English) was reading aloud passages from Kafka (*The Penal Colony*) as the preoccupied 45 filed, one by one, from the presidential suite to be arrested and escorted to police vans.]

2:25 P.M. Mr. Doty called and said Dr. Regan suggested that Dr. Brown and Bush-Brown (probably one and the same) were being sent to Pct. 16 with copies of the injunction and to observe booking procedures so that there would be no complaints.

(Platek 1970)

During these proceedings the final total of 45 was reached, and the demonstrators had not been influenced by either Doty or Bush-Brown. Another myth persists that History Professor Georg G. Iggers returned from the lavatory to rejoin the faculty just as the door was being locked on the last K-9 van. Iggers has been faithfully described over the years, as pleading with police to allow him to accompany his colleagues to the station. Not so, he says. "When I returned, a university security officer called me aside. He had noticed my accent and thought he should warn me that foreign nationals were in serious trouble if arrested under these circumstances." Although already an American citizen for twenty years, Iggers decided he had made his point and left. The thoughtful security officer overlooked a *bona fide* foreign national, South African John M. Coetzee, then an Assistant Professor of English. Now an internationally recognized author, Coetzee could not predict that twenty years later he would be awarded an honorary degree at UB's 1989 commencement, at which his relationship with the 45 would remain unacknowledged.

"I had a mistaken notion of faculty privilege at the time, and thought that the university would never consent to arresting its own faculty," Fleischer explained. "Most of us were operating within an American tradition of peaceful civil disobedience. . . . Most of the young faculty at the time felt that something of enormous importance was going on. Teaching 18th century poetry or the Victorian novel somehow didn't seem as important as what was immediately happening at this university and lots of others. It was as if the intellectual enterprise was put on hold for the time being. It was something that people got caught up in. The decade marked an incredible turning point in our culture." Philosophy Professor Kenneth F. Barber adds, "Some younger faculty really believed we were on the verge of a great revolution."

Initial booking at nearby Precinct 16 is described by Anthropology and American Studies Professor Robert K. Dentan as "almost jovial." One officer cheerfully announced, "Hey, these are professors—now they're arresting professors!" Anxiety levels heightened during the trip from there to downtown Buffalo, and especially after cell doors clanged shut behind them. "The Black Maria is threatening to most of us," suggests Wickert. For Dentan the trip "was more comfortable than I thought it would be—without the dogs, of course," but other interviewees complain about the K-9 vans. Barber, who "had no intention of getting arrested," swears that his van deliberately took a short cut down some railroad tracks, and Anthropology Professor Albert T. Steegman recalls that his vehicle made unnecessarily sudden and jarring stops.

"Aside from myself," Dentan observes, "I don't think anyone expected to be arrested or tried." He is still concerned that most of the faculty deliberately remained uninvolved and were "fundamentally unserious." There also was some "posturing—the professor who urged me to come to the sit-in did not himself show up." James H. Bunn "understood that the sit-in, as an act of civil disobedience, carried with it the possibility of arrest—especially after the five-minute ultimatum." Actively opposed to the Vietnam War since 1968, Wickert has no regrets and would do it again. "I participated more as an expression of protest rather than out of any desire to see the acting president." Snell, who hastened back to Buffalo a day early from New England to be at the sit-in, also anticipated arrests.

Feelings of "anxiety" and "powerlessness" were common faculty reactions. Most of them had never experienced such direct contact with police and didn't know what to expect. Steegman was among those who had doubted that arrests would occur. "In retrospect, had I known, I would have gotten out." He believes the police were outraged that such a privileged group would even consider breaking the law. "Although not physically abused, we were not treated like human beings from the moment we came under police custody." One officer told him, "You guys should have been lined up and shot." Another, pointing to the American flag on his shoulder patch, was overheard by Lawler telling another officer, "I'd feel better if this was a swastika." Dentan explains that the overwhelmingly male police force led an insular life and usually tended to associate with and talk to other police officers. "Like social workers, they often come to hate the people with whom they have to deal." Pops remembers that several faculty had tried to persuade their colleagues not to demonstrate and correctly predicted the arrests. ("They will kill you!" one shouted, in all seriousness.) "I believed arrests were unlikely; had I known I wouldn't have been so eager to visit Hayes Hall."

Federman "couldn't believe what was happening" and became more apprehensive as the net tightened. "Shit, this is the real thing," he told himself in the K-9 van. "You are abruptly caught in the machinery and really lose control of events around you. You are fingerprinted, hear the gates close, and suddenly you are a criminal." He wondered if his UB career might be finished. When an officer noted his accent and asked, "Are you an American?", Federman could not refrain from retorting, "Hell, I fought for you guys in Korea."

Several of the UB faculty today relate to Sherman McCoy, the main character in Tom Wolfe's novel *The Bonfire of the Vanities,* who suffered many indignities and much unwanted publicity during his booking in New York when he was charged for an act he did not commit. Although not handcuffed, the 45 were photographed, fingerprinted, searched (their pockets turned inside out), and all personal belongings, including belts and neckties, were impounded. The unkindest cut of all for those who relied on them was the loss of their spectacles. Lawler said that he "shuffled around myopically while holding up my trousers." Axelrod felt "helpless and disoriented," and Duggleby "couldn't walk three steps without my glasses." Unlike the fictional McCoy, the 45 were not deprived of their shoelaces.

Interviewees remember one surly turnkey—not the most coveted of police assignments—who handed out the evening meal, which was most charitably described as "a dry piece of bologna on white bread." Bunn and his cellmates were reminded of their good fortune: "Do you know what they would do to you in Russia? You wouldn't get anything but black bread and water." When the ubiquitous turnkey reminded several prisoners that they wouldn't fare as well in Russia, they half-seriously wondered if the food could be poisoned and settled for a glass of water. When a French-speaking faculty member exchanged a pun with Federman about the meager repast, "Ici on bouffe à l'eau" (here, one eats with water), they were ordered, "Don't speak that Russian in here!" Dentan wistfully remembered his attaché case that was now in a police vault—it contained an apple and a sandwich he had foresightedly brought with him that morning.

Federman felt it advisable not to inform his mother-in-law in California about the incident. His wife agreed, but neither anticipated a March 30 *Newsweek* photograph ("Buffalo Professors in Jail: New Guidelines for Campus Revolution"), depicting him with three cellmates peering out from behind prison bars. The irate mother-in-law telephoned to remind her daughter, "I told you not to marry him and that he was a communist." Another member of the 45 became fearful that ongoing adoption proceedings for a baby girl would be delayed or jeopardized by his arrest record. Axelrod's young daughter brought a personal note to the police station pleading for her father's release so that he could fulfill his promise to take her to a movie that afternoon.

The incident received national press coverage, and the 45 achieved instant notoriety in the Buffalo area. "The media, including the *New York Times,* viewed us like the students with whom the administration felt it was impossible to negotiate," Barber says. Faculty members engaging in such peaceable and honorable demonstrations on their own campus had not, it would be claimed by the 45, been arrested and jailed since fifteen Harvard professors were seized from protesting the Spanish-American War. In a plea for financial help the Buffalo Faculty Defense Committee (1970) charged in the *New York Times,* "For the first time in an American university faculty members peaceably assembled on university premises have been arrested and jailed." (Among the respondents to this advertisement was Margaret Mead.)

A headline story in the *Courier-Express* (1970b) was supported by background items and photographs. Names and addresses were prominently displayed in both papers, assuring harassment from irate readers. News accounts emphasized that the arrests took place only after efforts by Bush-Brown and Doty failed to convince the 45 to leave.

"Those arrested were charged with violating a preliminary injunction prohibiting trespassing in UB buildings and violence," the *Courier* reported. "Following the arrests," the article continued, "Dr. Regan said he would issue a statement. After keeping reporters waiting for two hours, he announced he would not make a statement."

Both the *Courier* (1970b) and *The Buffalo Evening News* (1970a) emphasized that Judge Joseph S. Mattina released the 45 without bail over the objection of District Attorney Michael A. Dillon, who would not entertain any university request for reduction of the charge against the faculty members and would not agree to the placing of lesser charges. The *News* fueled conspiracy theories by reporting (erroneously) that after the arrests were made and Hayes was cleared, "the building was cordoned off by police (who) turned away a number of persons who were carrying sleeping bags and walkie-talkies."

The *Courier* noted that the arrests "appeared to have given the faltering strike new impetus. Monday's demonstrations were about one-third larger than similar activities last week." Both papers carried the acting president's belated statement;

> Those members of our university who conducted the sit-in in the president's office Sunday were acting in the long and highly respected tradition of civil disobedience. While I disagree with their specific purpose, I recognize that they bore witness with their bodies and their liberties, and that they did so peacefully. I shall do everything that I can to see that the peaceful character of this action is given the fullest consideration in any subsequent proceedings. . . . (*Buffalo Evening News* 1970b; *Courier-Express* 1970c)

Each newspaper carried a page-one statement by the district attorney that UB officials should also declare the 45 in contempt of the Supreme Court injunction. "If the university does not execute the actual court actions within a week," he promised, "I will make every effort to institute such proceedings in my own name" (*Buffalo Evening News* 1970b; *Courier-Express* 1970d).

The outside community perceived the 45 as malicious conspirators of evil political intent—the malevolent cynosure for the confusing events of preceding weeks that involved police, administrators, faculty, and rampaging students. "An openly hostile media," Frisch maintains, "portrayed the 45 as extremists and hardcore radicals, blurring important distinctions between violent and non-violent protests"—and between disruption and peaceful dissent. He recalls one editorial page cartoon from the *News* (1970c) in which the backdrop depicts the university in flames while two evil witches—identified as "radical students" and "radical faculty"— vigorously stir the contents of a steaming cauldron labeled "Anarchy." Frisch also believes that SUNY attorneys escalated the charges by equating the non-violent faculty demonstrators with screaming, rock-throwing students.

Their only journalistic support came from the highly suspect *Spectrum*, the student newspaper that by now was entirely under radical control and clearly uninfluential outside the campus community. The March 16 lead article reported the arrest of approximately fifty full-time faculty members for staging a peaceful sit-in at Hayes Hall and concluded with an editorial cast:

Dr. Regan aided by several of his administrators have made this university into a battleground. The police are just his repressive arm. And this
university must remain on strike until not only that arm but the man pulling
the strings are off campus, until all charges by the university against its
protesting members are dropped, until all demands are met. Regan has
demonstrated on every level that there is no choice but to shut it down.
(*The Spectrum,* 1970)

Most of the 45 were upset and confused over hate calls. Telephone numbers were changed, and at least one family moved to Canada. "The media
authenticates your existence," Pops observes. "When you do something like
this you become identified as a real person." One of the original 45, who
left UB, claimed that when he purchased a bottle of wine the liquor store
proprietor, recognizing him from a television newscast, said, "If I had a gun
I would shoot you for what you did last week." The day after his name
and address appeared in both newspapers, another faculty 45 member found
a death-threat note on the door of his car; he left the driver's door open
and kept one foot on the pavement when he started the vehicle.

While the general public was not understanding, many previously neutral
faculty and students now turned against the administration. The feeling of
clannishness that binds disparate faculty members together when some of their
peers are attacked by outsiders should not be underestimated. A moral for college presidents: Do not forget how clans react in defense of their own, even
when their colleagues may be a little in the wrong. Anyone who has even remote-
ly been an organization man learns this sooner or later, often the hard way.

Most faculty members are generally suspicious about "the administration," a nebulous concept at best. A more measured response, including deans
and department chairpersons meeting with the 45 in Hayes Hall, might have
satisfied many uncommitted moderate faculty, now shocked by the arrests.
Several of the members of the faculty 45 who continue to teach at UB believe they would have been satisfied had the acting president talked to them,
if only to listen to their concerns about the continuing police occupation.
Liberal and moderate faculty—bewildered by the criminal contempt charges
lodged against the 45—immediately challenged both the administration and
the university governance structure. Thirty professors, deans, and department
chairs formed "The University Survival Group." A steering committee explained that they would constitute a third force in university affairs, a voice
to respond to the extreme polarization between students and the top administration, and issued a statement:

When both the administration and the faculty, as represented in the Faculty Senate Executive Committee, seem unresponsive to the state of emergency which has paralyzed us for nearly three weeks, when a group of
colleagues stage sit-ins to demonstrate their frustration and concern, and
when the violence which we constantly face shows no sign of ebbing, we

feel that we must act to restore some sense of trust and direction in the university community. . . . We must reverse the climate of hostility and confusion in which faculty and students are driven apart and our university is regarded across the nation as another academic war room. We must thwart those politically motivated external forces which threaten to turn our campus into open territory for a witch hunt. . . . As concerned faculty, we see this as our job . . . rendering the faculty effective and responsible and diffusing the hostility which threatens to destroy this enterprise. (The University Survival Group 1970)

On March 15, 1970, the 45 were charged with criminal contempt and criminal trespass in violation of Section 215.50 (3), punishable by up to one year in prison and a $1,000 fine and Section 140.1 of the Penal Code, three months and a $500 fine. Another criminal contempt charge was filed in the Supreme Court of New York under Section 750 of the New York judiciary law, which could result in six months in prison and a $250 fine.

> Now bringing scholars to justice is no easy task,
> They thought of three kind of contempt and criminal trespass,
> When it comes to pressing charges, they didn't have no shame,
> They were just so happy to finally have somebody to blame.

By March 20 The *Courier-Express* had received so many angry reactions from the local citizenry that it ran a full page of them to catch up with the volume. Included among twenty-eight letters were these references to the 45:

If people are wondering why students think and act the way they do today they only have to look to the 45 faculty members who were arrested. . . . They are the ones who should be charged with instigating all of the current trouble on the campus. . . . Other universities are also infected with the eggheads or "intellectual snobs" as Vice President Agnew calls them. . . . They should be fired.

Round up all of the commie professors and turn them loose on the corner of Broadway and Bailey. Give us 10 seconds to hold a kangaroo court in the neighborhood and then let the teenagers deal with them accordingly.

The protest should be halted by the National Guard and the school closed. Furthermore, every rebel student should lose whatever state aid he or she might be getting and every trouble-making professor should be summarily dismissed.

I certainly hope the state will not continue to pay the salaries of the so-called professors who must bear a large part of the responsibility for stirring up the whole mess.

These [the 45] people assume that there should be a complete and separate set of rules only for them, and in letting them get away [released without bail] with such horrendous actions we are condoning this wrong belief. Let's punish these unlawful perpetrators of destruction for the criminals they really are.

The Courier-Express deserves the thanks of the public for the fine pictures and stories of the protesting faculty members. All you have to do is read their statement and look at their pictures to know who started all of this trouble.

The 45 must be counted as deliberately malicious, or as stupid as the man who lights a match in a dynamite factory. In either case, the 45 must bear some moral responsibility—and they should be removed from our educational system. (*Courier-Express,* 1970e)

The 45 were never tried in the city courts, but from April 7 to April 17 stood trial for the third charge before Justice Hamilton Ward in the Supreme Court, Pruitt reports (1989). The defendants maintained silence. Their basic argument was that they denied the charges; since these were criminal charges there was a presumption of innocence and it was up to the state to prove them guilty. Justice Ward criticized them for not offering a defense, but he also did not require those submitting afffidavits to appear in court, thus denying the defense an opportunity for cross-examination.

"Going into the trial we were sure of two things," Frisch tells reporter Jeffrey Trebb (1990). "One, there was no way in hell we could be convicted. The prosecution lacked basic evidence and there is validity in the American Court System. Two, we knew we could be convicted on account of the community mood."

The affidavit of SUNY Attorney Thomas Winfield charged the 45 with refusing to comply with the preliminary injunction, although they had prior knowledge of its existence, Pruitt writes (1971). They were not charged with violating the injunction or with disrupting "lawful and normal operation of the university" (the language of the injunction) but fear was alleged that further disruptions would ensue if the occupancy of the president's office continued. The three attorneys representing the 45 argued that the language of the preliminary injunction was so vague and ambiguous that it inhibited speech and conduct protected by the First Amendment.

The state called on two campus security officers, who testified about previous, separate incidents in which student demonstrators threatened police headquarters and disrupted a basketball game, Pruitt reports (1989). The officers admitted that the 45 were in no way involved in the cited disturbance, but the Court refused to strike the testimony, which had the effect of suggesting that the professors were violence-prone and acting in concert with disruptive student activists. No other witnesses were called to prove allegations of criminal contempt.

On April 17 the judge found that the defendants, "individually and in concert with others," had failed to comply with the provisions of the preliminary injunction and were in contempt of court. He sentenced them each to thirty days in the Erie County Penitentiary, but execution of the sentence was stayed pending appeal to the Appellate Court. Justice Ward was as gen-

erally unable as the outside community to understand why the faculty did
not set a better example of behavior than students. The Buffalo 16 still resent
how the judge conducted the case and chastised them when he passed sentence. "When a court of this kind makes a clear order, those above all that
ought to comply with it are charged with the responsibility of teaching our
young people," Justice Ward observed, adding gratuitously, "I could order
you across the street right now. There are officers prepared to take you"
(*Buffalo Evening News,* 1970d).

> So we bowed our heads in court before Justice's sword,
> Then looked up and saw Judge Hamilton Ward,
> He said you're paid to know better, shouldn't lead your students astray,
> I don't want to hear no philosophy, I think I'm going to put you away.

Ketter (1971) describes the effect of the sentence as "electrolytic," and
increasing numbers of faculty who had tried to maintain neutrality were upset by what they perceived as an overly severe sentence. Faculty who believed
that the incident had been just another deliberate attempt to create new problems and further embarrass the acting president now expressed concen about
the fate of their colleagues. *The Buffalo Evening News* (1970d) also viewed
the sentence as extreme:

> No one can predict the final outcome of the case in the appellate courts,
> but it seems to us that Supreme Court Justice Hamilton Ward could have
> done no less than find the "faculty 45" guilty of contempt for their March
> 15 sit-in. . . .
>   We cannot believe that justice was well-served, however, in the 30 day
> jail sentence which he handed down for each defendant—at least not jus-
> tice in the sense of beeng tempered with mercy or even with a reasonable
> relevance to the seriousness of the offense.
>   The court was right to uphold the sanctity of court orders and to con-
> demn the defendants for their acts of defiance, undertaken in an effort to
> force the removal of Buffalo city police then on campus. . . .
>   But 30 days behind bars? Surely that is all out of proportion, in this
> particular instance, to the nonviolent nature of the defendants' single, brief
> protest action. Irresponsible as we believe the "faculty 45's" sit-in was, in
> defiance of the court order and a warning of arrest, we still feel it would
> have been more appropriate to combine a record of conviction and fines
> for contempt with a stiff courtroom tongue-lashing plus a warning of more
> serious consequences for any repetitions.
>   In these days of outrageous court defiance by everyone from cursing
> revolutionaries to public employee groups and grandstanding southern
> governors, it is no easy thing for a judge to draw an appropriately stern
> line in meting out contempt penalties. But if excessive leniency invites fur-
> ther contempt, so can excessive harshness tend to martyrize the guilty and
> radicalize their supporters.

Although an implacable opponent of police occupation, Connelly calls the action of the 45 "a hare-brained gesture, especially since none of them was in an influential position or an active participant in any form of university governance. They were idealists with no hands-on experience during the ongoing trouble, abstract rather than practicing liberals. Still, it was a serious error not to talk to them, not unlike the mistake by the British in the Easter Rebellion in Ireland, when they opened fire on protesters rather than conferring with them."

Ketter (1971) expressed similar reservations: "To praise the group as bold, young idealists ignored their mature years, their indirect methods and the dependence on legal counsel. . . . No statement of altruistic motives, no appeal to abhorrence of police control, no campaign or lapel buttons and fund raising overbore the fundamental mistake in judgment: an intentional flouting of a court order. Only those who had not watched the same thing happening when other campuses challenged the courts could have been surprised."

Engineering Professor Charles M. Fogel, who was then the Assistant Executive Vice President and one of the most trustworthy and loyal members of the Regan administration, has a different perspective: "The action that I was most offended by was the arrest of the 45. There had to be a collegial way to have handled this, even if it was just letting them remain there in the president's office. Their viewpoint could have tempered the administrative actions profitably for all."

The ruling to delay execution of the sentence afforded valuable and necessary time to prepare legal appeals and seek additional financial support.

> From here on it's the D.A.'s show,
> We got appeals to appeal, and two trials to go.
> And the Grand jury's looking to see heads roll,
> And in Buffalo, man, we wouldn't win no popularity poll.
>
> Now justice costs big money in the U.S. of A.,
> So if you got an extra dollar won't you put it in the tray,
> And we'll sing until the morning, til the break of dawn,
> And we'll dance the jurisprudence til the Hayes Hall Blues are gone.

(None of the 45 reported losing more than $250–$300 from personal resources. Advertisements, benefits, donations, poetry readings, and record sales raised enough money for legal expenses.)

In addition to maintaining a daily log about ongoing events, Pruitt followed the story of the 45, compiling the following arguments presented by defense attorneys in the fall of 1970 at the Appellate Division level. (Fifth Judicial District, Rochester, New York.)

(1) The Supreme Court failed to afford basic safeguards in the criminal contempt trial, thereby denying them, the 45, due process of law under the Fifth, Sixth, and Fourteenth Amendments of the Constitution. Neither

the right of confrontation of accusers and cross-examination, nor the presumption of innocence and the privilege against self-incrimination, were observed. The state's criminal pleadings were inadequate, and the 45 were not even positively identified as the same individuals who had occupied the president's office.

(2) The faculty could not be convicted of criminal contempt because they were not bound by the language "all persons receiving notice of this preliminary injunction," and the injunction's prescriptive language designed to prevent conduct which "disrupts the normal operations" or "the unlawful educational function of the university" was void because of vagueness.

(3) The 45 did not violate the terms of the injunction since their conduct on March 15 in no way disrupted or interfered with the normal operation of the university. (Pruitt 1971)

On November 5, 1970, the conviction was unanimously reversed by the Appellate Division, Fourth Judicial Department, Pruitt writes. The Appellate Court ruled that "the record in the instant case is devoid of any proof that the students violated the injunction, and the evidence is legally insufficient to establish that the faculty members either were agents or acted in collusion with them." Furthermore, the "too broadly worded" injunction was specifically aimed at the conduct of the students, and faculty members had not been parties to such disruptive actions, Pruitt explains.

The case finally turned full circle. A year later, *The Courier-Express* (1971) reported that:

criminal trespass charges were dismissed in City Court (June 3) against 45 University of Buffalo faculty members arrested following a campus sit-in last year.

Judge H. Buswell Roberts dropped the charges in the 14-month-old case on the recommendation of Dist. Atty. Michael A. Dillon. . . . The university administration, which had brought the civil contempt proceedings before Justice Ward, indicated that it would not appeal the Appellate Division findings.

Judge Roberts dismissed City Court criminal contempt charges against the defendants (Jan. 19, 1971) following the Appellate Court ruling. . . . The defendants remained free throughout the court action.

Immediately below the article, names and addresses of the original 45 were again listed.

The way the administration handled the episode still rankles members of the original 45 who remained at UB. "It was a siege mentality, and the administration quickly retreated into a law and order syndrome," explains Charles Keil, then an Assistant Professor in American Studies and one of the 45. "It became hard-core administrators against hard-core radicals, and the administration was unwilling to sit down and talk to anyone. Furthermore, the majority of the faculty were invisible—and they are even more invisible today." Haynie categorizes the administration as ineffective: "Spring vacation was coming and they would have been smart to ignore the whole incident." Pops suggests that "a visit from Regan would have helped—or he could have left us sitting there." Axelrod concludes that "there were no villains or evil persons, but the administration was guilty of fumbling and bumbling."

"It was childish for Regan to move so quickly and precipitously when he had time," Frisch maintains. "He might, for example, have insisted that faculty were welcome in the president's office at any time, but part of the difficulty may have stemmed from not knowing exactly who was there."

Local interviewees believe that little was accomplished by their symbolic gesture, although Fleischer and Bunn point out that the incident became a leading case in the Law of Trespass. "They learned that you can't enjoin the whole world, and the broadness of the injunction helped our case," Bunn says. "We were also made to realize that the university was part of the community, and not situated on the edge of the moon." Fleischer, who feels that some of the bad community feeling still exists today, also informed Continelli (1989) that some "people on the faculty didn't speak to one another for years."

Lawler wonders why the university never formally apologized to the 45 for the legal discomfiture to which he and his colleagues were subjected, but John Coetzee, now a Professor of English at the Univeristy of Capetown in South Africa, may have suffered the most. "After the sit-in I remained on the UB faculty until May of 1971, and passed through the same legal procedures as the rest of the 45," Coetzee writes (1989). "However, my status vis à vis the Immigration and Naturalization authorities was immensely complicated by the fact that I had been (until the appeal succeeded) conicted of an offense against the law. *Inter-alia,* the re-entry visa that until that time allowed me to leave and re-enter the United States was withdrawn, making travel impossible. This played a large part in my decision to resign and leave the U.S. in 1971." He does not regret his participation and agrees with those who feel the administration overreacted.

Some of the Buffalo 45 may still remember the final chorus of "The Hayes Hall Blues::

> Dance the Juris,
> Prudence.
>
> And we'll dance until the morning, til the break of dawn,
> And we'll dance the Jurisprudence til the Hayes Hall Blues are gone.

References

Axelrod, Seymour. (1989). Interview and Questionnaire.
Barber, Kenneth F. (1989). Interview and Questionnaire.
Buffalo Evening News. (1970a). "45 in UB Sit-in Ignored Warning," March 16.
———. (1970b). "UB Students, Facing Large Police Force, Cancel Amherst March," March 17.

220   *Dissent and Disruption*

Buffalo Evening News. (1970c). "Double, Double Toil and Trouble," editorial cartoon, March 17.
———. (1970d). "Right Verdict, Harsh Penalty," April 18.
Buffalo Faculty Defense Committee. (1970). Advertisement, *The New York Times,* March 29.
Bunn, James H. (1989). Interview and Questionnaire.
Coetzee, John M. (1989). Letter to the author, August 27.
Connolly, Thomas E. (1989). Interview and Questionnaire.
Continelli, Louise. (1989). "The Riot Squad," *The Buffalo News,* May 21.
Courier-Express. (1970a). "Judge's Writ Bars Disorders at UB," March 6.
———. (1970b). "45 of Faculty Arrested in Sit-in at Hayes," March 16.
———. (1970c). "Police Name 45 Arrested on Campus," March 17.
———. (1970d). "VFW Demands Rocky Crush Sedition at UB," March 17.
———. (1970e). "Citizens Offer Comments on Recent Disorder at UB," March 20.
———. (1971). "Trespass Charges Dropped in Hayes Hall Demonstration," June 14.
Dentan, Robert K. (1989). Interview and Questionnaire.
Doty, Edward W. (1989). Interview and Questionnaire.
———. (1970). Deposition, March 18.
Duggleby, Christine R. (1989). Interview and Questionnaire.
Federman, Raymond. (1990). Interview and Questionnaire.
Fleischer, Stefan. (1989). Interview and Questionnaire.
Fogel, Charles M. (1989). Interview and Questionnaire.
Frisch, Michael M. (1988). Interview and Questionnaire.
Goodman, Nicolas D. (1989). Interview and Questionnaire.
Haynie, Charles A. (1989). Interview and Questionnaire.
Iggers, Georg G. (1989). Interview and Questionnaire.
Keil, Charles M. (1989). Telephone Interview.
Ketter, Robert L. (1971). "Report of the President," *The Reporter,* February 11.
Lawler, James M. (1989). Interview and Questionnaire.
Platek, Frederick J. (1970). Police log, March 15.
———. (1989). Interview.
Pops, Martin L. (1989). Interview and Questionnaire.
Pruitt, Dean G. (1971). "A Note on the Disposal of the Faculty 45 Case," unpublished.
———. (1989). Interview and Questionnaire.
Snell, Fred M. (1989). Interview and Questionnaire.
Spectrum, The. (1970). March 16.
Steegman, Albert T. (1989). Interview and Questionnaire.
Trebb, Jeffrey. (1990). "Faculty 45, Their Protest Became an Enduring Symbol of the Time," *UB Today,* Spring.
University Survival Group. (1970). Statement, March 18.
The Vicious Vandals. (1970). Chorus and back-up group, "The Hayes Hall Blues: 45 Revolutions per Minute."
Wickert, Max A. (1989). Interview and Questionnaire.

Aftermath—The End of An Era

All modern revolutions have ended as a reinforcement of the power of
The State.

—Albert Camus, *The Rebel*

Every generation seems to go through this bloody ritual again and again,
and if not every generation, then every other generation—of demanding
of the world more than it can give, finding the world is not just unsatis-
fying but intolerable in some basic respect, and reacting.

—Irving Kristol from *Second Thoughts:*
Former Radicals Look Back at the Sixties

"By the early seventies the upheaval was over—as mysteriously as it had appeared, and as worldwide," writes Gitlen (1987). "The sixties receded into haze and myth: lingering images of nobility and violence, occasional news clips of Martin Luther King, Jr., and John F. Kennedy, Beatles and Bob Dylan retrospectives, the jumble of images this culture shares instead of a sense of continuous, lived history. The sixties: a collage of fragments scooped together as if a whole decade took place in an instant" (p. 3).

Maintaining scholarly objectivity about an era that severely disrupted higher education and continues to influence the outlook and judgment of those who lived it is difficult. Greeley (1972) concludes that the movement was over in early 1972, but there is general agreement that severe campus unrest essentially ended after the spring term of 1970. As the semester closed, the disorganized movement lost momentum. Anarchy cannot long be tolerated within any organization and the overturn of institutions by complete and sudden revolution in a large society was then almost unknown.

"In 1969, SDS at the peak of its size and militancy, with some hundred thousand members, hundreds of chapters, millions of supporters, and under the intense scrutiny (to say the least) of the White House and the FBI, broke into screaming factions, one of which, the Weathermen, began to build bombs," Gitlen reports (1987, p. 417). This faction, the Revolutionary Youth Movement I, considered itself the vanguard of violent revolution and tried to recruit students, workers, and blacks to present a united front. Its leaders endorsed terrorism and conducted workshops on sabotage, hastening the decline of SDS as college students became increasingly opposed to violence as an appropriate form of protest.

Gitlen refers to a 1970 Harris poll that reported the first drop since 1965 in the percentage of students calling themselves "radical or far left"—from 11 percent in the spring of 1970 to 7 percent in the fall. "From spring to fall the middle-of-the-road category rose from 26 to 34 percent, and the 'conservative' and 'far Right' groups, which had been sliding steadily since 1968, from 15 to 19 percent. Students were stampeding away from the New Left" (p. 417).

While higher education would not be entirely free from occasional unrest in 1970–71, the scope and intensity of 1969–70 levels were never closely approximated. The American Bar Association (1970) identified the nature of violent incidents during the 1969–70 academic year: Arson, willful destruction of property, including manuscripts and notes of faculty members, assault and battery, the occupation of buildings, interruption of classes, disruptions of meetings, barring entrances to buildings, holding administrators captive, violating injunctions, and other unlawful conduct were reported from campus to campus.

Student unrest became history. Overall, America was changed, especially in the tone and direction of higher education. At UB no buildings had been burned down, and university purposes were not altered beyond recovery.

And, what is most important, no lives were lost.

In a *New York Times* article Michael T. Kaufman (1970) reported that two campus security guards were fired upon at 12:30 A.M. Monday, March 16— the morning after the Faculty 45 episode—as they were investigating a report that Molotov cocktails were being made near Schoelkopf Hall. Five .22-caliber bullets chipped into the building facade while a sixth hit the back of a security vehicle. " 'What's happening here is a reverberation of escalations,' said a Hippie oriented sympathizer of a student strike that has disrupted the university," Kaufman continues. " 'First they brought the cops on campus, then the faculty protested, then heads were split last Thursday, then 45 faculty members sat in and were arrested and now there may be individual terror.' "

Activists claimed that the sniping incident—about which there was no further publicity—was a right-wing ploy to discredit the movement. That afternoon three hundred demonstrators appeared for the first time at the Ridge Lea campus facility three miles from the Main Street campus. Chanting "Pigs must go!" they clanged on kettles, broke several windows, and shook tambourines in what the University News Service characterized as a "fairly peaceful" protest.

The March 18 *New York Times* (1970) reported that police and community leaders were stepping up pressure on dissident students and teachers at the troubled campus, and sheriff's deputies had arrested Dan Bentivogli, the head of UB's chapter of Youth Against War and Fascism. He reports that he was placed on five-year probation with no jail time.

> Aside from a bomb threat and a student demonstration that was canceled, the two campuses of the sprawling university were relatively quiet today. Squads of city and campus policemen patrolled the grounds in riot gear. Opposition to the strikers in the largely conservative Buffalo community has been growing daily. In Albany, local legislators have been putting pressure on Governor Rockefeller to step into the crisis. . . .
>
> "City police on the campus also appear weary of their confrontation with the students. One of their first acts when they were called on the campus was to place an American flag on the bell tower of the Administration Building. . . . On the bulletin board of the police command post in Clark Gymnasium are pictures of student demonstrations with such comments as 'Freak Show' added. The board also contains several attempts to make an acronym out of the 'pig' epithet with such comments as 'Pretty Important Guys' and 'Pride, Integrity, Guts.' "

Two other items on the same page concerned meetings scheduled for March 18 with the governor, Republican legislators, and State University Regents to discuss the UB disorders.

"An early start on spring vacation . . . appears to have brought a measure of tranquility to the strife-torn campus," *The Buffalo Evening News* (1970) reported on March 19. "A demonstration slated for Wednesday attracted only about 40 students and the American flag was flying again on the campus flagpole in front of Crosby Hall." By the end of spring vacation on March 29 the police had been withdrawn from the campus. After the March 12 clash between police and demonstrators, Pruitt reports (1970), further organized physical confrontation was ruled out by the activists as unproductive, illogical, and too dangerous. "There were indications . . . that violence as a tactic in the university struggle is being rejected by all but a fringe group," *The Reporter* (1970a) verified. Local radical leadership, divided over this and other policy questions, disappeared.

Since presidents are usually blamed for whatever goes wrong, they are often the earliest casualties. The *Spectrum* (1970a) reported the acting president's resignation, to be effective on August 31. "In a press conference later in the day Dr. Regan felt that the problems which caused the recent turmoil are 'on their way to solution.' . . . He thought that he could have handled the recent situation better had he appointed his own men rather than inheriting them from President Meyerson." A 1970 American Council on

Education report by *The Special Committee on Campus Tensions* points out that the president is likely to be abandoned in times of turmoil. "One executive, who became the target of disrupters, observed angrily, 'No one was in sight when it came time for support. Everyone faded away into the background. It was like a gigantic live replay of the movie *High Noon*. All the so-called friends had reason to be absent on the day of the showdown.'" Other presidential respondents in this study identified the faculty as a major source of difficulty: "A number of presidents see the faculty as the entrenched voice of conservatism on the campus, while others are disturbed by the active role of faculty in promoting dissent and divisiveness."

In May UB was among the many colleges and universities shaken by violent and spontaneous, but disorganized and short-lived, demonstrations triggered by President Nixon's bombing of Cambodia and the Kent State tragedy. The nationwide reaction to the Cambodian adventure would eclipse all previous student protest. By the end of May 1970, 415 colleges and universities had been disrupted, writes Manchester (1974). "It was the first general strike in the country's history, and it was entirely spontaneous. At the end of the first semester 286 were still paralyzed, and while 129 others in 43 states had officially reopened, many classsrooms were empty" (p. 1211).

As Nixon anticipated, protests flared up after the Cambodian intrusion. Most shocking was the Kent State incident where Ohio National Guardsmen needlessly killed four students and wounded ten others at 12:30 P.M. on May 4. Within a week around two hundred colleges and universities closed after protest strikes and violent demonstrations. American militiamen had killed United States citizens, reinforcing the message that both police and protesters were capable of violent acts.

After Kent State "the dam broke," writes Gitlen (1987), who estimates that strikes were called for on about 30 percent of the nation's twenty-five hundred campuses. Although larger and more elite universities were disproportionately affected, demonstrations took place at over half of our institutions of higher education—large and small, public and private, secular and religious, four-year and two-year units. "At least a million students probably demonstrated for the first time in their lives in May," Gitlen believes. "On May 9 the mobilization drew over one hundred thousand people to rally in Washington on only ten days notice. . ." (p. 410).

Militant and violent protests spread. "Thirty ROTC buildings were burned or bombed during the first week in May," Gitlen continues. "National Guard units were mobilized on twenty-one campuses in sixteen states. Police were evidently overheated. On May 14 at Jackson State in Mississippi amid tensions apparently unrelated to the war, the police let loose a shotgun fusillade into a women's dormitory, killing two students and wounding nine—who, being black, inspired far fewer headlines or demonstrations than the killings at Kent State" (p. 410). Then a revolutionist's bomb tore out the sides of the Army Mathematics Research Center at the University of Wisconsin, killing a physicist and wounding four other persons.

These tragic events, according to Hayden (1989):

> spread a pall over what remained of the movement. There dawned a shocked sense that the times were driving people toward madness. The broad and creative energies once directed toward civil rights and peace were, for some, channeled into hardened "cadre organizations" cults whose members increasingly sought purity, fixed answers, and reinforcement. In addition to the Weathermen, the death throes of SDS gave birth to several tiny Marxist and Maoist organizations which named and renamed themselves as they splintered into the future. The Progressive Labor Party, which had lived like a fungus on the SDS body for several years, shriveled up as the body itself died. (p. 420)

In fact, "the post-Cambodia uprising was the student movement's last hurrah," says Gitlen (1987). "Activism never recovered from the summer vacation of 1970. . . . Demonstrations declined at the old centers of protest, and press coverage declined precipitously. . . . The general impression was that the campuses were 'quieting down,' " (p. 411). Once SDS imploded, Gitlen explains, "there was no national organization to keep student movements boiling, to channel anti-war energy into common action, to keep local organizers in touch with one another to provide continuity from semester to semester. . . . The spectacle of SDS factions hurling incomprehensive curses at one another was not inviting to newcomers. Neither was the turn to violence and mindless destruction" (p. 417).

"Student movements tend to be focused on specific issues or crises," explains Altbach (1991). "While the leadership may have a sophisticated ideological perspective, the rank-and-file demonstrators have less commitment and little understanding that political change requires a long struggle. Student leaders have a tendency toward factionalism and confusion, which cripples the movement and confuses the issues. The rhythm of campus life also does not lend itself to sustained activism. Even on Tiananmen Square, students were concerned about impending examinations."

In concert with other campus publications throughout the nation the May 5 *Spectrum* (1970b) published a front-page editorial calling for a national student strike and "ceaseless opposition" to Nixon's presidency. The same day Buffalo police used tear gas for the first time to contain around 2,000 demonstrators from the State University College at Buffalo, Canisius College, and UB who were attempting to march downtown on Main Street. Tear gas added a new dimension to the demonstrations. Gentile (1982) recalls spending the better half of an evening in what was called a fire watch. "I assume it was called that because from my office I watched police fire tear gas into mobs of students. I remember cheering, laughing, crying, and choking as students would cover their faces with handkerchiefs, run up to the smoking canister John Wayne style, and throw it back at the police. Those were the good old days—when relevance was supposed to be where it was at, when pigs were supposed to be off, when nostalgia was not yet in, and when assistant professors were out. If it hadn't been so dangerous, it could have been humorous."

On May 7 tear gas was launched once more from Main Street to disperse an estimated five hundred demonstrators near Baird Hall. A *Spectrum* extra edition (1970c) now charged Buffalo police with deliberately firing buckshot into crowds of these demonstrators. In *The Reporter* (1970b) Commissioner Felicetta responded that a thorough "prior study" did not even "suggest" such a thing. Dr. Paul F. Hoffman, Director of the University Health Center who personally treated two students reporting gunshot wounds, was quoted as saying, "There is no evidence to warrant a conclusion that the wounds were inflicted by a shotgun." Dr. Musselman (1991) reaffirms today that he personally examined other individuals who claimed to have been shot on May 7 but could not verify one instance of buckshot piercing the skin. A later FBI report failed to support claims about the incident, which is still cited today as another example of police brutality. (Demonstrators may have been hit by a pelletlike residue—not powerful enough to penetrate the skin—from exploding tear gas grenades.) Reports in *The Spectrum* about the extent and seriousness of injuries to students subjected to tear gas are uniformly dismissed by health service officials. Remaining on duty during the entire period, Dr. Musselman treated persons exposed to tear gas on the campus lawn near Norton and Baird halls. He never wore the gas mask assigned to him. "I wanted those needing help to be able to recognize me," he explains. "Treatment was routine and no one was seriously affected or hospitalized. I guess I suffered the most from the fumes because I didn't wear a mask." Lorenzetti (1990) recalls one co-ed on a residence telephone dramatically informing her parents that she and her roommates were "being teargassed, but we're still all right."

Misperceptions continued to plague UB with sensational reports such as one carried in the *National Review* on June 2. John R. Coyne, Jr. (1970) added his contribution to UB's image:

> With the possible exception of Cornell, no university east of the Mississippi has been so racked by turmoil. [Harvard? Columbia?] During the past academic year there was a riot a week, complete with arson, firebombing and, on at least one occasion, sniper fire. The grand finale came on March 15, when 45 faculty members marched to the Administration Building, Hayes Hall, and sat-in the office of President Martin Meyerson to demand the removal of four hundred Buffalo policemen from the campus. (p. 560)

Such overdrawn images of UB during the 1969–70 term will never be erased and are likely to prosper with time. As recently as May 21, 1989, Louise Continelli (1989) inaccurately summarizes "the high drama" for the *Buffalo News:* "In early 1970 . . . women were pulled to the ground from their hair by riot-equipped campus and city police who stormed the campus in late February crashing into the Student Union clubbing and macing bleeding students," and "Following more student beatings, some students had to be hospitalized. . . . On May 7, 1970, police filled the Student Union with tear gas and buckshot." Goldman (1983) also claims that "While students risked their lives (although none were killed) . . . at least twenty-one were hospitalized" (p. 262).

Chronicle of Higher Education reporter William A. Sievert (1971) visited UB to report his impressions:

A year ago the State University of New York at Buffalo experienced one of the first, longest, and most serious episodes in what turned out to be a very hot spring on American campuses. Today the 24,625 student university appears to be tranquil and operating routinely. Only a handful of militant slogans, painted indelibly on classroom buildings, remains as a physical sign of the turmoil that was. . . .

Mr. Meyerson has been credited with bringing the Buffalo campus to national attention for innovative programs, involving the university in urban problems and developing a more personal learning environment. His three years as president generally are looked upon as a period of expansion although some administrators who worked with him feel that he left the institution leaderless. . . .

Many residents of the Buffalo area dislike the university's long-haired students whose protests they do not understand, and they like even less the teachers who support the students, such as the "Faculty 45."

Because of Mr. Ketter's reputation as a conservative hardliner, many people on the campus doubted that the university would make it through the first week of classes without a major outburst from the students. But, after seven months in office, Mr. Ketter has faced several demonstrations of 30 to 300 students sponsored by such groups as Students for a Democratic Society and the Niagara Liberation Front. None included violent tactics.

University Vice President Richard A. Siggelkow says "the radical movement lost its momentum because it lacked a real program and a sound intellectual base. People also don't want to be in a state of chaos forever."

I had resigned at the end of the term before Ketter's appointment but accepted his invitation in July to return under his administration as Vice President for Student Affairs.

A conservative-moderate faculty coalition directly influenced Ketter's appointment as president, according to Economics Professor Michael Gort (1990). Although Bennis and Regan were also interviewed by the local governing board, the faculty group insisted to that body that only Ketter's name should be submitted to the SUNY trustees in Albany for confirmation. Three times the SUNY trustees rejected the single nominee slate, requesting additional names. The UB Council held firm, and representatives from the coalition began to hold private conversations with the governor's staff.

Ketter (1987), finally invited to meet with the frustrated trustees, recalled the chairperson's opening comments. The candidate was informed that as a formality a few questions would be asked, but that the responses would have no bearing on his foreordained selection—"because the governor contacted us early this morning." Ketter remained as president for twelve years, although it is rumored that the most optimistic of individual trustee estimates was that he would not survive the coming academic year.

After violence subsides people try to resume their lives, but those on both sides who were most involved know the institution will recover slowly. "They are sad and bitter—sad that the institution with which they had developed varying degrees of identity has been so sorely wounded—and bitter because they feel that it was all so unnecessary," analyzes Miles (1969). "If only 'the other group' had the sense to understand the issues and had acted promptly the whole thing need never have escalated into a catastrophe. The bitterness gets in the way of rational dialogue and postpones for some time the rebuilding stage" (p. 359).

The impact of the student movement on UB was mixed, but the great majority of faculty interviewed twenty years later identify largely with negative influences: the university's educational progress and international status were severely retarded; true academic reform, such as initially promising interdisciplinary programs, became impossible to implement; the humanities never fully recovered from the excesses of the period; anti-intellectual aspects remain; community relations were severely strained for years; faculty recruitment efforts were adversely influenced; academic careers were negatively affected; and many promising faculty left.

Serious curricular disruption resulted because too many faculty failed to uphold academic standards, charges Psychology Professor Norman Solkoff (1991), who is also Director of UB's Office of Teaching Effectiveness. "Too many professors decided to let the students do whatever they wanted and acceded to infantile demands of immature 18 and 19 year olds who really didn't know what was educationally appropriate for higher education."

More minorities and women now pursue formerly closed professional fields and previously restricted disciplines, but that legacy is also contradictory: Reflecting national trends, UB's undergraduate minority enrollment continues to decline, especially for black males. Incidents of campus racism are reportedly increasing. Current faculty minority and female recruitment procedures—despite regulatory efforts of Affirmative Action offices—require review and serious re-evaluation.

"Why are colleges and universities consistently unable to rectify minority imbalance in both student enrollment and professional staffing levels?" Siggelkow (1991) asks. "Future students in higher education will be increasingly derived from minority groups, but it is doubtful if even a modest number of appropriate role models will be scattered throughout our colleges and universities to teach these underrepresented and consistently neglected members of the student body. Why are administrators in higher education such slow learners that they are reduced to repeating statements made by their predecessors twenty years ago? Covert institutional racism is more insidious than overt prejudice by individual members of a student body. Higher education may be no more racist than other societal institutions, but potential for irreparable harm is greatest in colleges and universities, since this is where professional careers originate."

Women's studies and African American studies are offered at UB, but some faculty question the content and whether such courses should have been permitted to invade the traditional curricula. Valued relationships developed among some faculty during the unrest, but some former friends still do not speak to one another because of it. Opening up the campus bureaucracy gave students a voice in university affairs, but few undergraduates seem sufficiently interested to serve faithfully and with real commitment on academic committees. It has been suggested that the experience prepared leaders in higher education for coping with future disruptions, but most universities appear as unprepared today as they were then.

The status of women has partially improved, but unfinished business remains. American Studies Professor Elizabeth L. Kennedy (1991) emphasizes that the roots for Women's Studies programs nationally and at UB distinctly pre-dated the student protest movement of the sixties, as did the struggle for civil rights. She confirms that although the New Left greatly influenced the women's liberation movement, female activists at UB were soon disillusioned by its male-dominated leadership.

Faculty-student relations may have improved in the late sixties but faculty members have since distanced themselves further than ever from undergraduates. (Students uniformly complain about professorial indifference to their needs, poor teaching, and lack of faculty contact—all basic student concerns in the sixties.)

Nationally, the movement helped to mobilize public opinion against the war and alerted our citizenry, at least temporarily, to the dangers and manipulations of a warfare state. Youth challenged traditional patterns of American life and culture with mixed results, and some college students emerged from social, political, and cultural complacency. Others who were involved or merely observed what was happening learned something about legal rights, governance processes in complex institutions, and citizenship responsibilities on and off the campus. Although as yet inconclusive, limited research suggests that some student activists of the sixties who became sincerely involved in social issues are more likely to retain initial commitments as active, concerned citizens.

Altbach (1989) observes that the anti-Vietnam student movement is perceived as having been ineffective and a failure. The war did not end and the various student organizations ceased to exist. "Yet the movement had a profound impact on American society," Altbach contends. "It created an anti-war atmosphere that convinced Lyndon Johnson not to seek a second presidential term and eventually forced the United States to abandon the war. The student movement also had a lasting impact on American values and attitudes. Liberal views regarding lifestyles, music and drugs were pioneered by the student movement. Student activists of the 1960s felt that their movement was a failure, but in reality it had an impact not only on the politics of the period but on the values and attitudes of society."

Student movements, Altbach explains, are, on the surface, "paper tigers. Stimulated by idealism and an utopian consciousness, these movements inevitably collapse when faced with the power of the state. Yet, ideas do have power and students, more perhaps than any other group in society, have the ability to articulate social discontent and to focus on society's ills."

Another myth that requires further study is that former campus radicals who encouraged distrust of those over the age of thirty are settled into middle age, comfortably surrounded by the trappings of the middle class. Many dedicated activists of yesteryear may be struggling, like everyone else, to make a decent living, but exactly what they are doing merits investigation. UB faculty member Charles Haynie (1989) maintains contact with some students who joined him at protest rallies in the sixties while affiliated with Tolstoy College. He reports that many former activists are still deeply involved in important causes and still striving, in their own way, to resolve societal problems.

Different administrative actions might not have significantly altered the 1969–70 scenario at UB, but lessons may be learned by identifying factors that influenced and contributed to the university's ineffectiveness and inability to cope with campus unrest.

UB administrators would have profited from improved internal and external communication, careful planning, stronger consensus leadership, well-defined policies, more effective student relationships, closer faculty contacts, less reliance on outside police forces—and much better luck. The university was severely handicapped when it lost administrative continuity and Meyerson's established leadership. Regan, as acting president, was effectively shielded by a handful of confidants, and there was no visible chief executive to interpret the role, actions, and character of the troubled educational enterprise. Communication, the means by which purposes are transmitted into action, broke down among the president, other academic administrators, and key faculty.

How well problems are detected, solved, and prevented depends on the ability of staff members to relate to one another and their superiors. By-products of effective communication include teamwork, efficiency, and job satisfaction; without direction, administrators increasingly tend to act independently and without regard for the welfare of the system. Gradual rigidity was fueled by "misinformation," a problem identified as nationwide in an American Council on Education (1970) Study on Campus Tensions: "We were constantly having to reassure people that we were not planning to do things we have never dreamed of doing, in the face of supposedly informed rumors to the contrary," one respondent notes. Another administrator suggests in the same report that not all communication failures were unintentional: "Administrative and trustee statements are very frequently misinterpreted as the result of really paranoid efforts on the part of students and faculty to discover a plot when there is none. Students distrust trustees and administrators and faculty; faculty distrust students, administrators and trustees; trustees distrust faculty and students, and so on. All this happens despite the fact that there is an abundance of information, which too many people either choose to ignore entirely or twist to fit their preconceived notions."

Staff members should be free (at least in private) to express views that may differ from those of the chief executive, who needs different perspectives to understand complex developments. The president must be able to identify overt and covert sources of influence and understand how certain individuals impact on the organization. Only after consulting as widely as the situation permits should a president lock the office door, where—in private—information can be distilled into what becomes *his* or *her plan* for resolving campus problems.

Effective college presidents have a profound respect for and appreciation of the role of others in decision making, note Fisher and Tack (1985). "They see every member of the campus community—faculty, students and staff—as being capable of making a difference. They empower others by believing in them and by frequently demonstrating their confidence in them." Security for staff members exists if they know that ideas, rather than their proponents, are central in determining courses of action.

College presidents can provoke important constituencies from time to time and still survive, but coalitions spell trouble. The test of a chief executive's effectiveness is the ability to bring different groups together into creative working relationships to act in concert and achieve the purposes of large, intricate human organizations.

There is no such thing as a course of action without difficulties, for in avoiding one difficulty others are encountered by anxious college presidents. Chief executives cannot evade their ultimate leadership *responsibility,* but they must be able to delegate the *authority* that permits their deputies in designated roles to act on presidential behalf. Leadership energies should not be dissipated over events that have already happened, matters previously resolved, or minor problems unworthy of further concern.

At UB open communication between administrators and activists was underutilized. Administrators elsewhere who agreed to consider concerns of protesters often avoided violence regardless of whether change actually occurred, claim Margolda and Margolda (1988). This strategy was most prevalent in student power protests; some changes resulted from deliberations, but the outcome was often a decision against change. Strategies involving faculty mediation were often effective in resolving issues raised by student activists. "Thus, early and continuing communication seems to be the major lesson to be gained from a review of the impacts of various response strategies" (p. 15).

We failed to understand how prolonged administrative indecision generates confusion and disagreement among and between responsible staff and faculty. Conflicts developed within the academic community between those who believed that substantive dialogue on student demands should be established only after activists cease to be defiant, and others who believed just as sincerely that discussions should commence immediately. Regan and his staff, as Pruitt suggests (1989), distanced themselves so far from the student body psychologically, that they were unable to understand either the concerns or feelings of outrage that finally developed among large numbers of undergraduates. "The relationship between size of institution and incidence and type of student disorder may also be due to the reduced inhibition against conflict and violence and the difficulty of getting together for effective negotiation that often accompanies psychological distance" (p. 381).

Increasing pressures are fostered by lengthy periods of inaction. Tensions between factions flourish, real communication between dissidents and administrators becomes impossible, rumors are rampant, and the administration's capacity to face problems rationally declines rapidly.

While it might not have been effective, there was no attempt, after Meyerson withdrew, to try the potentially most effective persuasion strategy of agreeing to debate the issues, thereby avoiding the charge of unwillingness to consider concerns of protesters. "This strategy proves effective only when administrators enter it sincerely and are prepared to handle the debates effectively," according to Margolda and Margolda (1988). "Most persuasive strategies did not provide an adequate response because they focused more on reducing the intensity of the protest than on addressing the underlying issues" (p. 14).

The administration did not redefine and live by UB's established institutional values. We never articulated a clear and consistent policy, with which an involved campus community could relate, defining where dissent (a democratic right and means of societal renewal) ends, and disruption (illegal and impermissible behavior) begins. We imitated too many other colleges and universities, passively waiting with them for events to envelop us. We squandered what time we had and failed to develop and promulgate an unambiguous statement specifying actions the university would take—or risk —to protect the spirit of free inquiry.

Serious difficulties stem from the sheer organizational distance between decision makers and those affected by administrative actions. Unexamined institutional conditions can gradually erode the quality of life and spawn student discontent. There was a related failure not to realize soon enough how easy it is for a small number of dedicated and deeply alienated individuals to effectively undermine the credibility of large institutions. "A feedback system must be designed to provide objective evaluations to the administration on the psychological health of the organization whether the top authority wants them or not," advises Miles (1989). "There should be an institutional and regular mechanism for providing this type of evaluation" (p. 362). Impersonalism—not necessarily determined by institutional size—can be alleviated when meaningful relationships exist among and between students, faculty, and administrators. In any large institution, individuals—often lost in the crowd—should be singled out for personal attention.

Administrative indecision and a poor sense of timing heightened internal disagreement. We lacked the desire or ability to plan ahead, developing strategies only when emergencies demanded responses. Many faculty and students, and most of the outside community, correctly perceived the administration as either acting too late or overreacting too soon. We performed like insecure executives in any typical business establishment who think the world revolves around their decisions, and are unable to tolerate disagreement.

Faculty and administrators cannot satisfactorily respond to the needs of everyone in the academic community. Students remain the "now" generation, often demanding immediate relief and instant perfection. Their demands are sometimes incompatible with a thoughtful climate of shared power that should typify intellectual settings. Some student groups are determined to get what they want—immediately. Their leaders may appear isolated, but their numbers expand rapidly if university responses are improper, ill-timed, or poorly implemented. Martyrdom can create a rallying point for dissenters, and making examples of activist students through arrest or selective disiplinary action can produce greater heroes. A martyr can be perceived as a stronger leader by many followers, often generating increased enthusiasm and renewed spirit for the cause.

The administration failed to understand or capitalize on the attitudes of the faculty, who were overwhelmingly opposed to activist disruptive tactics. A 1972 random sample study by Francis, Lewis, and Rubin (1972), which tabulated ninety-eight faculty responses, reveals that over 90 percent of the faculty contacted neither condoned nor tolerated disruptive actions that undermined or interfered with basic educational functions or caused property damage. They were almost in total agreement that disruptive tactics threatened academic freedom, and over 90 percent "strongly opposed" the occupation of buildings and interference with classes or faculty meetings. Canceling classes or closing down the university were viewed as unacceptable administrative responses. The faculty preferred internal disciplinary action and traditional university dialogue and discussion to maintain calm. Over 80 percent opposed placing city police permanently on campus or even bringing them in temporarily to restore calm, a finding that would have alerted the administration to be more open about intentions to involve outside police. The use of campus security to arrest destructive individuals and sign complaints that would result in city court appearances was favored by 58.6 percent. Placing reliance on university security forces is more realistic today, since campus police nationally have profited most from the unrest. For them it resulted in higher salaries, better training, and improved leadership.

While faculty prefer dialogue and discussion as their favored approach to maintaining calm, they accept the need for outside intervention if a major crisis is clearly developing. The administration erred in not better educating the faculty about possible options before invoking a massive police presence. Outside force should be called on to handle a specific disruption rather than employed as an instrument for mass control. Those who maintained that calling in outside police as an occupying force would ultimately spark serious confrontations were prophetic.

Fifty-five percent of the institutions that experienced violence during 1968–69 had occasion to call in municipal police, but it was the timing and size of the force as well as the internal secrecy preceding their appearance that caused unnecessary problems for UB. Calling in police is justifiable when uncontrolled disruption is imminent, but in this setting platoons of patrolmen marching in Gestapo fashion around the campus was not the most effective maneuver. And once outside police take over, university officials lose control and become observers. It was never clear to the great majority of the faculty that such an extreme measure was called for.

Some faculty have an advantage over administrators in that they are often more inclined to view dissonant students as sincere in their own cause. They realize the importance of listening to positions that contradict those of the administration. We should always hope that there will be professors who treat students with respect and understanding when frustrated administrators view them only as the enemy and sometimes forget that the primary concern of the university is to meet the needs or even the perceived needs of the student body.

Professors, like administrators, are also unlikely to admit that pedagogical or human relationships with students need improvement. Fundamental to academic reforms that might reduce campus tensions and alleviate potential unrest is a change of attitude that causes the faculty to take greater interest in general education and student welfare. Many seem to feel that this would be viewed by colleagues as an attempt to turn the campus into a therapeutic community, but few undergraduates today can find a faculty member who knows them sufficiently well to take sincere interest in their academic progress or write a meaningful reference.

Something is seriously wrong if the university experience, which should be consistently exciting and challenging, degenerates into a depersonalized learning factory. Single factors of curriculum, professors, administrators, and facilities do not operate in isolation. Satisfaction or success of the university experience is a product of interaction between students and the total college environment. Students can be helped to achieve a consciousness of that environment and what it means to be part of it. They can engage in a process of self-discovery where they learn to react, observe, imagine, listen, make sound judgments, add value to their lives, and communicate effectively.

Improvement of undergraduate education requires recognition for teaching skills as well as research, admittedly difficult in "publish or perish" universities. Until faculty in all disciplines realize the importance of a teaching methodology distinctly related to human inter-relationships, higher education will continue to merit justified criticism. Concomitant with better instruction comes greater and more sincere interest in the recipient of the process, but faculty remain hesitant about having their teaching reviewed. Modeus (1983) suggests that they seem to fall into two general categories: those who already know their shortcomings and do not want obvious instructional weaknesses further exposed, and others who sincerely believe they are already "outstanding" teachers who could not benefit from any evaluation of their teaching effectiveness, especially at the college/university level.

Traditionally resistant to change, faculty, seemingly encapsulated in a plasticene bubble of academic immunity, must become serious about influencing directions of higher education and implementing desired institutional objectives. Educators are irresponsible if goals remain unformulated and their institutions are allowed to drift. Considering new directions and moving forward involves so much pain that administrators satisfy themselves with unrealistic and unattainable—but lofty—"viewbook objectives," or indefinitely postpone consideration of difficult issues. Many find it easier to list priorities without regard to goals, neither a sensible nor intelligent approach.

Miser (1988) advises college presidents to appoint a task force of students, faculty, legal counsel, and student affairs professionals to review current practices and procedures that relate to campus dissent. "Higher education authorities would be foolish to believe that outpourings of youthful idealism and campus militancy have passed into history," he warns. "Any review of past practices should include investigations of the institution's history of dissent, traditions of free speech on campus, and institutional values and philosophy regarding dissent and disruption. . ." (p. 76).

"An effective policy on dissent and disruption," he emphasizes, "must contain clear definitions of dissent and disruption" (p. 76). Miser points out that students involved in dissent need to be informed where the line is between permissible and prohibited behaviors and the consequences of disruption so that there is no doubt about what will happen if policies are violated, which institutional officials will have authority to act if disruption occurs, and the adjudication process that will be used in cases of students accused of disruption.

Confusion still exists about legal relationships between students and the university. Miles (1969) believes that probation, suspension, and expulsion of offenders for illegal actions if invoked promptly and with due process, are far more effective than legal sanctions applied by civil or criminal courts.

"The certainty and promptness of a penalty, not its severity, are the keys to its deterrent effect" (p. 363). Since the question invariably arises, there is no legal basis to support student complaints of "double jeopardy." The fact that a university student has been subjected to college disciplinary proceedings does not in any way preclude a subsequent trial by public authorities for the same conduct. Similarly, a trial in the criminal courts does not preclude the imposition of appropriate disciplinary sanctions by the university. However, the possibility of injustice resulting from the imposition of multiple sanction for the same conduct may be considered.

No educational institution can reach decisions on policy, programs, and services without accurate and comprehensive information. Questions about faculty, physical plant, financial policies, and future planning are related in some way to data about "the student." Success is dependent on research that should include surveys of student and faculty opinions and attitudes, observations of student experiences, and investigations of student frustrations.

Some observers believe that periods of student unrest run in cycles, but the world changes so rapidly that predicting future behavior by historical precedent is an uncertain business. The classic notice in *The London Times* cancelling the Clairvoyant Society's upcoming meeting because of unforeseen circumstances is pertinent, but student unrest in the 1990s appears inevitable. Protest demonstrations are being held on college campuses, buildings have been occupied, shanty towns have reappeared, and some student activists have been arrested. Items high on the agenda that could spark protests during the 1990s include the flawed civil rights program, poverty amid affluence, environmental concerns, racial strife, economic stability, and what role the United States should continue to play in resolving world conflicts overseas and almost anywhere in Latin America. Activism may relate to women's rights, hiring procedures, equal pay, and sexual harassment. Dissent may turn inward, crystalized by steadily rising tuition costs, faulty tenure decisions, and reduced levels of student financial aid. A decision to reinstitute the military draft is most likely to bring youthful marchers out in force.

Richard Reeves (1986), writing from Paris, discussed the possibilty of an American version of student demonstrations then sweeping France. While there was no Vietnam factor at the moment, Reeves warned that the Paris uprising—against proposed reforms in educational laws—could be a harbinger of similar student outbursts in America. "Modern educational systems are turning out more educated and trained young people than national economic systems seem capable of absorbing," Reeves predicts. "The same words ('What is going to happen to us when we get out?') seem to describe American students. They share the fears, too, as their learned elders tell them of inevitably reduced American standards of living. And disillusionment may set in as they figure out that they are the ones who will have to pay back the national debt that their parents spent on themselves during the Reagan years."

The 25th Annual Survey of Entering College Freshmen, conducted jointly by UCLA's Higher Education Research Institute and the American Council on Education supports the possibility of renewed student activism, according to Kenneth Eskey (1991) of Scripps Howard News Service. Responses from 194,182 freshmen at 382 colleges and universities suggest that thousands of eighteen-year-olds plan to participate in campus demonstrations to promote social change. "This year's college freshmen are a throwback to the 1960s—ready to march and protest for what they believe in."

"There is a rapidly expanding number of American college students who are dissatisfied with the *status quo*," says Alexander Astin, who annually directs the research (Eskey 1991). He notes in the article that the survey was conducted before the Persian Gulf War, but predicts that any similar, prolonged conflict might once again galvanize campus militancy. Nationwide protests were already far more extensive when the Persian Gulf episode began than they were at the beginning of the Vietnam War.

Findings reported by the American Council on Education (1991) reveal that a rapidly expanding number of American college students want to become personally involved in bringing about change in American society. A record 39.4 percent of the freshmen surveyed said they had participated in demonstrations while in their final year of high school. That figure compares with 36.7 percent who reported such activism in 1989 and more than doubles the number of freshmen who said they had participated in high-school protests in the late 1960s. Over 7 percent say they plan to participate in campus protest in college, also an all-time high, compared to 6.3 percent in 1989 and only 4.1 percent in 1968. The percentage who believe the government is not doing enough to control environmental pollution increased for the sixth consecutive year, reaching 87.9 percent. Nearly 14 percent feel it is "essential" and "very important" to become involved in programs to clean up the environment. Nearly four students in five (79.4 percent) disagree with the proposition that racial discrimination is no longer a major problem in America and 38 percent say they plan to do something about it.

A study of student activism in America reveals that during periods of dissent over foreign policy, domestic policy protests are often heightened as well. Margolda and Margolda (1988) point out that domestic concerns and government foreign policy in the Middle East, Central America, and South Africa have already resulted in the development of pockets of unrest on college campuses. "Previous periods of apathy about societal concerns have been followed by intense activism which suggests that violent student protest could emerge in the next decade," they assert (p. 21).

Foreign student activism presaged American unrest of the sixties. As then, student rebellion today is highly visible in other nations, including Mexico, France, North and South Korea, and most tragically in China.

Historically, students follow a cyclical pattern, oscillating back and forth between personal preoccupation and social engagement, Levine and Hirsch (1990) maintain. "Periods of student self-absorption followed World War I, World War II, and the Vietnam War. These were times in which the activism and student unrest of the progressive era, the Depression, and the 1960s gave way to self-government crazes in the 1920s; panty raids, telephone-booth stuffing, and general disinterest in politics by the 'silent generation' of the 1950s; and streaking, toga parties, and yuppieism in the 1970s and 1980s. These periods of self-absorption lasted a little less than fifteen years and were preceded and followed by periods of social engagement, lasting about equally as long. . . . In the next few years, then, we can expect to see a revival of political activism on campus and more student interest in the 'relevance' of college courses," Levine and Hirsch conclude. "We should also expect students to be more concerned about international and social issues and in campus governance."

Ketter (1988) believed that new waves of student activism could be triggered by the nation's involvement in an unpopular war that disenchants students, faculty, and the general public, a major depression, or a series of severe economic recessions. "Other factors, especially in concert with a military conflict, also could exist which would create the conditions for disruption—a major natural or manmade disaster, a significant national scandal, or a major breakthrough in automation techniques that would significantly reduce the required workforce."

The late Dr. Ketter argued that UB had failed, as it did in the 1960s, to address the question of what factors are primary and fundamental to maintaining a true system of higher learning. "The administration (along with many other campuses) has remained distant and remote from the ongoing educational process. . . . These exact same tendencies are still evolving on this campus today," he noted. "It is virtually impossible today for the average student, or for that matter the average faculty member, to obtain an audience with an upper level administrator to discuss issues of importance."

Because that is where most of them are, students will use the open and vulnerable university system as a power base. They will continue to see themselves as independent adults free from institutional controls, while parents and alumni prefer more supervision. The general public will not change its generally schizophrenic view of eighteen-year-old adults as "kids" who enter college. If activism returns, students confronted by psychologically threatening challenges will again avoid taking personal responsibility for moral choices. As in the sixties, they will choose the path of least resistance. Nothing has undermined Newcomb's (1962) conclusions that college youth have an especially strong need for peer acceptance and the nourishment group membership provides.

Some members of academe relish in focusing unwanted attention on complex local and national issues, but without such critics our society would stagnate and be incomplete. How do we know which ideas are dangerous unless we know which ones are safe? Should universities function as academic cloisters, detached and removed from social-political issues?

Dissent should occur on any American campus that values the exchange of ideas, encourages political discourse, and fosters open dialogue. Higher education is our greatest hope for democracy only if objective inquiry and unfettered thought are permanent hallmarks. Sensitive issues must be debated without fear of reprisal or intimidation. Freedom of inquiry is the most likely casualty if violence and disruption again overtake higher education and efforts are revived to politicize our colleges and universities. Unresolved is the problem of how to cope effectively with activists who successfully disrupt meetings and shout down speakers with whom they disagree.

Members of the academic community must be free to organize, pass resolutions, distribute leaflets, circulate petitions, picket, and take other actions that are lawful and consistent with university policies and procedures. Activities of any individual group of persons are not allowable in the name of free speech if educational processes are violated. The right to demonstrate is impermissible if university functions are disrupted. Students must be prohibited from blocking free entry into or free exit from buildings; interfering with or obstructing regular university functions; denying the proper use of offices or other facilities to students, staff, faculty, and guests; or engaging in behavior that endangers personal safety or results in the destruction of property. There may be confusion about what freedom really is, but it should not include "the right" to take over academic buildings. Educational missions in higher education will be seriously threatened if thoughtless actions and emotionally inspired conflict among persons holding opposing viewpoints again results in the physical disruption of educational programs.

Each member of a true academic community must be fully committed to preserve the rights of all. Protesting groups require some personal sacrifice and self-restraint if freedom for all is to endure. Harassment, innuendo and insult, and explicit or implict physical abuse have no place in a university where personal rights must be respected. Students and scholars should conform to standards of mutual respect that exceed those of the community at large. Freedom is not free without voluntary restraint; reasonable debate and legitimate social actions are the appropriate ways to change policies within a democratic society.

Student generations do not change but contemporary college youth reflect prevailing climates of opinion. The proportion of students sincerely involved in social action is invariably overestimated by the general population, but college youth should be encouraged to deal with change and uncertainty, prepared to resolve both current problems and unanticipated challenges.

Shared interests and cooperative interpretations of society and the world by students and their mentors preserve and transmit knowledge through successive chains of generations. Realization of human potential is achieved through the acquisition, transmission, and application of skills and knowledge. Learning results from a series of interactions among and between students and faculty, who may too often introspectively perceive themselves as living on islands of freedom surrounded by swamps of ignorance. Still, no other place is as hospitable to the exploration of ideas, or as dedicated to the fullest possible development of the individual.

No area of investigation is yet so thoroughly understood that new discoveries will not be made. Colleges and universities must provide their students with scholarly curiosity and a sense of values with the courage to defend them. The educational experience should be dynamic, stimulating, and challenging—and always subject to revision and honest evaluation. As new truths and new ways to think about old truths are uncovered, teachers and students will learn that there are no right answers—only better or worse ones. The best immediate answer, revealed only after great study and reflection, is transitory.

Some former radical New Leftists met in Washington in 1989 to talk about the 60s and the era since then. Influenced by what happened in southeast Asia in the aftermath of the U.S. defeat in Vietnam when the bloodshed they thought would never happen did in fact occur, they had changed their views about the movement. Their papers in *Second Thoughts: Former Radicals Look Back at the Sixties,* may not reflect the views of many former radicals who avoided the conference and likely disdained those who convened it. For those present "the history of the movement was a cautionary tale that should not inspire but rather give pause to the huddled millenarians awaiting the advent of the Next Left," Peter Collier (1989) writes about the sessions. "The 60s had failed them personally and had been a disaster for the country. And so they came to Washington to bury the New Left rather than to praise it" (p. xii).

And most radical activists of the 60s might not accept what Joshua Muravchik (1989), a former chairman of YPSL (the Young Peoples Socialist League) said about the United States at the meeting:

America is arguably the finest country on earth, the most socially equalitarian and the most generous and peaceful great power in history. . . . Whatever reforms America may need today—and its success is the product of constant experimental change—the highest imperative is not radical transformation of America, but the preservation and perfection of its values and the extension of its liberating model to as much of the rest of the world as possible. (p. 165)

Despite Muravchik's words, a true university must always vigilantly defend itself from assaults by insiders and outsiders who seek to dominate higher education and stifle youth. External and internal repression spawn depotism and the university must learn how to protect itself from those who would subvert the institution into a political tool to be controlled by the most clamorous factions. If truth and reason are displaced by power and politics the university will degenerate into anarchy, inviting the despotic rule from within and repression from without. There should be no place within a true university for groups and individuals that are not committed to academic freedom and who refuse to accept the responsibilities embodied in that principle.

Particularly vulnerable will be management-oriented colleges and universities that fail to govern themselves well through their constituencies and become increasingly willing to jeopardize—and lose—vital freedoms that are essential to their existence as viable educational institutions.

References

Altbach, Philip G. (1991). Interview and Questionnaire.

———. (1989). "Viewpoints: Student Movement Is Defeated But Its Goals Remain," *The Reporter*, July 6.

American Bar Association. (1970). "Report of Commission on Student Government and Student Dissent."

American Council on Education. (1970). "Report: Special Committee on Campus Tensions," June.

———. (1991). Higher Education and National Affairs Newsletter, "Survey Cites Rise in Activism," January 28.

Buffalo Evening News. (1970). "Campus Quiets Down," March 19.

Collier, Peter. (1989). "Why Second Thoughts?" *Second Thoughts: Former Radicals Look Back at the Sixties*, Peter Collier and David Horowitz, eds., (New York: Madison Books).

Continelli, Louise. (1989). "The Riot Squad," *The Buffalo News*, May 21.

Coyne, John R., Jr. (1970). "The End of the Multiversity," *National Review*, June 2.

Eskey, Kenneth. (1991). "Study: 91 Freshmen a Throwback to 60s," ACE/UCLA Twenty-fifth Annual Survey of College Freshmen (1990), Scripps-Howard News Release, *Daily News*, Naples, FL, January 28.

Fisher, James L., and Tack, Martha W. (1985). "The Effective College President," *Educational Record*, Winter.

Francis, Bruce; Lewis, Steven; and Rubin, Ira A. (1972). Faculty Attitudes Toward Student Revolt, (Survey) SUNY/Buffalo.

Gentile, J. Ronald. (1982). "Education and Other Social Diseases: A WAPOM Survey" (WAPOM is the acronym for Women, Assistant Professors and Other Minorities), *Newsletter for Educational Psychologists*, June.

Gitlen, Todd. (1987). *The Sixties, Years of Hope, Days of Rage*, (New York: Bantam Books).

Goldman, Mark. (1983). *High Hopes: The Rise and Decline of Buffalo*. (Albany, N.Y.: SUNY Press), p. 262.

Gort, Michael. (1990). Telephone Interview.

Greeley, Andrew M. (1972). "The End of the Movement," *Change*, April.

Hayden, Tom. (1989). *Reunion: A Memoir*, (New York: Macmillan), p. 420.

Haynie, Charles A. (1989). Interview and Questionnaire.

Kaufman, Michael T. (1970). "University Seeks Buffalo Snipers," *The New York Times*, March 17.

Kennedy, Elizabeth. (1991). Telephone Interview.

Ketter, Robert L. (1987). Interview and Questionnaire.

———. (1988). Letter to the author, May 4.

Levine, Arthur, and Hirsch, Deborah. (1990). "Point of View: Student Activism and Optimism Return to the Campuses," *Chronicle of Higher Education*, November 7.

Lorenzetti, Anthony F. (1990). Interview and Questionnaire.

Manchester, William. (1974). *The Glory and the Dream: A Narrative History of America, 1932–1972.* (Boston: Little, Brown & Company).
Margolda, Marcia B. Baxter, and Margolda, Peter M. (1988). "Student Activism: A Historical Overview," *Student Affairs and Campus Dissent: Reflection of the Past and Challenge for the Future.* National Association of Student Personnel Administrators, Inc., Monograph Series 8, Keith M. Miser, ed., March. Reprinted by permission of the National Association of Student Personnel Administrators.
Miles, Rufus E., Jr. (1969). "The Pathology of Institutional Breakdown," *Journal of Higher Education,* May.
Miser, Keith M. (1988). "Student Activities Policy: A Statement of Institutional Philosophy," *Student Affairs and Campus Dissent: Reflection of the Past and Challenge for the Future.* National Association of Student Personnel Administrators, Inc., Monograph Series 8, Keith M. Miser, ed., March. Reprinted by permission of the National Association of Student Personnel Administrators.
Modeus, A. S. (1983). *The Unmaking of a College President: A Fictionalized Case Study,* (Lexington, Mass.: Ginn Custom Publishing).
Muravchik, Joshua. (1989). "A Cure Worse Than the Disease," *Second Thoughts: Former Radicals Look at the Sixties,* Peter Collier and David Horowitz, eds., (New York: Madison Books).
Musselman, M. Luther. (1991). Interview and Questionnaire.
Newcomb, Theodore M. (1962). "Student Peer Group Influence," *The American College,* Nevitt Sanford, ed., (New York: Wiley and Sons).
New York Times. (1970). "Student Leader Seized in Buffalo," March 18.
Pruitt, Dean G., and Gahagan, James P. (1974). "Campus Crisis: The Search for Power," in *Perspectives on Social Power,* James F. Tedeschi, ed. (Chicago: Aldine Publishing Company).
Pruitt, Dean G. "A Note on the Disposition of the Faculty 45 Case."
———. (1989). Interview and Questionnaire.
Reeves, Richard. (1986). "Student Protests Center on Jobs Now," *The Buffalo News,* December 19.
Rosche, Richard J. (1970). "They Shoot Students—a Report on Police Misconduct," (Buffalo, New York), May.
The Reporter. (1970a). "Strikers Reject Violence After Fracas Injures 58," March 19.
———. (1970b). "Regan Asks Buckshot Probe, Officials Doubt It Happened," March 18.
Sievert, William A. (1971). "SUNY-Buffalo Appears Calm, but Old Issues Stir Distress Under a New Administration," *Chronicle of Higher Education,* Feb. 8.
Siggelkow, Richard A. (1991). "Racism in Higher Education: A Permanent Condition?" *NASPA Journal,* Winter.
Solkoff, Norman. (1991). Interview and Questionnaire.
Spectrum. (1970a). "Regan Steps Down—Assumes Faculty Post," April 15.
———. (1970b). "A National Call to Action," Editorial, May 5.
———. (1970c). "Extra: Fire & Vigilantes Add to Campus Confrontation," May 7.

Name Index

DATE DUE

#47-0108 Peel Off Pressure Sensitive

MAIN STREET CAMPUS
BUILDING INDEX (1970)